And How Does That Make You Feel?

And How Does That Make You Feel?

Never
Everything You ~~Ever~~ Wanted
to Know About Therapy

JOSHUA FLETCHER

WM
WILLIAM MORROW
An Imprint of HarperCollinsPublishers

FIRST EDITION

Designed by Bonni Leon-Berman

Library of Congress Cataloging-in-Publication Data has been applied for.

ISBN 978-0-06-331012-4

23 24 25 26 27 LBC 5 4 3 2 1

The author has disguised identities and recognizable details of patients, and in all instances has combined material and scenarios from many patients into one. Despite these necessary changes to preserve privacy, all stories remain true to the spirit of talk therapy.

I dedicate this book to all the therapists who
have completed hundreds of hours of training
to get to where they are.

I also dedicate this book to the brave people who seek
help for mental health all around the world. It isn't easy
to open up. I hear you. I see you. Thank you.

Contents

Introduction

If you have ever had the pleasure of meeting a therapist at a party (a good therapist, anyway), you probably found them to be very attentive. Therapists try our best to listen. We do this not to find evidence of all your wrongdoings or to see into a hidden part of you that you'd rather we didn't, nor are we trying to pin a personality trait on your issues with your parents. We don't look into your darkest thoughts or read your mind, nor are we actively lie-detecting. We are attentive because what we like to do is listen. It's what we are trained for.

When we're asking you—in the therapy room or in life—"And how does that make you feel?" it's because we really want to know. We're interested. We're curious. We want to understand.

Much like the interior designer who can't help but scan every room they're in or the builder who taps on the wall of someone else's construction project, therapists often find it hard to switch off from the day job. Especially when it's a job that defines a large proportion of your identity. In social situations I've found that many people become uncomfortable when I tell them about my profession. Their body language becomes subtly more defensive, often followed by the half-joking question "So I guess you're psychoanalyzing me now?" I recognize the wariness and, as a qualified and experienced therapist, let me assure you that this playful accusation isn't too far from the truth. However, my professional curiosity is not the invasive analysis that many initially fear—it comes from a place of compassion, positive intrigue, and habit.

Furthermore, when we listen, even at a party or a family event, we find it difficult to switch off the years of training, including bookshelves of counseling theory containing lots of psychological problem-solving. Every person's mind likes to automatically draw from its own reference library, and therapists are no different, but it doesn't mean we act upon or assume the suggestions that the brain proposes to us. Often, we would like this part of the brain to switch off when we're not working, particularly if we're trying to chill out in front of the TV with a glass of wine.

It's important to remember that therapists are as human as every-body else. It's okay to see them like any other human inside or outside the therapy room. Therapists don't have everything worked out. We are flawed, we have our vices, and we constantly work on our own personal stuff. Throughout this book, you'll see just how human we can be as I share my vulnerabilities, imperfections, anxieties, and inner thoughts with you. I do this not to bring my profession into disrepute, but to help people realize that therapists aren't as scary or holier than thou as you might have feared.

I promise that there is no omnipotent know-it-all waiting for you on the other side of the therapy-room door, ready to pounce at the first chance to judge or shame you. Instead, the person who awaits you is, ideally, someone who wants to listen and is willing to be a conscientious, nonjudgmental guest in your world for a short while, both of you knowing that you can safely part ways until the next time you decide to open the door again. I hope this is how my clients feel about me and my practice.

I'm a psychotherapist who specialises in anxiety, and I really enjoy my job. Anxiety is something we can all relate to on some level, and it is something with which I have struggled massively in the past. Even now, my anxiety hasn't gone entirely. Still, thanks to life-changing therapy and psychoeducation, I can confidently say that I live a happy and fulfilling life—a goal I wish for all my clients. Helping them get to a good place is what drives me as a therapist. Anxiety can feel crippling to many, but each time I see one of my clients lean in to uncertainty and face their fears, it fills me with the utmost admiration. They are not broken. *You* are not broken.

As a society we are making progress in how we talk about mental health, but there is still a long way to go. Instagram hashtags and cor-porate well-being days can get us only so far, and there are still way too many people who think that difficult emotions are best kept under wraps out of embarrassment or shame. I believe that therapy can help nearly everyone at some stage in their life, but I also think there is a great deal that is misunderstood about the therapeutic process. And I want to dispel some of the myths and misunderstandings in this book, to reassure you that talking about mental health with a professional needn't be either terrifyingly vulnerable or endlessly self-indulgent.

This book is my contribution to encourage more openness around mental well-being, as well as a source of insight into a field that is often left shrouded in mystery. In *And How Does That Make You Feel?* you will find out what it's like to live as a therapist, but also what it's like to exist as a very real and flawed human being. It includes spicy stories of conflict, tragedy, and mistakes. I include the stuff that's happening that few therapists would dare tell you about, as well as some stuff I wonder if I should have included at all. But if even a small part of you, after putting this book down, thinks that therapy seems more appealing or less scary, or that you're perhaps willing to mention therapy in casual conversation, then my main wish for this book will have been fulfilled.

And How Does That Make You Feel? is structured around four client case studies. Any therapists reading this may be gasping at this point, "Oh my God, this is heresy! What about confidentiality?!" Rest assured that the characters and story arcs have been fictionalized. Before writing about these cases, I underwent a rigorous ethical screening with my supervisor and publisher. Anyone who knows me will attest to my passion for ethical practices and I assure you that hours of consideration and professional reflection have been spent on this book before and after words were put to paper.

The Inner Voice of the Therapist

I'd like to introduce you to my inner voices—very vocal characters that feature prominently throughout this book. Training to be a therapist, as well as going through therapy myself, helped me to develop a strong sense of self-awareness. Part of my emotional development, including my anxiety recovery, was to identify the different thoughts and voices that my mind liked to throw at me throughout the day. One morning I took out a pen and decided to label them all as my week unfolded. Over time I began to imagine these voices as characters at a big round thought table—each voice squabbling, debating, and fighting for attention in my mind.

The voices you'll encounter in my inner dialogue throughout the therapy sessions are:

ANALYTICAL—The voice that sees things from the perspective of counseling theory.

ANXIETY—The voice of worry that focuses on threats and unlikely catastrophes.

BIOLOGY—Hunger, fatigue, pain, discomfort, toileting, temperature, et cetera.

COMPASSION—The willingness to understand and help.

CRITIC—A judging voice.

DETECTIVE—The voice that searches for clues and meaning.

EMPATHY—The attempt to imagine and experience how others are feeling.

ESCAPIST—The voice encouraging me to avoid difficult feelings.

INTUITION—A nudge from the gut that goes beyond rationale and reason.

IRREVERENCE—Bizarre and unexpected thoughts that creep into the therapy room.

SAVIOR—The desire to "save" a person outside the realms of professional duty.

TRIGGER—Jealousy, anxiety, anger, defensiveness, associated trauma.

VOLITION—Metacognitive intervention—or, in less technical language, choosing to listen to a more appropriate voice than the one that initially arises.

1

Daphne

I glanced at the clock as Tony took a moment to reflect on what he had just shared with me. This had been a particularly groundbreaking session, as Tony and I had been working hard on uncovering why he often felt uneasy when he found himself on his own. However, this deeply therapeutic moment was marred by my stupid decision, moments before he knocked on the door, to quickly down a large Americano.

> BIOLOGY: *You're going to piss yourself.*
> CRITIC: *Idiot. You should have gone before you started.*
> ANXIETY: *You do know holding it in is bad for your prostate, right?*

I awkwardly adjusted myself on the chair to try to ease the discomfort. There's nothing wrong with announcing that you need to take a break to relieve yourself, but with four minutes left and at such a crucial time, I couldn't allow this to halt the ongoing breakthrough. I kept my eyes fixed upon Tony and tried my best to be in the moment.

> Tony: It's been starting to make sense to me for a while now. Looking back, I realize I have very few happy associations with being alone. When we explore the feelings that come up from our exposure work, memories of the divorce come up. Sitting in my brother's flat. The smell of cigarettes and damp washing . . .

He paused and met my eyes.

> Tony: Even growing up, when I was alone it was usually to avoid the arguing going on. The continuous conflict happening downstairs. Or even to escape the nasty lads at school. I'd run around the back of the sports hall just to find quiet. To me, being alone means I'm escaping from danger, but at the cost of sitting with sadness.
> Josh: Perhaps it's not the feeling unsafe that we're now running away from, but the feeling of sadness itself?

Tony: Yeah . . . Yes, it's like I always put in plans to never be alone just in case
I feel that sadness again. I really like my life, but this feels like a really
powerful old fear. I'm understanding why I'm always terrified to be on
my own, even if it's for, like, five minutes.

Josh: What's our homework going to be then?

Tony: Easy. I've got to practice being alone.

Josh: Why?

Tony: Because I want to change my association with being alone. I want to
enjoy moments to myself and not have to be terrified every time Helen
goes out to see her sister. I don't want to be counting down the seconds
until the kids come home from school so I am not on my own. Wow, this
is weird to imagine.

INTUITION: *Remind him of the definitions you both covered.*

Josh: Remember when we said that there's a big difference between
being lonely and just being on our own? I think that sounds like great
homework to set yourself.

Tony smiled nervously but had an air of determination about him.

COMPASSION: *He's doing really well.*
EMPATHY: *This homework will be hard, but he knows it's a step in the
right direction.*
BIOLOGY: *You're definitely going to piss yourself.*
ESCAPIST: *You need to end this session, quickly.*

To conclude the session, I rolled out one of the oldest therapist tropes
in the book:

Josh: I'm *just aware of the time,* Tony, and that we're coming to a close. Shall
we see each other at our usual time next week? Perhaps we can discuss
the homework then if you'd like?

··

I ushered Tony out of the room more hastily than I'd have liked, but I
was desperate. Once he got into the elevator, I threw him a smile as the

doors closed shut. Like a bolting horse with a watermelon-sized bladder, I galloped down the corridor and shoulder-charged the toilet door. Horrifyingly, I discovered that the cubicle was occupied, and the only urinal was being used by Dr. Patel of the GP practice downstairs. It's amazing how highly attuned the senses become when you're desperate to urinate, as I was able to deduce from Dr. Patel's trouser sounds that he was unzipping rather than rezipping. Why the hell had he come upstairs to use this toilet anyway?

Everything was hurting. I couldn't wait. I glanced over at the sink and took a deep breath. "I'm really sorry, Doctor, but this is an emergency." Then I did it. I pissed in the sink. The large mirror above the sink acted as poetic punishment for my actions, as I had nowhere to look but at myself.

BIOLOGY: *Thank you.*
CRITIC: *Dr. Patel thinks you are vile.*
COMPASSION: *It's okay to make the best out of a bad situation.*

I could hear Dr. Patel immediately rezipping.

..

I walked back to my office batting away intrusive thoughts of children washing their innocent hands in the sink that I had just fouled. I had made sure to wash and disinfect everything but still felt a lingering feeling of shame.

VOLITION: *You can leave this now. Back to work.*

The typical duration of a session with a therapist lasts for a "therapeutic hour," although most therapists keep sessions to fifty minutes in length. This allows time for a break in between appointments to ground ourselves, write and save notes, or urinate in sinks. I usually spend this ten-minute gap taking some mindful breaths and reflecting on the previous session, or mindlessly scrolling through memes on Reddit. Now back in my office, I looked at my schedule to see who my next client was. I had a new client penciled in under the name Daphne; there as no surname provided. She was due to arrive in two minutes for her initial consultation. Typically, just mere seconds to prepare for a new client triggered panic stations.

TRIGGER: *You're going to be caught off guard. Impostor!*
ANXIETY: *You look like a scruff. What if Daphne thinks you are unprofessional?*

I rushed to my desk drawers and pulled out a brush to rake through my hair. Then I turned on my mobile phone camera and used it as a mirror to check if my face looked presentable.

CRITIC: *You could have shaved, man.*
ANALYTICAL: *You still judge yourself on appearances. Something to reflect on later.*

I remembered talking to Daphne over the phone and recalled her emphasizing that she wanted to remain anonymous, which isn't completely out of the ordinary with clients who are protective about their privacy. I'm intrigued about meeting any new client, but those who are especially adamant about being anonymous are always, to be honest, a little exciting to me.

IRREVERENCE: *I wonder how many people Daphne has killed . . .*

The clock ticked and reached five minutes past the hour. Still no Daphne. I paced the room and made sure everything looked neat and tidy—I straightened the cushions, made sure my plants looked less neglected, and double-checked that my personal phone was on silent. Then I sat down and waited. I stared at the door like a dog waiting for their owner to come home. Eight minutes had now passed. Still no Daphne.

CRITIC: *What the hell are you doing, Daphne? This is rude. Time is money.*
EMPATHY: *This could be her first time in therapy. Perhaps she's really scared? Give her a chance. You remember your own experiences of therapy, right?*
ANXIETY: *What if she was hit by a bus on the way here?*
IRREVERENCE: *Imagine if she was caught hitting the bus instead. "Die, bus, die!"*
ANALYTICAL: *You're on edge because you're nervous.*

BIOLOGY: *Your sympathetic nervous system is activated.*
COMPASSION: *It's okay not to feel calm right now. It's okay to feel uneasy.*
DETECTIVE: *The evidence suggests that she isn't going to turn up.*
CRITIC: *Wow, man, you love to overthink.*
VOLITION: *I am going to concentrate on my breath and the sounds outside.*
COMPASSION: *Good idea.*

Twenty minutes had passed, and it was at this point I concluded that Daphne was not going to turn up. This is okay and can happen (not just to me, but to all therapists). It's called a frustrating no-show. If you ever bail on your therapist, just know that their initial feeling is worry for you. They hope that you're okay, then they secretly mutter a curse as an outlet for their hate for you. Obviously, I'm joking—the hate is saved for themselves. No-shows are frustrating, but that temporary frustration is almost always outweighed by genuine concern for a patient's well-being.

To fill the Daphne-shaped hole in my therapy room, I watched some funny dog videos on YouTube, as well as emotional moments from the movie *Hook,* then closed my laptop and started to pack up so I could head home for the afternoon. I pressed the button for the elevator and watched the illuminated floor number count up as it climbed toward me. The doors opened and . . . my jaw dropped to the floor.

Unveiled like a prize on a nineties game show was one of the most striking-looking people I had ever seen. She was also instantly recognizable. She was A-list royalty, a celebrity, an award-winning actor, a person who had starred in some of my favorite TV shows and movies. She was . . . well . . . I couldn't possibly say. I wish I could tell you who was really meandering the corridors of my office building in Salford, but confidentiality ensures that it's just "Daphne" for this book. What the hell was she doing here and why on earth was she on my floor?

Daphne: Hey, Josh, I'm so sorry I'm late. I have an appointment with you that I think I have missed.

ANALYTICAL: *Fuck.*
ANXIETY: *Fuck.*
BIOLOGY: *Fuck.*

COMPASSION: *Fuck.*
CRITIC: *Fuck.*
DETECTIVE: *Fuck.*
EMPATHY: *Fuck.*
INTUITION: *Fuck.*
IRREVERENCE: *LOL.*
SAVIOR: *Fuck.*
TRIGGER: *Fuck.*
VOLITION: *Fuck.*

The Origins of Anxiety

I get asked a lot where I think anxiety "comes from." Anxiety is our body's *threat* response; it is a powerful overriding mechanism that switches us into *fight, flight, or freeze* mode, just in case a "threat" is imminent. What that threat might be is subjective to the individual. It can be a quite literal threat, such as an axe-wielding maniac charging toward us. It can be a threat to our self-esteem, such as failing to give a good presentation or failing an exam. Or it can be a social threat, such as the fear of being pushed away, rejected, or humiliated. Or it could be a world-famous actor arriving at my practice unannounced, nearly forty-five minutes late for her appointment. Whatever the threat, the anxious mind likes to look after us by filling us with the overwhelming feeling of *doubt*. When we doubt, we stop what we are doing and give the potential threat attention, so we can attack it, solve it, or avoid it.

This threat-response mechanism was superhelpful for our ancestors—like, seriously needed. They would have been screwed without it. Our ancestors grew up with a lot of predators prowling around, such as lions and wolves. Our ancestors weren't built to fight these predators in one-to-one combat, so instead, humans copied the meerkat by evolving a threat response that *preempted* danger. Like a meerkat, they would channel their threat response into scanning the horizon for dangers. This way they could notice predators first and have the advantage of planning the first move. Our ancestors could decide to walk around the pride of lions without alerting them, or forge spears and sneak up on them to attack and collect stock for the evening's *Lion King*–themed barbecue. Similarly, if our ancestors suspected that something dangerous might run out of a cave to attack them, then their threat response triggered a doubt mechanism that fixated their gaze on the entrance to the cave as they walked past it. Better to be one step ahead, right?

What I find remarkable is that, despite all the changes to our modern lifestyles, this part of our brain has never evolved. The very same threat response exists in our brains today. Threats themselves, however, have modernized. Of course, there are still predators and dangers around, but we live in a comparatively safe society where the focus of our anxious attention is on more conceptual things. The lions have been replaced with worrying about achieving, not being enough, placating others, and making sure we are presentable. The cave our ancestors fixated on has become our well-being, or relationships, our careers, or where we place ourselves in our own existential mind map. The brain mechanism remains the same, but the threat is different.

It's also been theorized that the reason the critical judgment of others feels so terrifying to us is that being rejected, ostracized, and abandoned posed a very real threat to our ancestors. Within tribes, people pleasing was an essential trait for remaining within the community, where every member relied on every other. Safety came from being part of a collective. It was advantageous to worry about what the leader of the tribe thought and felt, just in case they might be angry enough to banish us from the security of the tribe. Today this threat mechanism still fires off for everyone, but often within the confines of an office, second-guessing emails from the boss, not being able to relax at home, or finding it difficult to say no to people. Ultimately, the threat response has a part to play in social connections, as well as equipping us to deal with big, scary threats.

2
Levi

As the elevator doors opened a massive, intimidating man stretched his hand out to me. I met his handshake and allowed him to compress my bones and tendons to within an atom's space of each other. I tried not to show how much this hurt—an old shame of mine derived from a lifetime of growing up revering emotionless "masculinity."

Levi: All right, pal, I'm Levi.

ANXIETY: *This guy is scary.*

Josh: Hi, Levi. Welcome to my practice. Come with me—I'll show you which room I'm in.

I walked down the corridor alongside this giant and noticed an array of tattoo art over his forearm and neck. Some were faded, but the tattoo on his forearm was fresh, still covered in cling film. Levi walked with authority but with an air of well-I-suppose-I-must resignation, like a bouncer walking over to a young lad he's about to eject from the bar.

ANALYTICAL: *I can see he's clenching and unclenching his fists.*
CRITIC: *He's taking up so much space—you're going to end up mashed against the wall!*
EMPATHY: *He must be nervous, and people display nerves in different ways. It's not personal.*

We stepped into my office and I gestured for Levi to take a seat.

Levi: Which chair do *you* sit in?
Josh: I usually sit in the one next to the window, but feel free to sit wherever you like.
Levi: I think I'll have *your* seat.

ANALYTICAL: *A power move.*
DETECTIVE: *He feels threatened.*

Josh: Yeah, sure. Feel free to take some cushions. Make yourself comfy.

Levi sank himself into my chair and slid low, so that he was almost lying down. He clasped his hands over his stomach and rolled his head to gaze out the window. He clearly wasn't comfortable but was trying his best to convey the message that he didn't feel threatened in the slightest.

Levi: So, when you gonna start reading my mind? Tell me all my problems are because Daddy didn't hug me?

Josh: *(mildly chuckling)* It doesn't quite work like that. I can't read minds, unfortunately. A psychotherapist's main job is to listen and provide a safe space.

IRREVERENCE: *It's always the parents.*
ANALYTICAL: *Perhaps.*
DETECTIVE: *We obviously need to know more—will you guys shut up?*

Levi got back to his feet and began to walk around the office. He started to pick up objects from my giant IKEA shelving unit and hold them up to the light.

Levi: What's this?

Josh: That's a little sculpture of a buffalo I picked up in Zambia when I was younger.

Levi: Why have you got it in here? Trying to show off your "gap year"?

DETECTIVE: *He's trying to intimidate you.*
ESCAPIST: *I really want to get out of here.*
COMPASSION: *You've got this, just carry on.*

Josh: It's more a reminder for me that I have overcome my own fears and challenges.

He glanced at me, raising an eyebrow, while turning the sculpture in his hands.

Levi: *(smirking)* That, and I bet you thought it looks good in this fancy office. I know pretense when I see it.

ANALYTICAL: *Use this as an inroad into starting a personal dialogue.*

Josh: Are you good at spotting pretense?

Levi: In my line of work, you see it every night. You see it in the body language, the nonsense that comes out of people's mouths when they stroll up to the door, coked up in their rented outfits and hired cars. You can easily spot those with money and those on . . . borrowed money.

He sat down.

Levi: I'm head of security at Seneka. Biggest and oldest nightclub in the northern district. Glorified doorman. Bouncer of the bouncers.

He glanced out the window.

Levi: Fourteen years I've been there. The stuff I've seen you wouldn't believe.

Josh: I know it fairly well. I spent time there on student nights back when I was studying.

Levi: Yeah, well, I don't remember you. Don't expect me to. I see thousands of faces every week. Thousands of drunken, pilled-up faces. Did you ever get chucked out?

Josh: Thankfully not.

Levi: Good job you didn't . . . We don't do this anymore, but years ago there was an alley we took misbehaving "clientele" to if they caused trouble inside the club. We called it the Concrete Court, which was this hidden dark area behind some bins, where swift justice was served on those who wronged. We also *confiscated* illicit materials in the, er . . . name of public safety.

DETECTIVE: *Something tells me those drugs were not handed in to the police.*

Josh: Sounds like a lot of responsibility.

Levi: Well, you can't do a lot of that vigilante, sweet-justice stuff anymore. This new generation is pretty much untouchable. It used to be that a quick roughing up of someone misbehaving meant they never did anything bad again. Now, every night, *we* are the ones on trial. Trial by social media. All because we didn't get a bloomin' pronoun correct when asking for ID! Can't call someone "love" without being labeled a . . . what's it called . . . ? A misogynist.

Levi paused. Despite feeling anxious, I decided to model a relaxed posture in the hope that he would mirror it. Surprisingly, it seemed to work. He took a deep breath.

Levi: How does this work then? This therapy stuff?

EMPATHY: *It's hard to lower your guard when you feel threatened.*
COMPASSION: *Well done, Levi.*
ANXIETY: *Still shitting ourselves here, lad.*

Josh: It depends on each person, really. I always suggest using the first session for us to get to know each other and hear what you would like help with. Together—and only if you'd like to—we can paint a picture of what's going on and we can work together to map out a way forward . . . all in a safe, confidential space.

Levi looked at me with what seemed like a mixture of intrigue and frustration. Suddenly, from nowhere, he snapped.

Levi: Well, of course it's safe. How would it not be safe? Not as if you're going to attack me, is it? For fuck's . . .

He stopped and immediately diverted his aggression into standing up again and walking over to the window. He sighed and looked down at the street below.

Levi: I, er . . . I didn't mean to swear. I hate swearing.

EMPATHY: *He probably hears it all the time.*

Josh: It's okay. You probably hear it all the time.
Levi: Yes. It's vile.

I noticed that my anxiety level lowered the more I spoke to Levi. It's natural to be anxious with any new client, due to the unknown. I still felt uneasy, but the more I observed and listened, the more I could see a man who was burdened with an inner conflict. I respected him for being here, willing to face it.

INTUITION: *Allow some quiet to fill the space.*

After staring out the window, lost in thought, Levi walked over to my desk. I remained seated and patiently waited for him to reengage. He seemed calmer. Despite that, I still found him terrifying. He loomed over my desk and started to adjust the cling film that was wrapped around his fresh tattoo.

Levi: Do you have tattoos?
Josh: Just the one.
Levi: What is it?
Josh: It's an Irish Gaelic phrase that means "protection of the gods upon my brother."
Levi: Are you religious?
Josh: No, not really.
Levi: Then why have you got religious scripture on you?
Josh: Because I was eighteen and thought I was cool. It also placated my very Catholic grandma.

ANALYTICAL: *Be careful not to share so much of yourself. You're here for him, not you.*
INTUITION: *Go with it. He asked.*

Levi remained facing my desk, his back toward me.

Levi: This new tattoo is my favorite. Mal did a great job on it.
Josh: I noticed it when you arrived. What does it represent?
Levi: It represents Gaunab. Death personified. The embodiment of evil. It's from southwestern African mythology.

He paused and glanced at his raised arm.

Levi: He's really got the shading spot on.

DETECTIVE: *I wonder why he has such morose imagery tattooed upon his skin.*
ANALYTICAL: *Hmm, tattoos don't always have to contain deep meaning.*
IRREVERENCE: *Remember the "carpe diem" tattoo on that girl in college?*

Josh: Is there an inspiration behind it?

Levi dropped his arm to his side and locked his gaze on my desk lamp. He still had his back to me. I remained quiet and, as weird as it sounds, I'm sure I could hear the spinning cogs of his intense thinking. It appeared I'd asked an absolute cog whirler.

Levi: I . . . er . . . I liked the symbol . . . er . . .

From what seemed like out of nowhere, I could hear some gentle tapping on the desk, but Levi's arms remained by his side. I could only see his back, which was making gentle, stuttered, convulsing motions. Then it hit me: The tapping on the desk wasn't coming from his fingers but from falling tears. Levi was crying. The big scary man who emerged from the elevator was now silently sobbing.

COMPASSION: *He has a lot going on here. I feel for him.*
SAVIOR: *I'm going to find out what's troubling him and take it all away.*

Levi made no move to dab his tears; he let them flow from his face, and I did not intervene. He seemed to need this space, and I let him have it.

3
High School
Presentation Evening

When you become a psychotherapist who writes books, it is possible that you can be seen as someone who is "successful"—but also a cheap (or, let's be honest, "free") alternative to forking out for a motivational speaker at your old high school. A sea of extremely bored eyes looked up at me at the lectern in the assembly hall. My old head of year was still there, astonished that I was in a position of success and responsibility when he could remember suspending me for selling cigarettes out of the classroom window; but he was also strangely proud to see me back and doing well. It was almost like my appearance back there reignited a long-extinguished optimism in him about troublesome lads still managing to get somewhere in life—like he *did* have an impact in some way, which he did, to be fair.

My opening gambit was interrupted by the violent, catarrh-ridden coughing of a parent about four rows back, which only added to the anxiety I was already feeling at the blank faces in front of me. The week before, I had been paid a lot of money to speak at a corporate event where many of the attendees had read my self-help books. After that talk I was swarmed with enthusiastic questions and flattery and treated to a meal with lots of cocktails, which I wish I could say I turned down. This day there was a comical irony in giving a talk at my own high school where hardly anyone seemed interested in who I was or what I might say.

I stumbled on my words, awkwardly fiddled with the mic, then re-gathered myself. "Hey, everyone, my name is Joshua Fletcher and I used to be a student here. I grew up around the corner on the Abbey Lane estate. I'm so happy to be the guest speaker at your presentation evening."

Heads perked up in interest. The coughing stopped. Mentioning the Abbey Lane estate never failed. My old high school is situated in the middle of two giant public housing buildings—Abbey Lane being one of them. I had their interest. I was one of them. I was more than just a guy in a navy Primark suit that had seen more funerals than celebratory events. I was ready to drop inspiring truth bombs worthy of any premium LinkedIn account. The games could now begin.

I pontificated with some spiel about how I'd come from nothing and made something of myself. Standard stuff. The deputy head had made me promise beforehand not to mention my behavior record at school, which was understandable, as they obviously didn't want to imply that breaking rules in school leads to a prosperous and successful life. So I abandoned the stories of stealing and copying the school master key, "borrowing" science equipment, drinking beer in the woods, downloading nude pictures, fighting, and being caught cheating in exams. The whole truth just wasn't needed here. Instead, I spoke about how this rough-ass comprehensive school had taught me compassion, self-belief, a moral code, and a lasting feeling of common sense, which it had, brilliantly. Unfortunately, the UK Office of Standards in Education didn't have a metric of success to measure this at the time, so the school was often publicly criticized and underappreciated. However, I didn't forget. There are some things that exist beyond the curriculum that lie in the beating hearts of the caring people who run a school.

A strange sense of duty drew me back to my hometown, where I felt I needed to complete the wholesome story arc of a troubled youth turned tragic-but-noble therapist who "reaches the kids" with his words.

At the end of my school talk, a teenaged boy enthusiastically approached the stage. He presented me with the first page of the event leaflet, with the words "Special Guest Speaker: Joshua Fletcher, Psychotherapist & Author" but with his own annotations. The boy had cleverly deduced that, with the addition of three simple slashes between the letters, the word "psychotherapist" can be separated into the words "Psycho the Rapist." Proud of his handiwork, he just wanted to show it off. Nothing to do with my speech. No lasting words of inspiration. Fair play to the lad. In that brief moment, it felt like it was good to be home.

4
Zahra

My first session with Zahra started in dramatic fashion. A woman about my age was crawling on all fours toward the office sofa, her long dark hair almost reaching the floor, while her exasperated mother tried to explain the situation:

Faiza: She has panic attacks, you see. She is having one now. She hasn't left the house properly in months. I have had to drag her here! She . . . she's like this every day!

Zahra finally reached the sofa, then rested against it, gasping for breath. She had tears running down her face and she was clearly experiencing some form of terror. I crouched down to face her, trying to meet her eyes, although it was difficult as she kept rolling her head against the lip of the sofa.

COMPASSION: *Extra gentle here; she is suffering.*

Josh: Hey, Zahra, I'm Josh. I know you are panicking right now, but this is okay. You are safe. Your body will come to a state of calm soon enough. I know it feels like something awful is abou—

She lurched forward and startled me.

Zahra: Why won't this feeling go away?! Please, make it stop! I . . . I think I need an ambulance!
Faiza: *(exasperated)* We have called an ambulance so many times, Zahra. You are okay.
Zahra: Easy for you to say that, Mum! Arrgggghhh, make it stop!

The mother glanced at me apologetically. Zahra lifted herself onto the sofa and began to hyperventilate. She had one hand on her chest and the other on her forehead. Her legs trembled and she wheezed as she tried to breathe.

Faiza: I'm sorry. She's not normally like this. What's happening to her?

Josh: Zahra, do you have any medical conditions I need to know about?

Zahra: *(trying to catch her breath)* No . . . I'm supposed to be a doctor, yet I . . . I don't know what's wrong with me. I've . . . done blood work and had my heart scanned . . . I think . . . I think I have broken my brain. God, I think I'm losing control—I'm going to be committed. Oh God, please help. Make it stop!

ANALYTICAL: *Yeah, this is a panic attack.*

INTUITION: *Get her to focus away from the feelings and sensations.*

ANALYTICAL: *Perhaps she is stuck in the panic cycle?*

Faiza: We searched for anxiety experts on the internet and found you. Can you help?! I will pay anything. Please help my daughter.

Zahra continued to hyperventilate between sobs. She was really struggling. She turned to me pleadingly. Desperate.

EMPATHY: *She wants you to take it all away.*

SAVIOR: *I WANT to take it all away.*

Josh: Okay. Everything is okay. Right. Here's what we're going to do . . . Zahra, try to look at me. You are okay. You don't need to do anything. I assure you that this feeling will pass. What you are experiencing is safe. It's very normal for the body. You don't need to do anything other than keep your attention on me or anything in this room, the best you can.

Zahra nodded and placed her hands on the floor to support herself. I looked to her mother.

Josh: It's okay, Mum. We will be all right now. If you come back toward the end of the hour, that'll be great.

Reluctantly, Faiza nodded and headed toward the door after an anxious look at her daughter. Zahra was still hyperventilating but seemed a tad more composed. As her mother closed the door gently behind her, Zahra finally looked up at me.

Zahra: I'm . . . I'm sorry. I . . . I'm such a mess.

Josh: You have nothing to be sorry for. Thank you for taking time out today to come and see me. Would you like some water? The adrenaline will pass soon, don't worry.

CRITIC: *Telling someone having a panic attack not to worry—good one, Joshy.*

Zahra: How do you know it will pass? What if I'm like this forever? What if I'm going crazy?!

EMPATHY: *Ah, I remember these feelings well.*
INTUITION: *Use that then. But don't make it about you. Be clever with it.*
ANALYTICAL: *You are displaying a relaxed demeanor, this should help.*

Josh: Well, you don't look crazy to me. Have you had those "what if?" thoughts before?

Zahra laughed nervously and picked up a cushion to squeeze.

Zahra: Err . . . pretty much every day?
Josh: Oh . . . that sounds fun.

ANALYTICAL: *Risky . . .*
IRREVERENCE: *Love it.*

Zahra: *(smiling slightly)* Oh, it's been a huge party every day at my house. I've been a qualified junior doctor for just four months and I've already been signed off. And no, I didn't sign my own sick note.

I passed Zahra a glass of water and she took a shaky sip.

Zahra: Is it normal to feel like this? I can feel my heart thudding, and my brain is whirling at a thousand miles an hour. Surely, it's not normal? I asked my doctor colleagues and some even ran tests, and they tell me I'm all right, but how can I be all right? This isn't normal. I am not

normal. I've gone and done it—finally. I've sent myself crazy. It was
bound to happen eventually.

Josh: I wouldn't say panicking is out of the ordinary. You seem pretty sane
to me.

Zahra: Pretty sane?!

Josh: I can't say for sure that you are sane. I mean . . . you might steal my
plants or something.

She looked at me in utter bewilderment.

ANALYTICAL: *Her attention is becoming more external. Keep going; this
is working.*
DETECTIVE: *Her interest is shifting from evaluating her symptoms to
evaluating you.*

Zahra: I read an article that you became a therapist because you
experienced panic attacks . . . is that right? After something tragic
happened to you or something.

Josh: Yeah, that's right.

Zahra: Well, how do you know what I am experiencing is panic? It's not like
you're in my head or can see it.

Josh: Good question. Shall we do the magic panic checklist?

Zahra: What's "magic" about it?

Josh: Nothing, I just like to exaggerate as much as anxiety likes to. Got to
know what you're facing and match it.

In my office I have a large portable whiteboard that rolls on wheels.
It's a supply teacher's dream. I stood up enthusiastically and wheeled over
the whiteboard, trying to keep Zahra's attention away from her panic
symptoms to break the panic cycle. I started to doodle my commentary
on the whiteboard—a habit from once being a schoolteacher.

Josh: Panic attacks, or panic disorder, occur when we have loads of panic
attacks, then begin to *fear* those panic attacks. It puts us in a "fear cycle" . . .

Zahra: Who'd have thought that mansplaining was the answer to my woes?

Josh: *(chuckles)* Just go with me for a minute. You have told me this happens
pretty much every day, so I suspect you're in something called the "panic
cycle" or the "loop of peaking anxiety."

I drew a poorly illustrated loop diagram on the whiteboard.

Josh: It always starts with an initial panic attack—the "big one." The one where you often feel like you're about to lose all sense of control. You usually dissociate, detach, feel loads of physical symptoms, and your brain just feels like it's on fast-forward. It basically scares us so badly that we don't want it to happen again. Do you remember your first panic attack?

Zahra: Yes. It was at a medical conference. I was invited to present my research findings and I . . .

She became teary.

Zahra: I just left. I just went home like a coward. The whole room felt weird. I suddenly became hot and felt so spaced out. Every fiber of my being was telling me to run. And that's what I did. I ran outside and I called my mum. She rushed over and picked me up and has been worried about me ever since. I had to move back in with her because I can't cope on my own.

Josh: She seems to care about you a lot.

Zahra: She does. She's been through a lot. I hate burdening her like this.

Josh: Is Dad there too?

ANALYTICAL: *Presumptive.*
CRITIC: *Idiot.*

Zahra gazed to the side, still grasping the cushion.

Zahra: No.

DETECTIVE: *Abandoned? Dead?*
INTUITION: *Bring your attention back. This isn't necessary.*
COMPASSION: *That's her story to share. She'll share it if she wants.*

Zahra: I suppose that was my "big" panic attack. Ever since that day I haven't been myself. I just felt like I couldn't do it, you know? I just had so much stuff going on and I didn't want to humiliate myself in front of my peers and fellow medical professionals.

Josh: Mhm.

Zahra: It's pathetic, really. I'm supposed to be the person helping and curing other people. I can't even cure myself. I just make the people around me worry, which isn't helping their health either.

Zahra's body language seemed to loosen, and she slumped into a calmer posture. She looked tired. The adrenaline seemed to be passing. Her anxiety turned to an almost palpable sadness.

Josh: Well, there's nothing to say you'll be having panic attacks forever. I can see that your panic is slightly easing now. Have you noticed?

Zahra: It's calmed a bit, yeah. I still want to run out the door and scream.

Josh: Well, at the risk of sounding patronizing, you have done really well to tolerate the awful thoughts and sensations and stay here talking to me. I appreciate that. Notice how your anxiety lowered without running from the situation?

Zahra: Yeah . . . it has. But it'll just come back again later. It always does. I just feel . . . hopeless. I feel ill.

Josh: I have hope that everyone who walks into this room can get to a place where they'd like to be. I also don't see panic attacks as a sign of illness.

Zahra: Well, according to the *Diagnostic and Statistical Manual of Mental Disorders*, fifth edition, panic disorder *is* an illness.

IRREVERENCE: *Ha! You got burned by the doc!*

Josh: True . . . But also, research suggests that panic disorder has a very high recovery rate when working with it correctly. I personally see it as a phobia. A fear of fear itself. That's why I don't see it entirely as an illness.

Zahra paused and seemed to try to catch a thought. Something I'd said had resonated with her. She flattened the cushion on her lap and sat forward slightly. She looked at my diagram of the panic cycle on my whiteboard and squinted in thought.

Zahra: I see. I fear having a panic as bad as I did at the medical conference, don't I?

I said nothing.

Zahra: Yeah . . . I panicked, I retreated. I went home to work it all out and feel better. I haven't managed to feel better. I just keep panicking every day, but I do fear panic attacks. I'm constantly looking out for them all the time.

Josh: That's called threat monitoring. More specifically, "internal threat monitoring."

I put down my finger air quotes.

Zahra: I do that all the time. I wake up and check myself: my symptoms, my blood pressure, my blood oxygen. I am searching and scanning for my signs of panic all the time.

ANALYTICAL: *She's developing a metacognitive awareness of her thoughts and behaviors relating to her panic phobia.*
EMPATHY: *It feels illuminating, but remember, recognizing this can also be overwhelming for her.*

Josh: How often do you avoid doing things just in case you panic?
Zahra: Every day. Everything is about the anxiety.
Josh: And how often do you try to think your way out of anxiety?
Zahra: Every day!
Josh: While we're playing anxiety bingo, how often do you misinterpret physical symptoms as the first sign of your imminent demise?
Zahra: Oh my God. I've been convinced these heart palpitations are the sign of a heart defect, despite having three heart scans and being checked over by my friend who is a specialist. I also think these whooshing sensations are a sign of adrenal cancer.

She looked at me with renewed interest. I had her full attention, which was helped by her panic passing.

Josh: Do you feel that anxiety, or worrying about panic, is the central focus of your life? Do you plan around it? Factor it into all plans before committing to a decision?
Zahra: You're reading the blurb to my autobiography. That's been my mind for the past two months.

Josh: Well, that's the magic list completed. Congratulations, it sounds like you're struggling with panic disorder.

Zahra: I still don't understand what's "magic" about the list, but it does feel comforting to have my thoughts and feelings recognized as something that happens to others. Not that I want others to suffer; it just makes me feel less alone. Can you help me?

EMPATHY: *I remember what that feels like.*
SAVIOR: *I want to save her. I want to help another person with their anxiety.*

She looked hopeful. Expectant.

TRIGGER: *Responsibility.*
BIOLOGY: *I'm going to immediately release lots of cortisol.*
CRITIC: *You are fucking shit with responsibility, you absolute charlatan of a man.*
COMPASSION: *Don't engage with this. Your value is immeasurable.*
CRITIC: *Is it? This woman is a doctor. Who are you?!*
INTUITION: *Back in the room. Now. It's not about you.*

Josh: I can try to help you to help yourself. Psychoeducation is superimportant for any anxiety condition. I can teach you what I know and support you, but eventually you've got to do the hard work yourself to stop panic attacks and get back on the right track. Do you think that's something you'd like to do with me?

Zahra: Yes. Let's do it.

Panic Attacks

A panic attack is when we suddenly feel an overwhelming sense that something awful is about to happen. It begins with a rush of adrenaline and the stress hormone cortisol, which can give us an intense "whoosh" feeling that immediately grabs our attention. We are then overtaken by a feeling that something catastrophic is imminent, which is then followed by a flood of very loud "what if?" thoughts, such as "What if I'm dying?" "What if I collapse?" "What if I'm going crazy?" "What if this feeling never ends?!" to name a few. This is usually accompanied by an intense urge to escape wherever we are.

To add to this fun cocktail, panic attacks can also be served with an array of weird physical symptoms, such as a pounding heart, derealization (when we feel detached from ourselves and reality), a tight chest, sweating, struggling to catch our breath, digestion issues, sensitivity to light, dizziness, and pins and needles in our extremities. There are many more symptoms, but these tend to be the most common.

Panic attacks can be terrifying, particularly to those who are unaware of what is happening. People who endure panic attacks are incredibly resilient; they are not having them out of choice. Panic is also not a sign of weakness, and anyone who informs you otherwise is, in my professional opinion, ~~an idiot~~ an ill-informed person who needs just as much psychoeducation as those who are suffering the panic attacks.

The Modality Wars

The only difference between a psychotherapist and a counselor is that "psychotherapist" has five syllables and sounds way cooler. It's why "psychotherapist" is plastered all over my website, as opposed to peasanty "counselor." Either way, both can be called a therapist, so next time you see someone call themselves a psychotherapist, just know they're as pretentious as me.

Therapists are some of the most amazing people I have ever met, both personally and professionally. However, they can also be nauseatingly self-righteous and annoying. There's a lot about the world of therapists that the general public doesn't know about, but we exist in numbers and in collectives, usually found impulsively spending money that we don't have on new training or trying not to be too "counselor-y" when interacting with loved ones. Let me invite you to peek into the mysterious staff room where we all congregate, smoke cigars, and scheme against our clients (we don't really; smoking is bad for you).

Before entering the staff room, you must know that a therapist must be trained in at least one *therapy modality* to call themselves a therapist. A therapy modality is a school of thought, or training philosophy, that therapy students practice; upon completion of a reputable course they can be awarded the title of therapist and, in many countries, granted a license to practice. There are many different types of therapy modality, which means there are many different types of therapist. For example, you may be a therapist trained in cognitive behavioral therapy (CBT); a person-centered therapist (PC) trained in humanistic counseling; a psychodynamic therapist (picture Freud); a transactional analysis therapist (TA); a metacognitive therapist (MCT)—the list goes on.

It's confusing as hell for the general public, which is why one of the biggest tragedies in the world of mental health, in my opinion, is the assumption that every therapist knows what they're doing. They don't. They can only draw upon the modality in which they are trained. Their knowledge is limited. Sometimes it works, sometimes it doesn't. The client also needs to connect with the therapist. In my opinion, when it comes to the therapy modality and the therapeutic relationship, it *must* be a match. Yet, if I had a penny for every time I've heard the phrase "I've tried therapy and it didn't work for me," I'd have around £20. We're in a global mental health crisis, and unfortunately many people feel disillusioned after their first attempt at therapy. To me, saying this is the equivalent of saying "I tried sports and I didn't like it" when all you played was lawn bowling, once. Most people are unaware that the world of therapy has a breadth of choice and different therapy modalities, which isn't helpful considering that it takes a lot of energy and bravery to decide to seek help in the first place, and there is no guarantee that the first modality one finds will be the right fit.

Within society, you may notice that people generally drift toward a certain tribe. This tribalism can be seen most noticeably at football matches, within an office environment, in politics, arguing on Twitter, and so on. It also exists in the world of therapy. Training to be a therapist takes a hell of a lot out of you. I respect anyone who has been through the rigorous nature of a therapist training program. It requires you to challenge yourself and your beliefs, and the process seeps into your personal life in a way that's impossible to fence off. A therapy course tests your resilience by challenging the very building blocks of who you are, which can be terrifying. If you are a therapist reading this, then a sincere "well done" from me. You made it.

Training in any modality requires you to give your all to this way of practice, but in doing so it can create a whole world of cognitive dissonance when trying to view the world a different way, especially through the lens of another modality. A lot of therapy training providers are run by passionate and inspiring modality "purists," who believe that most psychological suffering can be solved using the one therapeutic approach in which they personally trained and are emotionally invested. For example, someone trained in the psychodynamic approach would most likely believe that the works of Carl Jung and Melanie Klein should be used to explore the unconscious processes that underpin behavior ("Stop trying to shag your mum and dad"). Whereas therapists who train in Carl Rogers's person-centered approach believe that the core purpose of therapy is for the therapist to facilitate the client's ability to self-actualize ("I'm going to sit here and say nothing till you speak"). Cognitive behavioral therapy (CBT) (Beckian and Third-Wave) contrasts heavily with person-centered by offering to deal with problems by focusing on current thoughts, feelings, and patterns in behaviors ("Let's conceptualize your suffering into numbers for my computer"). Then you've got transactional analysis, which looks at stances on intimacy and conflict ("My inner child wants a milkshake"). And let's not forget the "trauma-informed," who like to play detective and pin everything on a vague concept of trauma that lies beyond the definition of PTSD because they once read Bessel van der Kolk's *The Body Keeps the Score*. The list goes on.

You can't really expect anyone to understand the breadth of therapy available even when they are compos mentis, never mind if they're suffering from mind-crippling mental health issues. What you're left with is a potluck, roll-of-the-dice approach when someone finally decides to pluck up the courage to seek therapy. I wonder which modality they'll end up with. Ultimately, it often lies in the hands of the therapist and their chosen modality. Sometimes it works and it works well. At other times it does not. Yet *all* modalities promise to help with your anxiety, anger, and depression. The heartbreaking thing is that when a particular form of therapy doesn't work, the client is often left feeling like it's their fault, or that they're beyond help in some way. A good therapist is one who can recognize the limits of their own knowledge and modality, rather than blindly believing that their approach is the savior of all suffering; and one who is secure enough to understand that a client's lack of progress is not necessarily due to the client's failure to engage with the modality. Plenty of these therapists exist, and they are excellent people. However, I'd be lying if I said every therapist was like this.

When you stare into the open door of the therapy staff room, squint your eyes and note that, despite the smiling front, we all secretly despise each other. Okay, I exaggerate—we don't. But we *are* passionate about how much we have invested in our own pathway to becoming a therapist. So much so that once a year we all meet up in a field, don our modality colors, and fight to the bitter death—we call it *The Junger Games*. The last remaining modality color is crowned the "one true modality" (last year it was hypnotherapy). If you would like a betting tip, the trauma-informed are favorites to win this year.

Now, you're probably thinking: So which modality color does Josh wear? Well, this is where things get complicated.

Not every therapist is involved in *The Junger Games*. Watching all this carnage unfold on the therapy battlefield is merely entertainment for the high lords of therapy, the important people. These are called the "integrative therapists," and they are the most self-important of them all. And that is what I am, of course: trained in humanistic counseling and cognitive behavioral therapy so far, and excited to study more in the future.

Integrative therapists are counselors who have studied in more than one modality and, in theory, can choose to mix and match approaches to best suit their client. Integrative therapists believe they're above modality purists because, let's face it, we are. We'll watch on from our golden thrones while life coaches refill our goblets, then we command said life coaches to curl into human footstools for our leisure.

On a serious note, if you're seeking a therapist, or seeing one now, ask them which modality (or modalities) they have trained in. Some will tell you straightaway without being asked the question. Ask them what the aim of their therapy is and what their modality is all about. You can check if this aligns with what you'd like from therapy. There are loads of brilliant therapists trained in every modality—just make sure you feel like it's a match.

5
Harry: Portal

June 2008

Josh: That was the worst match of my life.

My little brother rolled his eyes.

Harry: I'm pretty sure I've seen you play worse.
Josh: I swear it's fixed. Maybe it's our internet connection.
Harry: No . . . you just suck at *Halo*.

I glanced over my shoulder and caught his cheeky grin. I couldn't help but laugh. I slid the controller across the desk in defeat.

Harry: Wanna play something else? Mum bought me *Portal 2* last week.
Josh: *Portal 2*? Never heard of it and I didn't play the first game. I'm also gamed out.
Harry: Oh, come on! You'll like it. It's a couch co-op . . .
Josh: I do like a couch co-op. Is there gratuitous violence that Mum would disapprove of?
Harry: No. There's no fighting. It's a puzzle game.
Josh: Well then, count me out . . .

Harry looked disappointed. I hated to see him sad.

Josh: Fine . . . pass me the controller.
Harry: I think you'll like it. We have to work together to solve the puzzles and to complete it.

The screen lit up. We wheeled and bumped our chairs together, resuming our usual gaming spots. Before we could start, Mum burst into the room.

Mum: Why am I not surprised to see that there's still dirty dishes on the side!? Whose turn to wash up was it?

Harry and I pointed to each other.

Harry: But I walked the dog!

Mum looked at me, waiting for my plea.

Josh: Yeah, well . . . I—shit . . .
Mum: Joshua!
Harry: Can we just play a few games of *Portal,* please, Mum? I have to go to Dad's soon.
Josh: Yeah, Mum, it's *Portal 2*! We've been waiting years for this sequel!

She glared at me. Harry stifled a laugh.

Mum: As soon as his dad picks him up . . . dishes!
Josh: Okay, I will. Sorry.

Mum walked downstairs, and Harry set up the game.

Josh: Okay. What do we do?
Harry: We each have a portal gun that fires two different portals: an entrance portal and an exit portal.

Harry pressed a button and a yellow oval portal appeared on the screen.

Harry: The yellow portal is the entrance and . . .

He fired his portal gun again. This time a blue oval appeared.

Harry: This is the exit portal. If you jump through the yellow one, you teleport to where the blue portal is located.

Harry's character jumped through the yellow portal and warped to the other side of the screen. I moved my character to peek through the yellow portal.

Josh: Whoa. I can see you through the portal. That's so cool!

Harry moved his character to stand in front of the exit portal. Our characters stood and stared at each other. We looked like two animated portraits.

Josh: That's some amazing programming.

Harry: The goal of the game is to get to the exit portal. But we have to work together.

Josh: Okay . . . I'm in.

I jumped through the portal.

6
Noah

My usual new-client nervousness was kicking in. Noah was due to arrive in a few minutes. He had seemed very polite on the phone. I quickly changed my sweater, since, not for the first time, I had spilled mayonnaise down the front of it during lunch. I have an "emergency" drawer in my office that's designed for such situations. It has a hair-brush, deodorant, spare key, dustpan and brush, face wipes, and my last will and testament. It also contains a jar of mayonnaise.

There was a knock on the door. I opened it to reveal a well-dressed man in his twenties.

Josh: Hi, is it Noah?
Noah: Hello, Josh. Yes, it's me.
Josh: Please, come on in.

Noah followed me into my office. He removed his peacoat jacket and deli-cately hung it up on my coatrack. I gestured for him to take a seat on the sofa.

Josh: Can I get you a drink of water?
Noah: Yes, please.

When I returned I could see Noah fidgeting nervously with his cashmere sweater. He shook slightly as he took a sip of water. I took a seat opposite him.

Noah: Thank you.

EMPATHY: *He's nervous.*
COMPASSION: *Let's help to make him feel more comfortable.*

Josh: Is this your first time in therapy?
Noah: Oh . . . er . . . definitely not. I've had more therapy than, er . . . how does the idiom go? Hot dinners?

Josh: Not your first rodeo, then?

Noah: *(smiling)* No, it certainly is not.

Josh: How have you found therapy in the past?

Noah: Helpful. I think. To a certain extent, anyway. I much prefer it to trying to find peaceful solace on social media, which is where I have found myself scrolling for answers lately. A pointless pursuit, really. It just makes me feel more anxious, more alone.

Josh: I hear you. What did you find helpful about your previous experiences of therapy? It'll help me to get a better idea of how we can work together.

Noah put his glass of water down and grabbed a cushion tightly to his chest.

Noah: I liked having a safe place to talk. I liked being able to have a space that was private. Utterly confidential. This is entirely confidential, right?

Josh: Yes, of course. The only way I would have to break that confidentiality is if there was a threat to life or a serious crime had been committed.

DETECTIVE: *This hasn't reassured him. He has slightly flushed cheeks and he's avoiding eye contact.*

ANALYTICAL: *This seems to have made him feel uncomfortable.*

Noah: What do you mean, a "threat to life"?

Josh: If I believe that you or anyone else is in immediate danger. For example, if you were hinting at taking your own life, or you declared plans to kill somebody. Would you say you've felt like that recently?

ANXIETY: *I really hope he hasn't killed anyone.*

Noah: Oh . . . no. Nothing like that. I certainly don't intend to kill anyone.

Josh: And . . . what about harm to yourself?

Noah paused and looked out the window.

Noah: I have never planned to do anything like that. I do, however, have some personal traits that, er . . . have raised alarms in the past. I am not going to kill myself, but . . . are you sure this is confidential?

Josh: Yes.

Noah sat forward, and I noticed he was trembling. He slowly lifted one sleeve of his sweater to reveal a heavily scarred forearm. It looked calloused, blistered, and sore. I'd seen signs of self-harm before—I'd been trained to look for them—but he'd really done a number on his arm here and I'd be lying if I said I wasn't shocked.

ANXIETY: *Damn.*
COMPASSION: *This man has been suffering.*
EMPATHY: *It couldn't have been easy to show you this.*

Josh: Thanks for showing me. I appreciate your trust. Has any of this happened recently?

Noah slid his sleeve back down to his wrist, then rested his arms back on the cushion.

Noah: Last one was a few months ago. I, er . . . showed my last therapist and she seemed quite shocked. Then she announced that she felt that working with me fell outside the scope of her training. I felt a bit stupid, as I'd told her a significant amount about my personal life. Next thing I know, Mum and Dad are finding me a new therapist. And here I am.
Josh: Sounds like an abrupt way to end therapy.
Noah: Yeah. I liked her. I just felt even worse when I couldn't go anymore. Like I was beyond saving. It was quite disheartening.

He looked at me for the first time.

Noah: Are you going to turn me down? It's okay if you do. The reason I showed you this is that I don't want to have to go through everything again only to be referred on.

SAVIOR: *I can save you! I'm a kick-ass therapist!*
VOLITION: *Remember your professional boundaries.*
ANALYTICAL: *You know next to nothing about this young man.*

Josh: Well, I've certainly not seen any reason why we couldn't work together. I believe we all carry scars in some form or other. Also, I believe scars can be seen as a symbol of restoration, because . . . well . . . they are.

CRITIC: *Don't turn into one of those "healing" types you see on Instagram.*
COMPASSION: *Ignore them. Just go with it.*

Noah nodded. He started to calm a bit.

Noah: Do you have scars?

The question surprised me.

Josh: I, er . . . yeah, I do. Some physical, some mental. I think the majority of people have at least one form of scar.
Noah: What caused yours?

VOLITION: *Redirect.*

Josh: Certain things that happen in life. Remember, this room is a space for you to talk about *your* needs. While I'll answer questions, just bear in mind that I will keep a professional boundary as your therapist.
Noah: It always baffles me that therapists expect you to divulge everything—to the core of your soul—yet they somewhat hide from sharing their own. It's a bit of a disparaging power dynamic.
Josh: I can empathize with that. I think there's always a power dynamic in the therapy room, though, because one person is getting paid for being an "expert"—even though we're not—and the other is asked to be vulnerable. Also, if a therapist started exploring their own pain with their client, then they would be failing at their own job, which is to facilitate a space entirely for you. My job is to earn your trust through my professionalism, not through revealing all aspects of me personally. I believe we can't have a safe space without boundaries—this applies to both of us.

Noah pondered for a moment, then seemed to accept my explanation.

Noah: Yes. It would also explain why I get frustrated with my friend Richard. Every time I have tried to open up to him in the past, the conversation always seems to end up being about him. If you've lost your grandma, then he's lost two. If you've got a cold, then he's got COVID. If your relative has cancer, then all his family have become lepers.

I chuckled.

Josh: I think we can all relate to knowing a Richard. If you choose to continue working with me, what would you like to get from therapy?

Noah: *(after a pause)* I want to feel brave enough to tell a secret that I've held for a long time. I've never told anyone. I feel I need to build to it, though. I feel like I'll fall apart if I release it.

DETECTIVE: *Interesting . . .*
EMPATHY: *Holding secrets can feel cumbersome and crippling.*

Josh: Okay. Well, if you ever feel safe to share it, then know that I would appreciate how much that would have meant to you.

Noah nodded. Then he relaxed into his chair.

Insta-therapy

Why have actual therapy when social media has all the answers? Where's the value in seeing a professional who has invested years of time in training to help people with complex needs, when you can scroll the deluge of misinformation on Instagram or TikTok? Of course, social media is free and therapy is often not, but hear me out on this one.

Not sure if your partner is a narcissist? Well, here's "Five Signs Your Partner Is a Narcissist" from someone completely unqualified, who's about to tell you how much your girlfriend is a narcissist while body popping to Harry Styles. Perhaps you're feeling sad at work? Well, this is obviously "trauma" from childhood, not the fact that you've probably got stressful things going on right now. Someone not agreeing with you? Well, according to Insta and TikTok, this is because you're being gaslit . . . by your gran (who's also a narcissist who's sleeping with your traumatized boyfriend). I know this only because it was at the end of a video telling me "I am enough," after which I was offered a link to an expensive coaching course that could make me, as my friend Drew Linsalata puts it, "more enougher."

In my professional opinion, there's a lot of mental health advice on social media that is not helpful, and I'd even go so far as to say it's counterproductive. I acknowledge how egocentric this sounds, given that I also provide advice on social media, but as an expert on anxiety who has studied hard and also lived through a lot of it, I can and have seen the neurotic vortex into which one can be sucked by social media.

My advice is not to lose your critical lens when browsing social media for mental health help. If someone is telling you to use ice cubes on your wrists to cure your panic attacks, step back and consider why this may not be a sustainable coping mechanism going forward. Don't just assume that your problems are due to "trauma" because you blink in the morning and people please in the evening. Trauma can be complex, and post-traumatic stress disorder (PTSD) should be identified through trained professionals, such as your doctor. If someone suggests that they have the secret answer to all of your woes in their Patreon subscription, then I'd really look carefully at what you're paying your money for. Don't let my grumpiness ruin your experience of social media, just be wary of misinformation.

7
Mayfield Depot: Manchester

July 2015

The walls of the portable toilet shook violently to the bass line of the music, a passing strobe light fragmented through the ceiling grate providing the only light. Someone banged on the door for the third time. I ignored it. My sense of gravity was skewed; I was heavily inebriated. Balancing this powder on my front-door key in limited light *and* with the whole booth shaking was a bit of a task, but I savored the challenge because I felt like an absolute hero—a god, even. My friend Amos shouted through the grate from the adjoining Portaloo:

Amos: Oi! You done with that bag yet? Don't drop it down the toilet like I did last time.
Josh: Yeah, one sec.

COMPASSION: *Do you not think you've done enough of this for tonight?*
ESCAPIST: *Ignore them. You deserve this. You work a hard job. People don't understand. Have more. Have as much as you like!*
BIOLOGY: *The exchange is all set up for you, sir.*

I lifted my front-door key to my nose and inhaled the powder vigorously through my right nostril. The smell of petrol and a sharp stinging sensation spread through my nasal cavity like the back draft of a raging fire. My eyes grew wide. The strobe light scanned through the grate once more.

IRREVERENCE: *This is what bags of rice must feel like at the self-service checkout.*

I immediately felt attuned to the relentless thudding of the music. I was me, but 110 percent! I was loving it.

ESCAPIST: *BOOM! Party on deck.*
BIOLOGY: *I can confirm I have made a further withdrawal from your dopamine overdraft. Debt to be repaid over ten days. I have kept a percentage of next week's serotonin as a deposit.*

I fizzed inside. I reached up to the grate and passed the small bag of powder to Amos.

Josh: You got it?
Amos: Yeah, cheers!

The door of the Portaloo banged once more. This time I opened it, then stepped out into the sea of lights and pounding electronic music. A disgruntled guy in a Ramones T-shirt shot me a dirty look, then quickly stepped into the toilet, locking the door behind him.

CRITIC: *I bet he doesn't even listen to the Ramones.*
ESCAPIST: *Shut up. Let's keep partying!*

Amos bounced out of his Portaloo and joined me in the main dancing section of the giant warehouse. We both felt euphoric. I tilted my head back and let the waves of bass crash against my chest. We were both shameless, hedonistic bags of self-scanned rice having a wonderful time!

..

We filed out of the club at four in the morning, talking and laughing with some new friends we'd just met.

ESCAPIST: *This party isn't over. Let's keep it going!*
BIOLOGY: *This isn't good for us. You're overclocking the system. You're not twenty-three anymore.*
CRITIC: *Come on. You used to be more fun than this!*
ESCAPIST: *Come on, let's do it!*

We continued the party at Amos's apartment in the city center. His place was soon a hotbox of smoke and powdered drugs on mirrored trays. I didn't want the fun to stop. Someone took hold of the aux lead and provided music. I noticed the guy in the Ramones T-shirt sitting on the kitchen counter, flirting badly with a young woman. Amos was kissing an attractive young guy on the sofa. Another guy sat down in front of me.

DETECTIVE: *I swear I've seen this guy before.*
ANALYTICAL: *Yeah, from the club. He's called Daryl. You're high as hell right now.*
ESCAPIST: *Damn right.*

Daryl passed me a mirrored tray with a rolled-up note and gestured for me to use it. I obliged.

Daryl: Hey, that was the most surreal chat I've had in a long time. It's so cool to see that you're, like . . . normal. Like, you're human. What a night, eh!?
Josh: What do you mean? Forgive me, I don't remember our conversation.
Daryl: *(laughing)* Which one? The one in the club? I suppose it would be a long shot for you to remember our chats from a while ago.
Josh: From what? Have we . . .

Horror struck me . . . an awful, overwhelming horror.

DETECTIVE: *Ah, yes! This is a client from your training days. His name is Daryl. Came to see you about jealousy or something many years ago.*
IRREVERENCE: *Oooooooooooo . . .*
CRITIC: *You've just snorted a White Christmas in front of this guy without even acknowledging him. Is he not worthy of being recognizable to you?!*
TRIGGER: *You've just done drugs with an ex-client.*
BIOLOGY: *Yeah, the stomach can't handle this. Up we go!*

I projectile-vomited on myself. The pressure from vomiting, as well as from sniffing drugs all night, burst a blood vessel in my nose and caused blood to stream from my nostrils all over my T-shirt and onto the floor. The room spun wildly. Everyone fell into an awkward silence.

Amos: Okay. Music off. I think it's time for people to head home now.
Thanks, everyone! Off, you fuck!

He looked at me with the concern of a new parent witnessing his baby throw up for the first time. I was grateful to have a friend like him.

Everyone eventually filtered out, including Daryl and the guy Amos was kissing. The Ramones guy left a fancy lighter on the counter, which I saw Amos pocket. He came over and passed me a glass of water and two paracetamol. I removed my shirt and strolled to the bathroom to clean up. I stared into the mirror and began to cry. I felt pathetic. I *was* pathetic. Amos knocked on the door.

Amos: You all right, man? Hit it too hard?
Josh: Yeah. Just realized that Daryl was an ex-client of mine.
Amos: Oh my God . . . no way?!

He started laughing.

Amos: Right, let's get you into bed. You can tell me about it when you buy me brunch in the morning. You know you can always talk to me about anything, even if it's about Harry. You're not burdening me or anything like that. I understand it's tough.
Josh: I'm sorry, man.
Amos: Yeah, you will be. You cockblocked me, you total mess. You owe me one.

8

Daphne

Daphne was sitting in my office again. The previous night she had been in my living room, although not in person. I decided to watch my favorite movie of hers in an attempt to desensitize myself to having her sitting in my office. This turned out to be a ridiculous idea, which only left me feeling starstruck and childishly giddy. My anxiety was high but mixed with a feeling of excitement that this legend of movie and stage had ended up sitting opposite me in my unremarkable therapy room.

It won't surprise you to hear that my hair was brushed, I had shaved, and I'd ironed my shirt that morning for the first time since a friend's wedding last year. Daphne placed her bag to one side and smiled at me. She was an expert at holding herself in response to being seen, and it was incredibly difficult to discern what was performance and what was authentic. An aura of soft regality veiled her as she sat perfectly straight.

Josh: Would you prefer to be called Daphne or should I use your real name?

Daphne: I don't believe I told you my name isn't Daphne.

ANXIETY: *Shit.*

CRITIC: *Outstanding start.*

My face flushed immediately. I fidgeted and tried to keep my composure.

Josh: I, er . . . I apologize . . . I . . .

Daphne: *(smiling)* It's okay. I'm not naive. I know you are aware of who I am. In fact, a friend recently showed me an impression you did of me on social media. You might not remember it, as it was a while ago. I must admit, the resemblance was uncanny.

ANXIETY: *Oh . . . You do remember it . . . You thought you were hilarious at the time.*
ANALYTICAL: *This is why you're told to be careful what you share online.*
DETECTIVE: *Outstanding detective work, Daphne. A real pro.*

My face continued to burn to what I imagined to be a blazing red. I could feel sweat budding on my forehead. The impression that Daphne was referring to was a video I'd uploaded to my Instagram page a couple of years before. It involved me pretending to be one of my favorite movie detectives, which coincidentally was played by the woman in front of me. Playing a stoic and cool detective in a male-dominated film noir, she would break the ice with intimidating characters of the criminal underworld by flicking her Zippo lighter and asking for a cigarette. "You got a boon for my light?" she would say in an icy, smooth tone, while holding the flame inches away from the subject's gaze.

VOLITION: *Just be honest. Congruence is important.*

Josh: I do remember. I just want you to know that the impression was done out of admiration for the character you played in the movie. I apologize and will remove it immediately if it caused offense. I will be more careful . . .

Daphne: There's no need for the dramatics. Leave that to me, Joshua. I found it quite amusing, although the intonation could have used some work. Surely it's obvious that if I took offense then I wouldn't be sitting here paying for the privilege of your services?

Josh: True.

Daphne smiled at me and let her hands clasp together over her crossed knees. I felt like I was the sole focus of analysis. She was a mighty presence in the room. This was not a dynamic I was generally used to.

Daphne: My name is Daphne. This is the name I use outside of the acting world. Many of us have stage names. My other name is the one that my success is pinned to. It is the name I wear when I am doing my job. I suppose, for this context, Daphne is the appropriate name to use.

Josh: Okay. And what brings you here, Daphne?

Daphne: I'm in town for several weeks directing and performing my latest play as part of the international festival.

Josh: That sounds great! I actually meant what brings you to my therapy room. It's genuinely interesting to hear your reasons for being in Manchester, though.

She looked down and broke character for a second, an actor who was surprised that they had forgotten a well-rehearsed line. She looked back at me and smiled. Composure regained.

Daphne: Of course. I apologize—I often get pulled into pleasantries. I'm here because I need some help with negative feelings. I often dwell on them. I was told you were a safe person to talk to by a good friend of mine.

DETECTIVE: *I really want to ask who it was.*

VOLITION: *Don't ask. Remember your professional integrity.*

COMPASSION: *It's great that someone recommended you.*

Josh: Well, there's no better compliment than a personal recommendation.

Daphne studied me for a moment. Then she pulled a tube of lip balm from her bag and applied it delicately.

Daphne: The negative feelings get in the way of my personal pursuits. I'd like you to help me get rid of them. They obstruct everything I'd like to achieve, and they are a waste of time. I just . . . I don't wish to go digging around in my past or to do anything that induces gazing of the navel; I just need your help in fixing me. Preferably in five weeks, as that's when the show concludes and I'll be returning to London. Or just do whatever you can.

Josh: "Fixing" you? It sounds like you feel you're broken in some way.

Daphne: Of course I am. My heartbeat wakes me up at three thirty every morning. That isn't right. My doctor tells me it is anxiety, but how can it be anxiety when I'm asleep?

She paused and looked out the window. Across the way there was another office block. Through the window we could see a staff room birthday party, with office workers donning paper party hats and blowing whistles.

Daphne: I am anxious. I . . . have been struggling recently.

EMPATHY: *This is difficult for her to say.*

Josh: Well, I appreciate your sharing this with me.

I still couldn't get my head around the fact that this famous acting star was sitting in front of me. I felt a bit numb, and I admit that some of me was committed to keeping up appearances. That said, the more we spoke, the more I was being drawn into Daphne's frame of reference, which is the phenomenon that occurs when you step inside a client's world and start to see and feel their experiences as if you were in their shoes.

ANALYTICAL: *It's understandable that you're in shock, but this person is still a person. She is your client, and she is paying you and trusting you to be a therapist. Keep working on stepping into her frame of reference.*

And I did.

..

Daphne spoke about the pressures of her career: the constant media spotlight, the striving for more success, the exhaustion that comes from working sixteen-hour days and traveling around the world. While it sounded amazing as a concept, I sensed that Daphne pined for stability, stillness, and a sense of home. She had two teenaged children whom she missed deeply. For twenty minutes I absorbed myself in Daphne's world; my shoulders and chest tightened up, unconsciously mirroring her body language as I began to *feel* the pressure she was under, a process the psychodynamic heads call transference.

Daphne: There are *other* pressures I feel . . .

She looked sullen, and the animated persona she had used to describe work pressures faded. Daphne stared at her lap. Her upright posture had wilted a little, and she began to nervously play with the rings on her fingers.

Daphne: They go beyond that of work. Oh my, just saying all of this out loud brings a lot of it to light, doesn't it?

Josh: It sure can. For me, it's part of the wonders of therapy. Saying things out loud can suddenly put worries into context.

Daphne: Do I have to tell you everything for therapy to work? Is it needed to fix—I mean, help me?

SAVIOR: *The more you tell me, the more I can help you!*

ANALYTICAL: *Absolute nonsense. Remember your training.*

Josh: I am a firm believer in the power of talking about things that are difficult. Especially when done with someone you can trust and in a safe space. That said, I don't see any benefit in sharing things if you don't feel ready. You certainly won't be getting that pressure from me.

Daphne: I only trust you because Abosede trusted you.

DETECTIVE: *It was Abosede! An old client of yours. She kept this friendship quiet! Case closed.*

Daphne: I struggle with my sense of self. I . . . I'm not sure what I mean by that.

Josh: Well, would you say you are confident in knowing who you are?

Daphne: I know I am a talented performer. I have enough accolades on my wall to prance around with to prove that. I just . . . When I sleep at night I just feel like I have borrowed this body and mind as a temporary vessel. My body feels like a giant puppet and I have taken control of its strings for a day.

EMPATHY: *Disconnected from her own being. Feeling her authentic self when alone.*

ANALYTICAL: *Powerful, disconnected language.*

Josh: That sounds lonely, Daphne. For me, when I imagine a puppet show, I can picture the audience enjoying the puppets onstage, but at the expense of suspending their disbelief. Everyone forgets the puppeteer behind the performance. No one really cares about *who* is making the puppets move when the show is on.

Daphne: Yes. I . . .

She glanced through the window, and we both watched as a giant cake was carried into the office party across the way, to noisy cheers.

Josh: I'm sorry. I'd close the window, but it gets so hot in here.

Daphne: Looks like a good party.

I said nothing. Daphne continued to talk but didn't avert her gaze from the distant celebration. She looked sad.

Daphne: I once acted in a picture about a soldier coming home from war . . .

TRIGGER: *Exciting! No White Flag! Great movie. You still have it on DVD.*

IRREVERENCE: *WOOO, and now the star is in your office, Josh! You made it, buddy! She has such amazing skin.*

CRITIC: *Just shut up!*

Daphne: . . . to her family. She arrived home to nothing but . . . love. Even her brother, with whom she had a very fractious relationship, began to shed a tear. I really enjoyed being a part of that movie. The set team, the actors, even the director, all were so lovely to work with. The critics and IMDb slaughtered it, but it meant a lot to me . . .

Josh: Sounds like there were elements to the movie that are close to you that we didn't see on the screen.

She looked at me.

Daphne: "We"? You've seen it?

ANXIETY: *Not again.*

Josh: Yes. I have.

Daphne returned to gazing at the office party. A temporary wave of apathy had overcome her, like she had dissociated and forgotten where she was. She appeared to be staring at a jolly middle-aged woman who was blowing out the candles atop the giant cake.

Daphne: I . . .

She began to stutter. Her cheeks and chin quivered. But once again she regained composure. She was amazing at pulling herself back from emotion.

Daphne: You see? Even then. I'm here trying to fix myself, and just staring at that party made me feel awfully morose. Why is this happening to me? Can't you prescribe me some pills or something? Gosh, this is worse than agent meetings with corporate clients.
Josh: I'm a psychotherapist. *Psychiatrists* are the ones who can diagnose and prescribe medication.
Daphne: There's a difference?

IRREVERENCE: *Yeah, psychotherapists have personalities.*

Josh: Yes. Psychiatrists train and study for years in psychology and the effects of medication. Psychotherapists are trained to listen and apply therapeutic modalities. We're back to the quick fix, huh?
Daphne: Ideally. How would you fix me, then?
Josh: Again, I don't think you are broken, Daphne.

I sat up straighter, ready to get on my righteous soapbox.

Josh: The way it works in here, if you'd like to continue, is that we work together to identify what you *feel* the problem, or problems, are. I'm an anxiety specialist, so I will help you with my knowledge in every way I can. But I don't paper over any cracks in here. I believe that anxiety can exist because of unhelpful personal belief systems. It can happen because of stress and significant life changes, or because of hurtful things happening to us. What those are, well . . . you'll have to help me.

Daphne studied me again, as though she was the one analyzing me instead of the other way around. She relaxed as if she was content with the conclusion of her quiet consideration. Then she dropped what I like to describe as an unexpected therapy truth bomb:

Daphne: My mother . . . fucking . . . hates me.

BIOLOGY: *Whoa. That was shocking.*

Daphne unfolded her legs and slumped back into the sofa, exasperated. Her hands rested with the palms facing up. After forty minutes of keeping the illusion together, it had suddenly crumbled. Even I was surprised.

Josh: Okay. What makes you think that?
Daphne: Oh God, Josh, it's so bloody obvious. Octogenarian bitch couldn't muster a smile with a gun to her head. Probably praying for the gun to go off so she never has to speak to me again. Is it awful that I speak like that about my own mother?
Josh: No judgment here. I'm here to listen and to go with your feelings. No prizes for guessing anger toward Mum arising?
Daphne: She's abhorrent. The most superficial woman to walk the planet. Unbelievably judgmental. Well, judgmental toward me, anyway. My brothers, well, that's another story. A cock and balls give you a pass to unconditionality. My flaming labia, however, have been the constant excuse for eternal scrutiny since she dropped me from the womb.

Her eyes frantically scanned the floor, as if something invisible was scurrying across it.

Daphne: Honestly, she should write a book titled *How to Successfully Live Vicariously Through Your Children*. She's an expert. A genius at it, Josh.

INTUITION: *I think you should remain quiet here and give Daphne the floor.*

Daphne: I really don't know how I've tolerated it all my life. Fifty-three years! Actually, no, she was different when I was little—but when I hit puberty, everything changed. I became the object of her disdain, only to become a project with the aim of being molded into something socially "acceptable."

Her face burned with anger. The party across the way had quieted and Daphne began an attempt to regain the air of composure that she had lost. It was too late. Her eyes glazed with tears, but none fell.

Daphne: Why? Why does she hate me? . . . I'm sorry. I hate showing
weakness. I told you I was broken. I don't know why I am telling you this.
I just want to be able to sleep without my pounding heart waking me up. I
just want to be able to go out to dinner and enjoy myself with my friends.

COMPASSION: *Despite her success, Daphne has a lot to unpack here. She
is really going through a lot. She is burdened by a lot of pressure, anger,
and sadness.*

Josh: On the contrary, I think what you are showing me is beneficial for this
room. For this therapeutic relationship. Thank you.

Daphne: Why are you thanking me?

Josh: Because what is said in here lies beyond the defensive walls we use
to protect us from judgment. You made a decision, despite not knowing
me, to share a side of you that I imagine isn't shown to many people.
That is something rare and invaluable. That is exactly what belongs in
this room. I appreciate that trust was helped by the recommendation,
but the sentiment remains the same.

Daphne: Thank you. Although I just feel like a spoiled brat moaning about
my mother. Gosh, I have become a therapy cliché already!

Josh: *(chuckling)* Perhaps.

She grinned and seemed to relax.

Josh: You mentioned that you want to go out with your friends. What's all
that about?

Daphne: Oh, I have stifling anxiety when I attend anything social in my
personal life.

Josh: Your personal life?

Daphne: Put me in an interview chair or in front of the cameras, and I can
do that on autopilot. Cut to my personal life, and there I seem to have a
problem—to put it lightly. Part of the reason I've come to see you.

Josh: There's a contrast between you in "work" mode and you existing
outside of work?

Daphne: *(without hesitation)* Yes.

Josh: What happens when you interact with people in your personal life?
Sounds like two different personas, almost.

Daphne: I just seem to freeze and overthink. Even with my friends. Most of my family. Everything becomes . . . less automatic. More uncertain. I suddenly seem to be hyperaware about what people think. I just want to escape to silence and be alone. It's madness. Broken madness.

I sat and listened.

Daphne: Take this morning, for example. My family, including my mother, are coming to visit next week. Even just thinking about it makes my stomach flip and my heart begin to skip. It's so silly. I'm an established woman in my fifties. This is absurd . . .

She leaned forward and clasped her arms around her stomach in a self-protective pose.

Daphne: But it's not just my mum. It happens . . . anywhere. Even when grabbing a bite to eat with my agent, or visiting my cousins at their house or my friends in the Cotswolds. This anxiety is always there. Everyone always expects me to be this confident person. I have the money; I was lucky to be gifted with the aesthetic; I can read Latin, for God's sake. But put me at a table where I am not required to be a narrative-defying heroine and I crumble. I just crumble. Oh God, I'm off moaning again. I'm sorry.

COMPASSION: *You are not pathetic, Daphne.*
ANALYTICAL: *If she stays, we have to challenge these beliefs.*

Daphne started to zip up her bag, readying herself to leave. I felt I needed to say something quickly.

Josh: You are not pathetic. I believe that sharing vulnerability is a form of bravery. One that doesn't often get the plaudits, unfortunately.
Daphne: You're only saying that because you like my movies. Because of what I am. I only get praise for what I pretend to be.

DETECTIVE: *Good self-observation.*
INTUITION: *Mirror the earlier narrative.*

Josh: When did I say I liked your movies?

She looked abashed.

Daphne: You said you held admiration for my detective character when you
did that god-awful impression of me and shared it online.
Josh: I did, but the movie was . . . all right. I respected your performance,
though.
Daphne: Do you possess that level of judgment for my performance in here?
Josh: Absolutely not. I would also hope you don't perform in here.

Daphne stared back out at the now-empty office room. Birthday bun-
ting remained tied to the window as an ode to the lunchtime party that
had now dispersed.

Daphne: I find vulnerability difficult to show.

DETECTIVE: *Interesting. Daphne has performed some of the most
heartfelt scenes in modern cinema.*
VOLITION: *It may be worth drawing upon personal observation here.*
ANXIETY: *I'm scared, but I'll do it.*

Josh: Forgive me for bringing attention to this. You're aware I have
watched a significant amount of your work. But from my perspective,
you managed to perform powerful expressions of vulnerability on the
screen and on the stage.

I paused. Daphne locked her eyes on me in anticipation.

Josh: I suppose what I'm asking is: How come you find it difficult to show
vulnerability when, from an outside perspective, you're really damn
good at it?

Her eye contact did not break, but I could see she was mulling the question over in her mind. Then the salty glaciers that encased her eyes began
to fragment slightly. Still no tears. Not now. Not yet.

Daphne: Vulnerability is easy to show when it's not you. When it's not . . . me.

..

I escorted Daphne out of the room after rescheduling another appointment for the following week. I sat down, let out a sigh, and allowed my muscles to relax. I lit an incense stick and tried to tune in to the present. It was difficult.

COMPASSION: *You did well to navigate that. It's not every day something like that happens.*

CRITIC: *There're plenty of better therapists who could help her. You were too preoccupied with putting her on a pedestal. Fool.*

COMPASSION: *Let him have this one. He did well.*

IRREVERENCE: *"Got a boon for my light?"*

Frame of Reference

Have you ever had a conversation with someone who you felt was just waiting for you to finish talking so they could get on with what they had already built up to say? Perhaps you know someone who immediately diverts a topic about your experiences back to their own? "Oh yeah, that happened to me . . ." followed by a monologue of their own phenomenology. Have your feelings ever been dismissed in favor of the listener's frustration? "Other people have it worse"; "I don't need to hear this right now"; "You're negative and bringing people down!" Well, I introduce you to the *frame of reference*. This is the magical, transparent floating picture frame through which we gaze at the world. We all have one. Mine has gargoyles on the corners.

There are lots of frames of reference in the world at any one time. Around 7.8 billion—one for every person on the planet. Imagine that: 7.8 billion little picture frames bobbing around the planet. Each frame has its own lens and perspective, and it can capture experiences only in the direction in which it's facing. You're going to have 7.8 billion different perspectives. Some will look very similar, some will appear almost the opposite. Like I said, it depends on which way the frame is pointing.

We all contextualize and make sense of our own existence by drawing upon our own frame of reference—or, as the idiom goes, by seeing the world standing in our own shoes. A huge part of a therapist's training is to learn how to step out of our own portraits, our own shoes, and try to imagine what it is like to see the world standing in somebody else's loafers. What perspective are they seeing, and feeling, through the lens of their own portraits? In short, therapists do this and communicate it with clients to help them feel understood—to feel seen.

This is why people easily bond over shared experiences. The shared frame of reference means they can relate to how difficult or thrilling the experience felt. That sense of camaraderie and togetherness can make people feel less alone. Personally, when someone could relate to my own crippling anxiety disorder, with its constant state of dissociation, scary "what if?" thoughts, and frequent heart palpitations, it made me feel ten times better. Whatever the experience, people often come together to share a commonality among their frames of reference, whether it's joy, outrage, anxiety, hardship, or just a shared enthusiasm for the latest show on Netflix. When frames of reference overlap, it can make it easier to bond with people.

One of the most admirable human traits—and something I believe to be a sign of peak emotional maturity—is the ability to step *outside* of our own frame of reference and attempt to see the world through someone else's. "I wonder how this will make them feel"; "She will be sad on this certain date"; "He will appreciate this gesture because of . . ."; "I am struggling to imagine how they feel but I am trying"; "Maybe I should just shut up and listen because it's likely that this is what they need right now."

People who possess the skill of stepping outside of their frame of reference are often seen by others as considerate, empathetic, thoughtful, good listeners, and a comforting presence. They may also get put down for being "sensitive" or "soft," yet these people will often be on the receiving end of people opening up and confiding in them. It's a gift. To some people this ability to step outside of themselves comes naturally. To others, well, it needs practice. You can tell if you need to practice stepping outside of your frame of reference if you respond to someone's personal story with thoughts (or worse, comments) such as: "But what about me?"; "How do you think this makes *me* feel?"; "This is going to really inconvenience me and my feelings."

If I'm being honest, the skill of stepping outside my own frame of reference did not come naturally to me. I'm not saying I was incredibly selfish in the past, but it took a lot of self-development, training, and just plain growing up to be able to see things easily from someone else's point of view. I cringe when I look back and see how neurotic I became when the world did not bend to fit into my own frame. But it's all part of growing up. Every time I meet someone who can step into another's shoes, I try to keep a connection with them, even if it's just a friendly association. Strong connections are formed through empathy, or even just attempted empathy. I endeavor to convey this empathy with all my clients because we often share many relationships that are perhaps lacking in empathy. All the best therapists do this too. If you're in therapy or considering it, just know that your therapist is waiting to ditch their personal portrait frame and slippers; they're ready to jump into your frame of reference with you. For you.

9
Levi

ANXIETY: *Why is he staring at me like that?*

Levi was sitting across from me on the office sofa, cracking his tattooed fingers. He was waiting for me to say something. I was relieved that this time he had decided to sit down rather than pace around my office. Our previous session had been an emotional whirlwind, but I felt honored that he'd returned to attend this appointment. Something must have gone right.

Most of the last session had been spent allowing a space in which Levi could cry. He'd sobbed cathartically for around twenty minutes. He'd then disclosed that he felt his brain was "possessed," which I gently disputed. Levi's fresh tattoo was uncovered today. It had almost completely healed, aside from some mild swelling. I let the silence sit between us, and he continued to stare at me with impatience. It was almost comical, like he was waiting for me to finish a magic trick. I cracked first.

Josh: How have you been, Levi?

Levi: With what?

Josh: How was your week?

Levi: Like many other weeks. Town was quiet this weekend, which makes the nights drag on for longer. My colleague Ray had to be taken to the hospital for appendicitis, so we were a person short for an evening. Thankfully an old colleague, Mandy, stepped in to help.

Josh: Is Ray okay?

Levi: Yeah. Although I fear the most likable part of him has been removed.

Josh: His appendix?

Levi: Yes. It's a joke. Do you shrinks not understand jokes? Or is it all feelings and tissues with you lot?

Josh: *(chuckling)* Okay, I see.

ANALYTICAL: *Perhaps it would be an idea to refer to your last session. There were some key moments that may be worth exploring.*

Levi continued to stare at me. It was the stare that you would give to a friend who was about to tell you an embarrassing story of your previous night's antics. He was wary, fearing humiliation.

Josh: I recall from our last session that you believed you were "possessed" in some way. Perhaps this is something we could explore today? It's up to you.

Levi: I *am* possessed.

IRREVERENCE: *WTF? This is gonna be great.*
DETECTIVE: *I'm just gonna reach for my notepad.*

Josh: What makes you think that?

Levi: My brain shows me stuff I shouldn't see. I think stuff I should not think. Safia thinks it's the work of a demon.

I nodded, encouraging him to continue.

Levi: Safia is my wife. We have been married for twelve years.

EMPATHY: *I wonder what it's like to be married to a possessed doorman.*
COMPASSION: *Have some compassion for this man who is opening up.*
CRITIC: *You think the stuff you took to therapy was "normal"?*

Josh: Safia also thinks you are possessed?

Levi: My wife was the person who first noticed it. She doesn't miss anything. I trust her. She's been with me every step of the way to try and . . . what's the word . . . exercise . . . *exorcise* the demon.

ANXIETY: *We may be in way over our head here.*

Josh: Okay. And what does exorcising demons look like in your household?

Levi: In my household? Are you mocking me?

BIOLOGY: *One hundred and twenty beats per minute is the new seventy.*

Josh: No. Sorry, just trying to normalize the situation for us both. I don't often hear stories of people being possessed in here. Just know that it's absolutely okay to share it.

He seemed to accept my explanation. It was honest.

Levi: We've tried a few things to rid myself of the demon. Best we could do is keep it at bay. Allows me some peace.

Josh: It's encouraging to hear that you're managing to cope with your feelings around it.

Levi: You don't believe I have a demon, do you?

Josh: I . . . I would like to hear more and understand what it's like for you to feel like you have a demon.

Levi: The demon takes over my brain when I am not distracted. Thanks to Safia and our doctor, I can manage it and stop it from hurting me at night.

ESCAPIST: *Well, I'm glad there's a doctor involved.*

Josh: Okay. Before I ask why you think it's a demon taking over your brain, can I ask what you are doing to manage it?

Levi stood up like it was his turn for show-and-tell.

Levi: I can show you. Let me turn around.

Levi began to lift his shirt to reveal his back to me. It seemed like it was happening in slow motion, but I think this was because of the shock I was about to experience.

Levi's back was a flayed and calloused war zone of wounds, blistered, scabbed, and red raw. There were scars overlapping scars, and the middle of his back pulsed with flesh where skin should be. Dried blood congealed in the cavernous crevices of his abused skin. It was a collage of reds and pinks and a palette of bruises.

ANXIETY: *This is a lot.*

BIOLOGY: *I'm sorry, we don't have use for the contents of your stomach right now.*

ESCAPIST: *You're gonna have to leave!*
INTUITION: *Do NOT leave yet.*
ANXIETY: *Say something.*

Josh: Levi, your back is . . . heavily scarred. How has that happened?

DETECTIVE: *You know how this happened, but good of you to confirm.*

I managed to swallow and tense my abdomen to keep the vomit at bay.

Levi: I know, right? It's the only downside of keeping the demon at bay. Every night I have a ritual. For ten minutes I expel the demon. It helps me sleep.

COMPASSION: *This poor man.*

There comes a time when every therapist must question the limits of their training, their knowledge, and their competency. This session with Levi was quickly nearing that time.

ANALYTICAL: *I think it's time to start considering a referral for Levi to more specialized services.*
COMPASSION: *This man has severe psychological needs that require intervention. There's no shame in referring someone on.*
ESCAPIST: *We didn't get into this job for this. Tissues and feelings, Josh!*

Levi sat down again and smiled. He seemed relieved to have shown me the wounds on his back.

INTUITION: *Calm down. Let's just see how this plays out.*

Josh: And what is this ritual, Levi? Are you hurting yourself to stop unwanted images in your mind?
Levi: What?
Josh: Are you self-flagellating because you believe it's stopping the . . . demon?
Levi: Self-what? Talk in English.

Self-flagellation

Self-flagellation is the act of someone inflicting pain on themselves using specific ritualistic instruments, usually by whipping or flogging themselves. Picture someone holding a spiked whip and flicking it over their shoulder as hard as they can. This inevitably hits and pierces the back. Self-flagellation is associated with radical religious practices and is seen as a spiritual discipline. It is often a devotion, which can be seen as a form of penance. As a therapist, I see this as nothing but self-harm.

Levi: We believe penance needs to be paid because of my thoughts. When I attack the demon, the thoughts leave for a bit. It's proof in my eyes that I am possessed. I know you don't believe me, but it must be.

DETECTIVE: *So the doctor and Safia are in on this?*

Josh: What thoughts are these? What makes you think they're so bad?

A vein pulsed at Levi's temple as he locked his eyes on mine. I was nervous, but this fear was outweighed by personal and professional curiosity.

Levi: They are unspeakable.
Josh: It is safe in here. Remember, I am bound by confidentiality.
Levi: No. You have a duty to report certain things to the police. I know because we security staff can't ignore certain things.
Josh: Having thoughts is not a crime, Levi. No matter how horrible they seem to be.
Levi: These . . . are.

He began to tear up. He rubbed his latest tattoo. It seemed to me that he was gently self-soothing.

SAVIOR: *Come on, Levi. You can say it.*

There was a long pause. Levi composed himself.

Levi: The demon tortures me with these images of . . . there's too many to say.

I remained silent, listening attentively. After a minute, he continued.

Levi: Before I tell you, you must realize that it's not me who wants to think these things. It's the demon. It's punishing me for something. My penance has not been paid.
Josh: Okay.
Levi: I get inappropriate images in my head of all the things that belong in hell. Like hurting my loved ones, inappropriate stuff with children, putting stuff in my mouth that I shouldn't. Horrible stuff like that.

ANALYTICAL: *Intrusive thoughts?*

Josh: Okay.
Levi: What do you mean, "okay"? I just told you I have horrible thoughts about kids, and you think that's "okay"?!

His arm went upward in an automatic motion, as if he were about to attack himself. He stopped when he realized what he was doing.

Josh: I'm not saying your suffering is okay, but I'm acknowledging that what you're experiencing is what is commonly known as intrusive thoughts. They are intrusive because it sounds like you clearly don't want to experience them.

Levi looked down at his knuckles and seemed to contemplate what I had just said.

Levi: The thoughts are disgusting. I don't want them. I'd rather put a bullet in my head than for them to be true. It's the work of the devil inside me. Safia says they will leave eventually. Please don't call the police.

He looked incredibly vulnerable. Guilty.

Josh: I'm not going to call the police.

I paused for a moment, bracing myself to ask a necessary question. As I spoke, I could hear that my tone was almost apologetic.

Josh: I have to ask this, Levi, but do you intend to act on any of these thoughts? Or have you done anything to act on them?

DETECTIVE: *If he admits to anything, you know you have to report him to the authorities.*
SAVIOR: *Please don't say yes.*

Levi's face filled with blood. All of his knuckles cracked at once as he clenched his fists. He began to shout.

Levi: I am not a pedophile!!

I wasn't shocked at this reaction, and so I kept my composure. It wasn't the first time, nor would it be the last, that I would ask that question in this therapy room.

Josh: Well, I think that clears that up. Apologies: I have to ask questions like this from time to time. It's for safeguarding purposes. Thanks for answering.

I got up and fetched my whiteboard. I felt excited all of a sudden. Levi looked baffled.

Josh: Now, let me tell you about intrusive thoughts . . .

Obsessive-Compulsive Disorder

Obsessive-compulsive disorder (OCD) is a crippling and vastly misunderstood anxiety condition that often comes with *intrusive thoughts*. Unfortunately, OCD is often misused as an adjective to describe overly clean, tidy, and organized people. *"Oh wow, I'm so OCD!"* should not be a statement used to describe a preference for symmetry on your work desk, nor a way to be mildly self-deprecating because all of your DVDs are in alphabetical order. OCD, especially untreated and misdiagnosed OCD, can be an extremely life-hindering anxiety disorder, which can cause high levels of debilitating worry and often leads to depression.

OCD presents itself in so many ways and is a sneaky condition. Most OCD clients with whom I have worked struggle with intrusive thoughts, which are often nasty, taboo ideas and images that come into our mind when we don't want them to. The thoughts are often shocking, repulsive, and bizarre in nature. An intrusive thought is defined as anything that is unwelcome, involuntary, and distressing. Some of the most common intrusive thoughts people with OCD experience are:

- **VIOLENCE**—thoughts about losing control and hurting people for no reason, usually loved ones, like kids, partners, strangers, or the self. "What if I stab myself?'; "What if I drown my baby?'; "What if I poison my elderly mother?"
- **SEXUAL**—inappropriate thoughts about doing taboo sexual things. This can involve adultery or engaging in sex with a gender to which we are not usually attracted, family members, minors, or animals.
- **CONTAMINATION**—intrusive thoughts around contaminating the self or others with something—germs, bacteria, or poison, for example.
- **ORGANIZATION**—the thought and feeling that something bad will happen if things aren't done or organized in a certain way.
- **CHECKING**—thoughts about burning the house down, leaving the oven on, carbon monoxide poisoning, leaving without locking the door, et cetera. This can lead to excessive and compulsive checking.
- **SOUNDS, SONGS, AND MOVIES**—intrusive thoughts can be a random sound, a word, a song, or even a movie reel that replays over and over.

It is so important to understand that people with OCD do not choose to have these thoughts. They are often brilliantly intelligent, creative, and courageous people. In short, what happens is that the brain's threat response becomes confused and decides that these thoughts could be a possible danger. This has even been seen on brain scans. Personally, I see OCD as an offshoot of profound intelligence—a side effect of having a wonderfully creative mind that unfortunately doesn't stick to its remit of using the imagination only for good. In the case of Levi, I suspected that what he may have been experiencing was a form of OCD . . .

9
Levi (cont.)

Levi: So what you're saying is that my brain has a part that is similar to my ancestors'? To spot dangers?
Josh: Yeah, that's right.
Levi: And these . . . thoughts . . . are not the work of a demon?
Josh: I'm pretty confident they're not.

Levi mulled it over but looked confused.

> **INTUITION:** *Make an analogy he can relate to.*
> **VOLITION:** *Good idea.*

Josh: Have you ever had some serious incidents at the nightclub? Say, for example, you needed to break up a fight?

Levi looked at me as if I'd asked an ice cream vendor if they sold ice cream. He raised an eyebrow, but I could sense I was getting somewhere with this.

Josh: Okay, can you remember a time when it was really challenging? Where you and your colleagues were perhaps in a bit of danger? I know your job has high risks.
Levi: Yes. It doesn't happen a lot. We usually have things under control and can call on help from door people across the city. But I remember a few times it got dicey, yeah.

He looked up at the ceiling as he dived into the memory bank.

Levi: There was one time where a local gang pulled up in a blacked-out car. They came to threaten my colleague Ray, the appendix guy. He threw one of them out of the club for dealing drugs in the open. The arrogance of it. Anyway, this car pulls up and out jump five guys with huge machetes . . .

I could see his body tighten as if he was reliving the moment.

Levi: . . . there were four of us on the door and we quickly radioed in some help. I remember stepping out toward the thugs to try to de-escalate the situation. My chest was pounding and I felt sick. I just thought of Safia, my daughter, and my colleagues, and hoped I didn't die that evening.

He exhaled slowly as the memory dissipated.

Levi: That was a scary time.

Josh: Thanks for sharing that with me. I noticed that your body tensed up as you were reliving it. Sounds terrifying.

Levi looked down at his posture. His abdomen was tight, his shoulders were raised, and one leg was bouncing. He looked surprised.

Levi: Yes. I . . . suppose I did react to that memory.

Josh: And THAT is your threat response. It is anxiety. If you are going to understand intrusive thoughts, you must remember that the threat does not need to be real in order for it to *feel* real. Your threat response is reacting to the thought or memory because it took center stage in your imagination.

Levi: All right. But what has that got to do with these . . . thoughts? And who's to say it's not a demon? I've got my wife, a doctor, and our pastor saying it is.

DETECTIVE: *Who on earth is this doctor?*

CRITIC: *We could share some words with them, couldn't we, Joshy?*

EMPATHY: *If they don't know about OCD and anxiety, then you can't expect people to understand it like you do. People will draw their own conclusions from what they know.*

Josh: I do not believe that demons possess our thoughts, Levi. I believe . . .

ANXIETY: *You sure you want to say this?*

INTUITION: *Do it . . .*

Josh: . . . that a part of you may think this too. Why are you here, Levi? Surely you must know that I am a psychotherapist—a person who doesn't perform exorcisms or banish demons or spirits. It seems to me that what you've been doing so far isn't helping and you have bravely come here for help.

IRREVERENCE: *Josh, the demon slayer!*

Josh: From what you've said about your thoughts and . . . your reaction to them—the self-harm . . .

Levi: I didn't say I self-harmed. Watch it.

Josh: Levi . . . your back is gravely wounded. I believe you have done this because it gives you temporary relief from the thoughts. A lot of what you have said so far sounds like OCD, but I'd like to explore this more with you, if you would like to. I can tell you how your thoughts are very common, how many people struggle with OCD, and how we can tackle it.

Levi looked at me but didn't say anything. In that moment I saw him as a person who was struggling—forgetting my own anxieties from my own frame of reference. He looked scared. A scared person living in a huge, lifelike wrestler costume. Except I no longer felt as intimidated because I felt I could see the person inside the costume.

Levi: I have to leave early today. We have a meeting at work. New regulations and stuff.

Josh: Oh, okay.

Levi stood up. There was a gentleness to his movement as he walked to the coatrack to fetch his bomber jacket.

Josh: Would you like to catch up next week?

Levi: Maybe.

He opened the door and began to walk out.

Josh: Oh, Levi . . .

Levi: Yeah?

Josh: Please go to your doctor . . .

VOLITION: *Really? Specify a qualified one, perhaps?*

Josh: Please go to your general practitioner about your back. I'm worried about it.

He narrowed his eyes at me. Then he left.

Introjection

One of my favorite terms that I learned during my studies to become a therapist is the concept of an *introjection*. Derived from the work of the great Carl Rogers, an introjection is an absorbed belief system that we can infer from any life experience. For example, I'm a child who comes home from school and no one greets me or asks about my day; I may *introject* that I am not an interesting person because my parents don't seem interested in me. To rub salt in the wound, perhaps my sister comes home five minutes later and my parents jump out of their seats to laud her for her latest sports medal. I may introject that value is achieved only through winning and sporting achievements, or that I am less lovable than my sister. Imagine getting praised for achieving straight *A*'s but criticized for getting *B*'s; we may introject that we have value only when we achieve perfection—that we will be judged on outcome, not intention. We can introject beliefs from anywhere and absorb them as part of our belief systems. Most introjections happen when we are younger, as we have yet to develop our sense of critical interpretation—in other words, the part of ourselves that can say "This behavior might have to do with them, rather than with me."

As a therapist, I'm on the lookout for unhelpful introjected beliefs all the time. This is why the common cliché exists in TV shows where the therapist is poking around in your childhood. It's because a child can introject something that is incorrect and, unfortunately, it is often left as an unchallenged fact as they grow up. Here are some examples:

1. A child cries at a funeral because they have lost their grandmother; this is completely natural and healthy behavior. The child's uncle leans over, puts a hand on their shoulder, and says, "Don't cry. Be strong for your grandma." The child, who respects their uncle as an authority figure, then stops crying while simultaneously introjecting a belief that hiding one's emotions equates to strength. If someone you know has died, you are allowed to cry. It's what that basic biological function was designed for.
2. A girl grows up with her physical appearance being the constant focus of scrutiny from people around her. Comments such as "You've put

on weight," "Your figure looks great," or "Are you sure you want to eat that?" are commonplace, alongside societal introjections seen in the media and the glorification of unrealistic body types. She introjects that she has value only if her body is deemed acceptable to everyone else.

3. A young person grows up questioning their gender and sexuality but is surrounded by family members and friends who use homophobic and sexist slurs. They introject that being gay, or any questioning of gender, should be suppressed so they have a better chance of fitting in with their peers. They may also introject the same prejudices.

4. A parent walks out on their family and doesn't return. The child introjects that the parent must have left because of them, or that they are not good enough to deserve love and attention.

5. A man gets praised by his peers for having sex with multiple women. He introjects that sleeping with women is a form of achievement. In contrast, a woman is labeled as shamefully libidinous for sleeping with the same number of men.

6. A person introjects that it is sinful to do or think certain things due to the codes of their faith. When and if these incidents occur, they are left feeling bad about themselves.

As adults we are an amalgamation of our introjections. These introjections may be personal, religious, moral, logical, or just derived directly from personal experiences. Those who are "people pleasers" become this way because of an introjected belief. Perhaps it's because they have learned that they need the validation of others for their esteem, or maybe it was introjected as a safety behavior because they have been in abusive relationships: "If I keep this volatile or emotionally fractious person happy, then I am less likely to feel hurt."

It's worth noting that most introjections are helpful. For instance, I always remember that it's important to look both left and right before crossing a road. And I learned in school the importance of kindness and forgiveness. Thou shall not kill, thou shall not steal. Celebrating victories and praising effort. I'll always thank my mum for praising me on intentions, not output. However, the positive introjections are not what get my therapist alarm bells ringing. The ones I'm looking out for are the unhelpful introjections, which the client believes to be unquestionably true because they have held the beliefs for so long. Many therapists, including myself, subscribe to the Jungian belief that, in his words, "until you make the unconscious conscious it will direct your life and you will call it fate." Becoming consciously aware of my own introjections was a large part of my own personal growth. To realize that my reactions and behavior were influenced by my beliefs and experiences was a real eye-opener.

Introjections can begin before we have even left the womb. Gender reveals in blue for a boy or pink for a girl are regurgitations of introjected beliefs usually steeped in tradition. Baby dolls for girls, action figures for boys; strollers for girls, footballs for boys; crying is for girls, being tough is for boys: These are all introjected beliefs that can get passed down from previous generations. Again, many introjections can be positive, but I use these as examples that can often go unquestioned for both the individual and within a culture.

Rogers believed that anxiety and depression are the result when our belief systems rely *solely* on unhelpful introjected beliefs, instead of being mitigated by beliefs derived from our own experience. If you're suffering from any mental health concerns, I'd always suggest gently reflecting on why you think what you do about yourself and where those thoughts may have come from. We are all a result of our introjected beliefs, but it is up to us to challenge those that obstruct the path to contentment.

10
Zahra

It was ten minutes before Zahra was due to arrive for her second session.

> **INTUITION:** *For some reason I feel like it would be a good idea to meet Zahra outside, in front of the building. Just in case she is panicking again.*
> **SAVIOR:** *Yes. Let me get the white knight armor.*

I walked out the front door of the main building onto the street to be greeted with some rare Manchester sunshine. I noticed that my hand automatically went to reach for my back pocket to pull out a lighter, even though I hadn't smoked for five years. An old habit from when I first moved into this office and used the entrance as my place to light up.

> **DETECTIVE:** *God, I miss smoking.*

A light blue SUV turned the corner and pulled up next to me. The passenger door immediately swung open and out stumbled Zahra, puffing her cheeks as if the car had been starving her of oxygen. She looked up at me, clearly still struggling but significantly less panicky than the last time she arrived here.

> **Faiza:** Do you need me to come with you?
> **Zahra:** No. I'm okay. Thanks, Mum.

Zahra closed the car door, composed herself with a deep breath, and straightened her blazer. It was kind of comical. Endearing.

> **Zahra:** Morning, Joshua.
> **Josh:** Good morning.

We walked into the foyer and stopped in front of the elevator. I gazed at it performatively, as if it was a museum exhibit that I was seeing for the first time. Zahra's face dropped.

Zahra: No.

Josh: Why not?

Zahra: I'm not ready.

Josh: Have you never been in an elevator before?

Zahra: Of course I have.

Josh: Okay. This one is no different, I promise you.

Zahra: But what if my panic gets worse in there?

ANALYTICAL: *Remind her of what you discussed last session.*

Josh: More reason to go and do it. Also, don't make me take the stairs. I'm proud of never hitting my watch's daily floor target.

Exposure Therapy

Exposure therapy is a process used in cognitive behavioral therapy to reduce fear and avoidance. Our brain's fear center is controlled by a tiny almond-shaped part called the *amygdala,* which is the fastest but also the dumbest part of our brains. If our mind perceives a threat, our amygdala will release stress hormones such as adrenaline and cortisol that immediately flood the body. You know the amygdala has triggered this release when you feel your stomach flip (or you feel butterflies), your heart races, you feel weird, dizzy, detached, and apprehensive of something awful about to happen. This is usually accompanied by the need to immediately scan and analyze the situation and decide whether to stay, fight, or solve.

The amygdala is important for encoding memories, particularly ones that could potentially be dangerous. This is helpful to warn us against re-petitive threats and was excellent for our ancestors. For example, let's say a bear attacked us the last time we bumped into one. The amygdala helps to encode this memory and store it in the memory bank under the file name danger.zip. The next time we see something that even remotely looks like a bear, our amygdala will associate this with the danger section of the memory bank, then immediately release adrenaline and cortisol faster than we can will it. You have probably experienced this sensation yourself: perhaps when a friend has startled you as a joke, or you had one of those "falling over" dreams as you're drifting off to sleep. It's the very same process for phobias. If you're afraid of spiders, think about how it made you feel when one suddenly startled you. What happened is that the amygdala saw it first and, just in case you were in danger, released a lot of stress hormones, sending your heart rate soaring.

The key phrase to remember here is "just in case." The amygdala will trigger anxiety if it senses any sign of threat *just in case* it could be harmful. The amygdala's motto is always "Better to be wrong and alive than lacka-daisical and dead!" This is why it is really hard to be rational when under the effects of a misfiring amygdala. Zahra is a doctor and understands biology better than most, but she still doubts her safety in an elevator thanks to her overzealous amygdala. Furthermore, the amygdala can decide that certain nondangerous things can now be a danger. This is where exposure therapy comes in.

By exposing ourselves to the supposedly dangerous threat, we can *show* the amygdala that certain situations are *not* dangerous. It has been scientifically proven that if you expose yourself to an anxious trigger, while removing safety behaviors and anxious compulsions, then the amygdala rewires itself. We can turn off the amygdala in situations where we don't need it. In the case of Zahra, I will try to use exposure therapy in situations that challenge her own fears—places where she must face panic and the fear of fear itself.

Zahra (cont.)

Josh: It's your choice. I won't pressure you.
Zahra: Are you joking? You've literally just pressed the call button.
Josh: I've told you I'm not taking the stairs. Come and join me if you'd like,
   or you can take the stairs.
Zahra: I think I'll take the stairs. I'm not ready. The panic will be too much.
Josh: The panic is never too much. You can handle more than you think,
   Zahra.

I stepped into the elevator but kept my arm over the sensor to hold the door open. I stood to the side, inviting her to join me.

Josh: Oh, I forgot to tell you that my office is now on the eighth floor. That's a
   lot of stairs. The elevator would be so much easier.

ANALYTICAL: *Liar.*
DETECTIVE: *Liar.*

Zahra: Liar.
Josh: Come on. You can do it! Let's practice being anxious. That's the whole
   point. Let's teach that amygdala that we can tolerate it and it's no longer
   going to dictate our life.
Zahra: Okay, screw it. Just hurry up. Please press the floor button.

She stepped in and stood in the corner, grasping the elevator's leaning rail.

COMPASSION: *She's doing well. Fair play.*

Josh: You're doing really well. You're probably having loads of "what if?"
   thoughts right now, like "What if I'm trapped?" and "What if this panic
   becomes overwhelming?" That's okay.

Zahra was stooped forward but held the elevator bar as if she was traversing a narrow ledge on the side of a skyscraper. She was breathing shallowly, and her long black hair covered her face. She nodded in agreement but didn't look up. The elevator began its ascent.

> Zahra: I . . . I'm so scared.
> Josh: I know. Be honest: How scared are you on a scale of one to ten?
> Zahra: Twelve.
> Josh: *(chuckling)* Really? I know you're scared, but you seem a lot more composed than the first time you came to see me. If that was a ten, then what is this?
> Zahra: Okay, I'm an eight. Maybe a nine.
> Josh: Nice one.

> ANALYTICAL: *You used subjective units of distress [when we measure the intensity of anxious feelings] derived from CBT.*
> COMPASSION: *Well timed.*
> IRREVERENCE: *In the kink world, CBT stands for cock-and-ball torture.*
> VOLITION: *Shut up.*

The elevator doors opened. Zahra was the first to leave, in a similar fashion to how she left her mother's car—hyperventilating. I followed, and we made our way to my office.

> Josh: Well done! That was really courageous of you. The amygdala won't forget that.
> Zahra: Nor will I!

On entering my therapy room, Zahra took time to brush her hair and compose herself. She looked assured—hands clasped in her lap. Seeing her like this, I could imagine Zahra as a doctor sitting in her own office. She gave little away, but I hoped that she felt proud of her exposure to her fear in the elevator.

> Zahra: I was considering what you said last time. The word "tolerance" stuck with me.

I placed two glasses of water on the table and sat down opposite her.

Josh: What do you mean?

Zahra: You spoke about recovery being judged on the willingness to be tolerant or something?

Josh: Ah, yes. With anxiety disorders, the path out is always practicing the willful tolerance of uncertainty. This is what you did when you decided to enter the elevator.

She looked slightly embarrassed, but then she continued her point.

INTUITION: *Perhaps stop laying it on so thick.*

CRITIC: *Agreed. Want some pom-poms to go with these superlatives?*

Zahra: I've been wishing for the anxiety to go away. I've tried everything to make the anxiety and panic feelings disappear. Honestly, I've spent so much money on things my colleagues would laugh at me for.

EMPATHY: *When you're in the clutches of the panic loop, you'll try anything.*

Zahra: It's ridiculous. I have a gallon of CBD oil in my kitchen. Rescue Remedy in all forms. I spent money on these stupid online techniques made by internet cowboys. I just fell for the quick-fix bullshit because I wanted to believe it would make me better.

Josh: Hey, there's a multimillion-dollar industry surrounding anxiety and mental health. It sounds like you were only trying to ease your suffering.

Zahra: But I just feel stupid.

I sat and held the space in silence.

Zahra: Anyway, this willful tolerance you spoke of: Your technique really made sense to me.

Josh: It's not my invention—it's from psychology and counseling literature. Tell me why you feel it makes sense to you.

Zahra: The other day, I was due to have a meeting to discuss my return to work. This triggered a horrible panic attack. As well as guilt and all the rest. Anyway, when that happens I usually run to the bedroom and close myself away. You know, to wait it out. But this time I was so frustrated that I decided to join the meeting anyway.

Josh: You left the house to go to a meeting?

Zahra: No. It was over Zoom. I was panicking and the screen was blurry, but I managed to navigate to the meeting. I decided not to hide my panic and show my bosses what I was experiencing.

Josh: Okay, that's good.

Zahra: Turns out they could hardly tell I was panicking. They just said I looked impatient!

She leaned forward toward me.

Zahra: All this doom and terror was going to happen anyway, but I noticed that when I was trying to concentrate on the meeting, my anxiety felt . . . less? It was still awful, but the edges were smoothed slightly.

BIOLOGY: *Diverting focus can lessen the effects of negative sensations such as pain and discomfort.*

Josh: Where your focus lies is important. It sounds like your previous coping strategy of hiding and hyperfixating on the sensations didn't help.

Zahra: No. I've come to realize this. It's a bit like when you're about to receive an injection. You can stare and focus on the moment the needle hits, or you can turn and chat with someone while it's happening. The latter usually makes the process easier.

ANALYTICAL: *Nice analogy.*

Josh: That's a great analogy to use while doing exposure work. It's important we do as many exposures as we can to break the habit of avoidance.

Zahra: But why did I end up like this? I never thought I'd end up with an anxiety disorder. I thought I was strong.

Josh: Having an anxiety disorder says nothing about how strong you are. Being anxious does not equate to weakness.

Zahra: Oh, save the altruism, Gandhi. You know what I mean. Why is this happening to me?

Josh: I have a theory.

Zahra: Does it require you to use that whiteboard again?

IRREVERENCE: *Haha.*

Josh: No . . . but I can if you'd like?

Zahra: What did they say in school? I'm an audio and kinesthetic learner. I'm okay.

I remained seated.

Josh: I'm a believer in the theory of the *stress jug*—also known as the stress *bucket, balloon,* or any similar receptacle. The stress jug represents our ability to manage stress. The size of the jug is dependent on genetics. So if both our parents are anxious, it's highly likely we will inherit a nervous system that operates in a similar way. A smaller jug. It doesn't mean that we inherit disordered anxiety, though.

Zahra frowned in concentration. She was listening.

Josh: Often people who experience panic attacks will claim it "happened from nowhere," but this is rarely true. Panic attacks occur when our stress jug overflows. What's *in* our stress jug is different for every person.

I mimed the outline of a giant jug. I don't know why. Then I started pouring imaginary liquid into the imaginary jug.

Josh: Different stressors from our personal life fill up the jug. This could be money worries, parenting stress, career issues, health conditions, grief, traumatic events, self-esteem issues, et cetera. The stress jug fills up and our friend the amygdala—also known as our threat response—takes notice.

Out came the hand puppets. My thumb and fingers turned into mouths. I was on a roll.

Josh: The amygdala has never really evolved since our ancestors, so it doesn't understand modern, subjective stress. It gets confused.

So, *just in case* there's a danger, it'll trigger loads of anxiety and adrenaline.

Zahra: My jug fills up, my threat response takes over, I see.

She looked deep in thought.

Zahra: It makes sense. The threat response releases the stress hormones and gives me all these strange symptoms. Over the last few months, it seems like the threat response . . . the amygdala . . . has identified the anxiety as a threat in itself. I see . . . I get it. It feels like I'm going around in a loop because as soon as I get any sign of anxiety, I begin to worry about it, which then turns into panic. It's like anxiety equals threat, then my mind and body go bananas.

COMPASSION: *That's a really good way of describing it.*

Josh: That's a good way to describe panic disorder. Except you're not going crazy. It can just be uncomfortable.

Zahra: How do I turn off the amygdala then?

Josh: We *show* the amygdala that "normal" situations are not dangerous. Until it turns off or quiets down significantly. Then I believe we keep it turned off by emptying our stress jug. This is where therapy really helps, in my opinion.

CRITIC: *And how you love your opinions.*

Josh: The trickiest part is identifying what's in the stress jug.

Zahra: Is this all a ruse to try to make me cry about sad things? I'm not here for that, I just want the panic attacks to stop.

DETECTIVE: *She's on to you, sir.*

Josh: We have already spotted the most obvious thing filling up the stress jug and we're already one step ahead with that.

Zahra: My anxiety significantly lowered when you stopped moving your hand like a mouth.

She grinned.

Zahra: It's my fear of panic, isn't it? It has stressed me out so much. Then I'm worried about not being able to return to my practice. Worried about losing my job. Worried about the impact I'm having on my mum. There's a lot in my jug.

Zahra suddenly looked despondent.

Zahra: Does that mean I have to go through everything in my jug to get rid of the panic attacks?
Josh: Not necessarily. That's up to you and what you feel comfortable with. Once we're better with the fear of panic itself, I always recommend taking a preventative approach. Making more room in the jug to be able to tolerate life's other stresses.

There was a long pause.

Zahra: My father died ten months ago.

TRIGGER: *Death.*
BIOLOGY: *Thud.*
ANXIETY: *Whoa.*

Zahra: I . . . I don't want to talk about it. It just needs to be said. So you know.
Josh: Okay.

Zahra disclosed this bombshell as if giving a workplace presentation. Her voice was steely and far removed from emotion. I stayed silent.

Zahra: In fact, he didn't just die. He was murdered. He . . .

EMPATHY: *This is so difficult for her.*

Zahra: He was killed by my brother. Stabbed to death. Twelve times.

I did my best to remain calm, composed, and within Zahra's frame of reference. I kept eye contact and listened intently. My heart was racing because of the shock, but you get this in the therapy room from time to time. This is what I am trained for.

Zahra: So I suppose that's in my jug. Aside from fearing the panic attacks. And yes, I was very close to my father. My brother is mentally unwell and has learning difficulties. It was a . . . tragic event.

Her resolve and demeanor barely flinched, but I could sense a maelstrom of emotions simmering under the surface.

Zahra: So, Joshua, how do I get that shit out of my jug?
Josh: You have already started to.

11
Harry:
Staying Up Late

July 2008

Mum: Five minutes and he's got to go to bed.
Josh: Okay, no worries.

I turned to Harry.

Josh: Five minutes, mate. Let's hit the save point and call it a night.

We always pushed our luck. We played for around fifteen more minutes before Mum walked in and reprimanded us.

Mum: He needs to sleep. You probably could do with some rest as well.
Josh: You know me, Mum. I'm a night owl.

She raised her eyebrows and left. Harry brushed his teeth and got into his bed. My bed was across the room. We had always shared a room growing up and still did any time I was visiting home.

Josh: Good night, mate.

Harry smiled.

Josh: Oh, I forgot . . . Harry?
Harry: Yeah?
Josh: Smells.
Harry: That's mature.

He rolled over and went to sleep. I walked across the landing and tapped on my mum's bedroom door.

Josh: You off to bed? Good night. Love you.
Mum: Love you. Don't stay up too late.

I took the games console downstairs and fired up *Call of Duty*. I was the perfect image of a young man in his twenties with no girlfriend. But who needed a girlfriend when your kill/death ratio was as sexy as mine? There was a shuffling behind the door, then it quietly opened. Harry tiptoed through.

Josh: You're incurring the wrath of Mum here, mate.
Harry: I can't sleep. Can I play with you?
Josh: What's up?
Harry: Just . . . stuff happening at school and things.
Josh: Someone giving you trouble? They need a clout?
Harry: Nothing like that. I just . . . I don't want to talk about it. Can I just play
    Portal with you for a bit?
Josh: Course you can. Keep quiet, though. I'm not getting blamed for this.
Harry: Can I have a sip of your beer?
Josh: No.

He smiled and joined me on the sofa.

12
Noah

Noah was considerably more relaxed at the beginning of this session and seemed happy to talk. We had spent the remainder of the previous session talking about his life as a young accountant and his hobbies and interests, and afterward he seemed to trust me. It's not within a therapist's remit to try to "like" a client, as each client should be treated with the attitude of complete acceptance and support outside the realms of judgment. Carl Rogers called this Unconditional Positive Regard. However, we are human, and I'd be lying if I said that I didn't find Noah quite endearing.

Noah: . . . and it's wonderful to feel part of the team. It took some time for them to warm to me, though. I needed to pluck up the courage to talk more and assert myself. This Friday we've got after-work drinks in town.

BIOLOGY: *We like beer, don't we, Josh? Picture it now. Delicious and crisp.*

Josh: This is really encouraging. Do you feel like being part of the team has helped your mood recently?

Noah: Yes. I suppose it has. This city is still new to me, so it's nice to lay down some roots, so to say.

I smiled and nodded.

Noah: My apartment looks less like a prison cell now. I managed to acquire the help of two handymen to help shift my aunt's old sofa up four flights of stairs. I've put a lick of paint on the walls, and the broadband is going to be installed tomorrow.

Josh: Excellent.

Noah: I have also assembled my bed. My hands are blistered from turning a blasted Allen key all evening.

IRREVERENCE: *Hexagonal prismed death rods.*

Josh: IKEA, by any chance?

Noah: Yes. I'd never been! It was my first time. My parents always turned their noses up at it. Their loss, really, I actually loved it. What a magical land of semi-assembled furniture.

Josh: "Magical" is one way of putting it.

VOLITION: *Come back to Noah's frame of reference. He doesn't need to hear your disdain for walking around that maze.*

BIOLOGY: *The meatballs and that mental fruit jam, though?*

DETECTIVE: *You're hungry. Stop thinking about food.*

CRITIC: *Why didn't you eat at lunchtime? Also, you're a therapist—you can't use the word "mental."*

BIOLOGY: *Guys, you MUST listen to this rendition of Enya.*

Noah: Is that your stomach rumbling? Or is it mine?

Josh: I'm so sorry. It's me.

Noah: Oh, do you need to eat? Please don't sit there hungry on my account.

COMPASSION: *Bless him.*

Josh: No, seriously, I'm okay. It just rumbles from time to time. I really appreciate that kindness, though.

I gulped down the rest of my water to fill my stomach.

Josh: So, what would you like to discuss in today's session?

He shrugged his shoulders.

Noah: I don't know, really. I'm currently quite happy. Don't really feel like bringing myself down.

Josh: That's understandable. Sometimes feeling good can give us confidence to look at things from a different perspective. I'm not saying you should come here to feel miserable, but muddy waters can be easier to wade through when you've got a spring in your step.

Noah: Hm. Okay. What do you want me to talk about?

Josh: What comes to mind?

DETECTIVE: *What about that juicy secret, Noah?*
INTUITION: *Something tells me we should leave that for now.*

He paused to focus.

Noah: I . . . All that's coming to mind is this staff night out this weekend. It's exciting. I hope that I can forge stronger relationships with them.

Social Anxiety

Social anxiety is fear and worry that surfaces around social interactions with other people. In the moment, this can feel like a hyperawareness of the self through a critical lens: "Did I say something offensive?" "Do they think I am boring?" "Can they see that I'm anxious?" "What if they think I'm weird?"

Interestingly, most social anxiety occurs in the *anticipation* of socializing or ruminating on what happened long *after* the event. People can spend weeks in nervous anticipation of a social event, playing through scenarios and conversations in their minds before the event has even happened. They can also spend hours afterward dwelling on the interactions that occurred during the event. This is the threat response bringing attention to our perceived "performance" and picking holes in it. We can convince ourselves that worrying about and overanalyzing our social performance can make us perform better in the future. It's sad that some people feel they need to perform when I bet they're just excellent as themselves.

Social anxiety is usually anchored by a fear of judgment or rejection, or the need to placate other people in order to feel safe because perhaps we've been bullied or abused in the past. We can also just naturally be shy (which is totally okay). I used to struggle with social anxiety when I was younger because I was desperate to feel a sense of belonging. Whatever the trigger for social anxiety might be, a critical hyperfixation of the self is the behavior that is universal across all aspects of social anxiety. When I work with social anxiety, I often look out for unhelpful, introjected beliefs (see page 70), and I incorporate them with strategies derived from cognitive behavioral therapy.

12
Noah (cont.)

Josh: It sounds like making these new relationships is important to you.
Noah: Yeah. I feel lonely a lot of the time.

EMPATHY: *Must be lonely living in a new city.*

Josh: Since moving here?

He hesitated.

Noah: Yeah. Well . . . kind of.

His expression turned forlorn.

CRITIC: *You've gone and made him sad!*
ANALYTICAL: *This is therapy. It's often the place to discuss difficult things.*

Noah: I've always felt lonely—if I'm being candid.

I remained silent. Noah curled the ends of his sleeves within his palms. He stared over at a potted ficus tree on my desk, as if confessing to it.

Noah: I've had friends and . . . I get along with some family . . . but there's been no one really that I've had a connection with. I've . . . never had a partner. I suppose I feel pressure to perform at the work event because I'm so desperately wanting a connection. I've also signed up to volunteer at an outreach center for the homeless just to meet new people . . . and also to feel valued.
Josh: Okay. Loneliness—and a pressure to ease that loneliness?
Noah: Yes.

I readjusted myself on the chair.

Josh: You mentioned you "had" friends and get along with "some" of your family?

Noah: Yes. I grew up with boys who lived around me and we formed a sort of friendship group where the camaraderie was based entirely on geographical location. Since higher education we all seemed to go our separate ways. Start new lives. Lots of us in different parts of the country.

Josh: Naturally drifting apart?

Noah: At first, I thought so. But, on reflection, I think it's because of my sexuality.

Josh: Okay.

Noah: Growing up, I was attracted to both girls and boys. I believed myself to be bisexual. But I'd say I'm more pan now.

He stopped talking to the potted tree and looked back at me.

Noah: I started to notice them pulling away from me toward the end of school. I started to develop traits that differed from the norm. I hated myself for it. The irony is, I wasn't the only queer in that group; I just wasn't as good at hiding it. Except when I was at home. That's when I became an outstanding actor.

ANALYTICAL: *He's getting into a flow—following his thoughts and feelings via his memories.*

Noah: I'd shake when walking down the garden path. That house . . .

I saw him shudder slightly, and his hands grew even tighter. His sleeves were stretched to their limit.

Noah: That house, Josh. Let's just say that being a homosexual wasn't the only banned ideology under that roof.

He took a deep breath and sighed. He sipped some of his water and then lifted and shook his head, as if waking himself from a semilucid trance.

Noah: It's weird. It would explain why *I* am weird. But I am not weird compared to what's in there.

COMPASSION: *You're not weird.*

Josh: Not gonna lie, there's a part of my mind that really wants to hear what happened in that house . . .

DETECTIVE: *That would be me.*

Josh: . . . but I can also see you're becoming distressed recalling it. Just know that if you'd like to explore it, then this is a safe space to do so.

Noah took a deep breath.

Noah: It's fine. I knew I'd have to talk about this at some point in therapy.
Josh: Did you discuss this with your last therapist?
Noah: Yes. It was tricky enough to do it that time, so forgive me if I'm a bit cumbersome navigating the past again.
Josh: Take your time. I don't like whistle-stop tours anyway.
Noah: Okay . . . My father could be described as an abusive man. He could be very controlling. He would control me as best as he could. He would also control my mother. He could be a loud, volatile, opinionated beast who terrified the daylights out of us.
Josh: "Could"?
Noah: The peculiar thing was, his abuse was completely incongruous to his general day-to-day personality. He was and is capable of being a perfectly nice person. It's like he has two personalities: one a calm, measured, and, dare I say, empathetic man, and the other an angry, possessed one.

He grew pale.

Noah: Actually, his amiability was a performance. He was never genuinely kind. He only felt kind when he was totally in control. When my mother and I were compliant. When we conformed to his way of living.
Josh: What did that control look like?
Noah: Mostly emotional blackmail. Forcing our compliance by telling us how much we were hurting him. He'd throw stuff, smash things, and

sometimes beat us. He'd call us worthless. Repeatedly. It was worse when he drank, but the rage could come at any time.

Josh: That sounds terrifying. You and your mum must have been on eggshells.

Noah: I was. I tried my best to avoid the house, or at least keep out of the way if I had to be there.

He suddenly frowned.

Noah: Don't be under any illusion that my mother and I were some kind of team formed through mutual oppression. She spent the majority of the time placating my father, which often meant throwing me under the bus. God, I hated her for it, but I suppose she was only doing what she could to survive.

Josh: There were times when you felt both of your parents were against you?

Noah: All too often. When my father was away for work I would see some form of loving from my mother. But when he was around it was obvious that she just prioritized her need to feel safe. Only twice in all of my childhood did she suggest leaving, but it never happened. She was just too scared.

EMPATHY: *Tricky situation. Anger and yet empathy for Mum. Must have been so difficult and confusing growing up in that house.*

Noah: Anyway, I developed strategies to get by. I concentrated on my studies and had my outlets if I needed them. I just had to accept that my parents were not going to help or be there for me in ways I needed them to be.

ANALYTICAL: *Remember the first session when Noah showed you his scars?*

Josh: One of these outlets was cutting your arm?

Noah: That was one of them, yes.

Josh: Do you still speak to your parents now?

Noah: I do. Over the phone a few times a week. I know I shouldn't, but I feel so lonely. I'm also scared about being cut off by them. I think deep down that I still want their affection. Their approval. Oh God . . . this sounds pathetic. I *feel* pathetic.

Tears started to fall down his face.

VOLITION: *Pass him the tissue box.*

Noah: Thank you.

.. .

Noah spoke in more detail about the abuse he received from his father, including times when he was beaten around the head with a porcelain mug, made to urinate outside in the rain as punishment, and forced to watch his father drag his mother up the stairs by her hair. He often had to witness his father sexually assault his mother, as well as "stand watch" while his father slept with other women downstairs.

BIOLOGY: *I'm releasing stress hormones to help process the intensity of all this.*
COMPASSION: *Make sure you take some time for yourself after this session to breathe and relax.*

Noah: He's a lot calmer nowadays. But I still do fear for my mum. Weirdly, my dad became calmer when his own father died.

ANALYTICAL: *Generational cycle of abuse, perhaps?*

Noah: I think he was beaten by his own father. My mother told me. I also know his uncle was sent to prison for sexually assaulting young boys. I can only imagine what impact that had on him growing up, but the way he breaks out into rage and drinks himself into unconsciousness suggests to me that it wasn't sunshine and rainbows. Even so, he's a coward who just copies his own father.
Josh: What impact do you think all of this is having on you now?

He contemplated the question.

Noah: The obvious thing to say would be that it has affected my confidence. But I fear it has affected me in other ways too.

I nodded, signaling to him that it was okay to continue.

Noah: I . . .

He began to sob.

COMPASSION: *Ah, man. Must be a lot to go through all of this.*

Noah: I am afraid . . . I am afraid that I am my father.

He grabbed another tissue.

Noah: I often get rage. Outbursts. Moments when I don't feel in control . . .

He was really sobbing now. He grabbed a cushion and held it tightly, rocking back and forth to soothe himself.

SAVIOR: *Reassure him.*
VOLITION: *Be careful.*
COMPASSION: *Reassure him.*
ANALYTICAL: *Reassure him for what? You don't know enough.*
DETECTIVE: *Agreed.*

Josh: You are not your father, Noah. Perhaps you can identify some similar traits in yourself, but you are your own person. In this session alone I've heard lots of care and empathy from you. Are these traits you would associate with your dad?

He loosened his hold on the cushion slightly.

Noah: No.

We sat in silence for a few minutes.

Noah: I'm nervous because I won't have any control over the situation. The night out with colleagues, I mean. I can't control the chances of being rejected. I can't control my sexuality. I just . . . need this one night to go well.
Josh: Hm . . . Have you thought about what you *can* control?
Noah: Er . . . I can control how I look? What time I turn up? What I say?
Josh: Well then . . .

He smiled.

Noah: You asked me what impact I think everything with my dad is having on me now . . .

I raised my eyebrows to show an enthusiasm for his recall.

Noah: It has left me feeling powerless. I am powerless. I am useless. A burden, even.

Josh: I can see how maybe you could have come to that conclusion given what you have told me about growing up. But do you think those beliefs apply now? Someone who is successfully starting up a new life in a new city? Nailing down a job and meeting new people? Taking responsibility for his mental health by seeking therapy? None of those seem like the traits of someone powerless and useless. For me, it rings the bell of assertion and personal responsibility.

There was a pause. I could feel the low thud of my pulse in my ear.

Noah: There're just some things you can't come back from, Josh.

DETECTIVE: *Hmm . . .*

13

Daphne

I flicked on the kitchen TV to add some background noise as I chopped my vegetables. I was ordering way too many takeouts of late, so a homemade vegetable curry it was for this evening. The unnecessarily dramatic intro music of the local news program burst out of the speakers as I squeezed a tube of tomato purée. The main headline focused on a visit by the prime minister, who was pictured pretending to have fun with local schoolchildren.

Josh: Prick.

There was a satisfying sizzle as the vegetables skated around the non-stick pan. I added spices and coconut milk. The third headline on the news was a featured overview of the Manchester International Festival, with Sunil Gupta, Salford's finest, reporting on the popular event:

Sunil: . . . and there is already hype at the sold-out matinee performance of *Lyrebird* at the Exchange Theatre. Tickets sold out fast and critics are already lauding its celebrated star—who both acts and directs the play—for staying faithful to her passion for the stage.

Then I heard Daphne's real name. I looked up at the television to see her beaming with enthusiasm.

Daphne: Everyone is so happy to be here and we're so excited to be performing in Manchester for the next few weeks. This area has such a rich tradition and love for theater, and we hope that *Lyrebird* brings as much enjoyment for the audience as it does for us performing it.

Sunil: I must say I was fortunate enough to watch the preview and your performance was incredible.

Daphne: Thank you so much. I can only be as effective as the brilliant actors and stage team around me. It has all come together beautifully. They have been outstanding.

Daphne was so composed and convincing, yet since meeting her I wasn't sure if this interview was her authentic self or a performance. How much of this was her show business self and how much her real self? Suddenly, a burning smell hit my nostrils. I looked down and saw that my curry had started congealing and burning on the sides of the pan. By the time I'd saved it, the news had moved on from Daphne's interview.

..

Josh: You look pretty deflated. Are you okay?
Daphne: Yes. I'm just tired. Opening a show can take it out of you.

Daphne was sitting on the sofa in her usual upright pose. She looked spectacular in an orange dress. In contrast, I had to resort to wearing a faded *Back to the Future* T-shirt because I'd accidently shrunk all of my shirts in my new washer-dryer. I'd also spilled tea on my white trainers. Thankfully, Daphne didn't seem to notice.

Josh: How's the show going?
Daphne: Excellent, really. An effective way of not getting wound up by
    directors with profound control issues is to just become one yourself.
Josh: You are now the director with control issues?
Daphne: One hundred percent.

We both smiled.

ANALYTICAL: *A good way to ease into the session and remind her the
space is safe.*
INTUITION: *Ask again.*

Josh: You sure you're okay? I only ask because you did look quite sad.
Daphne: I looked quite sad? For a moment there I forgot you were a
    therapist who is trained to spot this kind of thing.
Josh: It pays the bills.

Daphne took a deep breath.

Daphne: My mother visited last night. She brought the family, of course. We went out for a late dinner.

Josh: Family?

Daphne: My eldest daughter, my stepfather, my brother, and my sister-in-law, as in my husband's sister. Well, she used to be; I'm not sure how it works now that I'm divorced. We went to an Italian place and the usual antics happened: Mother dictating the mood, the conversation—the judge, jury, and executioner on every topic at the dinner table.

She sighed.

Daphne: It's my fault. I have placated her all my life and modeled the same cowardice toward my daughters and my brother. Now we're all left with the strict conductor and us the lame orchestra.

ANALYTICAL: *Very self-critical.*
EMPATHY: *Sounds like behavior deriving from fear.*

Josh: When people placate it's usually from an anxious place.

Daphne: I'm absolutely terrified of her. It's ridiculous. I just curl up and freeze at any sign of her disapproval.

Fight, Flight, Freeze, or Fawn

The *fight or flight* response is a term most of us have heard of at some point. If you were listening in lower-school biology, you'd have learned that it is an innate response we all possess that responds to stress or a threat—prompting us to stay and fight potential threats or run away. For example, if a bear was running toward you, the fight or flight response, triggered by the amygdala, would kick in and you'd either stay and fight the bear, or run like hell. Personally, I'm hard as nails and I'd fight the bear. Winnie can meet his maker.

Since then, the fight or flight response has had a twenty-first-century hipster upgrade. It is often now referred to as the *fight, flight, freeze, or fawn* response. The freeze response describes people who seem to shut down when faced with a threat. This could involve having an unnoticeable panic attack, becoming speechless with nothing to say, freezing during a presentation, feeling immobile in response to shock, or completely dissociating due to the reminder of a traumatic event.

The fawn response is when our sense of threat persuades us to people please to avoid potential conflict. People pleasers can slip into a fawn response usually due to introjected beliefs growing up—perhaps to curry favor with an irrational authority figure to whom they look for approval, or they may fawn as a safety behavior because of emotional and physical abuse, either from growing up or from an abusive relationship.

Daphne (cont.)

Daphne: That would describe my relationship with my mother very well. I'm a freezer and fawner. Desperate for her approval.

> **ANALYTICAL:** *It might be worth exploring the origins of this response.*
> **IRREVERENCE:** *Isn't she, like, eighty years old?*
> **EMPATHY:** *Exactly. A lifetime to construct terrifying associations and introjected beliefs and to condition a threat response that would be on autopilot by now.*
> **COMPASSION:** *Agreed.*

Josh: Why do you think your mother's approval holds so much weight?
Daphne: I don't know. I just . . . perhaps this is why I'm in therapy.
Josh: Maybe.

I sat and listened to a shouting strand of my brain as it reminded me of something from the last session.

Josh: I recall you saying in our last session that you wanted to be "fixed." You want to fix the negative feelings. Have you considered that the feelings might just be a natural product of what you are experiencing?

Her eyes fixed on me like a cobra's.

Daphne: Joshua, please don't be under the illusion that my mother is the only issue in my life. That would be wonderful, wouldn't it? Let Daphne cry about Mummy and magically heal myself?

I said nothing.

Daphne: I admit that I could perhaps work on all the baggage that I have accumulated via Mother. But there are many things that . . . what is it that you say . . . ? Fill up my stress jug?

Josh: Okay.
Daphne: One thing at a time, perhaps.

Daphne applied her lip gloss. She instantaneously became a famous actress rather than the client, and I had to remind myself not to react.

Daphne: Nice to see you've made an effort today. I swear, last time you had a formal shirt on.

ANXIETY: *Busted.*

Josh: Apologies, my nice clothes shrank in my dryer.
Daphne: Oh, I didn't say the shirt was "nice."

We sat there for a while in silence.

Daphne: Fine.

I raised my eyebrows.

Daphne: During dinner, at the restaurant, I experienced an anxiety attack. I was suddenly overwhelmed by this sense of doom, and I felt light-headed. I hurried to the bathroom and . . .

She bit her bottom lip in shame.

Daphne: I hid in a cubicle.

I waited for her to continue.

Daphne: It felt like my chest was being sat on by a mule. I couldn't get a full breath. My sister-in-law, or whatever she is now, came in ten minutes later to ask if I was okay. She was then followed by my mother, who started lambasting me from the other side of the cubicle door. "Anything to get out of being with your mother!" and "You can't go five minutes without acting up, can you?!" followed by "I've come all this way and you've made me come in here even with my bad knees?" She said, "Grow up, Daphne. You're a fifty-three-year-old woman. You can't be expecting hugs in restaurant toilets because you're not capable of handling a simple family dinner."

EMPATHY: *Ouch. That's hurtful.*
CRITIC: *This is good stuff: I'm writing this one down.*

Daphne: The sad thing is, Joshua, she was right. I did want a hug in that
moment. From that horrible bag of a woman. I . . . wanted to be held.

Her eyes twitched with emotion, and she responded quickly by narrowing
her gaze to a steely squint to regain control of her reaction. It was like she
was the sole player of her own bodily Whac-A-Mole game, where each
chirpy, jumping mole was a negative emotion, with Daphne wielding the
toy hammer to silence it. She regained her composure.

Daphne: Anyway, the episode subsided, and I rejoined my family at the
dinner table. I think my eldest daughter guessed what was going on.
She is very perceptive. I transformed into my best self very quickly
and became charming again, despite my mother shooting me daggers
between smiles. I think I folded her into the taxi myself when it was time
to go home. Is this enough to fill a stress jug, Joshua? Pining for an old
woman's affection?
Josh: I'm saddened to hear that you felt so lonely during your anxiety
attack. Sounds like you are very resilient, Daphne. From what I've
heard so far, it sounds like your mother holds power over you. Over
your self-value.
Daphne: Don't pity me.
Josh: I don't.

There was a pause, and Daphne stared at one of my plants on the shelving
unit. I noticed that her neck and chest became red and blotchy, but her face
was as motionless as ever.

Daphne: Answer me this, please: Why can't some people be pleased?
Why . . . why was I never enough?
Josh: Who says you were never enough?
Daphne: My mother's approval meant everything to me growing up. It was
like a drug. My father was a rather meek man and served only to please
my mother. He was very loving to me, but the value of his love was, let's
say, less potent than what she could provide. She had such a powerful
gift, her love, yet she shared it sparingly. Why? Why was I never enough
for her to share all of it?
Josh: I can't answer that. Only your mother knows and . . . even she
might not.

Daphne looked at me as if she had expected this answer.

Daphne: I'm so sorry. I shall stop all this whining, it's preposterous. I'm a successful, prestigious actor with enough money to buy a new mother if I'd like. I'm sorry for wasting your time—you must have people with actual needs who require your help, rather than the first-world neuroticism of an actor who still craves to dangle from her mother's teat.

> **CRITIC:** "... dangle from her mother's teat." Got it. What was the first bit you said?

She suddenly faked an upturn in positivity, which was one of the few times I could discern that she was purely acting.

Daphne: Lovely session! Thank you. I don't need to stay the full hour, do I? I feel that's enough for today.

> **ESCAPIST:** She wants to leave.
> **ANALYTICAL:** Persuade her back if you can. But obviously don't push it if this is sincere.
> **COMPASSION:** Let's help her feel the validation she deserves.

Josh: You said that your mother's love was like a drug. I took from this that she is capable of being loving? That she has given you her approval in the past?

> **DETECTIVE:** Hunting out introjections are we, Fletch?
> **ANALYTICAL:** We're learning more and exploring with Daphne.

Daphne stopped assembling her things to leave. There was a moment. She was transported somewhere long forgotten in the deepest echelons of her memories. I couldn't tell where she'd gone, but it seemed like it was a happy place. The steely-faced veneer broke to allow a smile: the smile of someone who felt safe enough to be happy, even if just for a moment. I really wished to be part of it, to feel it, but something told me I wouldn't find out what the memory was.

Daphne: My mother adored me as a child. She would brush my hair, sing to me, take me to the theater, dress me and show me off to all our family and her friends. I think she wanted the best for me, but this became convoluted and enmeshed in her own hopes and dreams. The admiration became . . . transactional . . . like I had to earn it as I grew older. The intimacy slowed down unless it was the day of a performance, or if I pleased the director of a show. I had to constantly practice—my singing, my physical theater, my posture . . .

As she described her past, Daphne's body language loosened. The curtains of her own stage parted slightly, allowing me to see briefly what was in the wings. I appreciated this. I also did not want to bring attention to it in case Daphne stopped.

Daphne: I recall one day when she hadn't said anything nice to me for weeks. I was fourteen. No physical contact, no praise, nothing. I didn't wish to be infantilized, just acknowledged. Come the day of my theater company's successful production of *Richard III*, and my mother's wall of coldness abated for a brief period. My part as Lady Anne Neville drew a rousing reception. The pride in her eyes as the audience stood and clapped. I was paraded around dinner evenings for weeks. She held me close, showing me off, like a trophy.

> **EMPATHY:** *I imagine this felt amazing for Daphne after feeling like she was being starved of love.*
> **ANALYTICAL:** *Conditional affection, mind you.*

Josh: This affection sounds very . . . conditional?

She looked at me.

Daphne: It's what I'm coming to realize.
Josh: The affection is being given on the *condition* that you perform well. That you are successful and please others around you. That you are— for the want of a better summary—*worth* giving intimacy, praise, and love, but only when you are being *extraordinary*?
Daphne: Yes.

A tear threatened to fall. She dabbed it away quickly.

Daphne: I think she wanted the best for me, but in a strange, cutthroat way. If it wasn't for her, I wouldn't be where I am today. I wouldn't have attended drama school. She funded everything, pushed me to my limits. She . . . helped to create everything I have achieved today. I do appreciate it. I'm not a spoiled bitch taking things for granted—I really do appreciate it. I appreciate her . . .

Josh: It sounds like it was easier for your mum to acknowledge her pride for what she helped to construct—in this instance, your public persona. A configuration of yourself that has brought you incredible success. You also sound grateful for her help. She sounds very influential.

Daphne withdrew another tissue from her own handbag, ignoring the box I'd placed on the table.

Daphne: She had a difficult time growing up. I know my grandmother was incredibly harsh. According to my cousin, she sent my mother to a boarding school run by abusive nuns. I also know that, before she met my father, she was beaten for years by a drunken boyfriend. When she went to my grandmother to say she was leaving him, Grandmother sided with the abusive boyfriend.

EMPATHY: *She's stepping into her mother's frame of reference.*
ANALYTICAL: *This usually helps to contextualize.*

Daphne: I think that two things have happened.
Josh: Yeah?
Daphne: I think that she is living vicariously through me. I think my mother is envious of my access to opportunities, to success, but at the same time extremely passionate about providing them for me. She knows what it's like not to have them. I think she also sees my achievements as her own—she parades me around with the intent of showing people "Hey, see? I can do things and be successful—look at my daughter!" I think she poured all her love into providing me a life that she could never have, but at the expense of being a cold, matriarchal nightmare.

Josh: So when you have needs, like having an anxiety attack, this isn't
   delivering the life your mother wishes she could live vicariously?
Daphne: Yes!

   ANALYTICAL: *You captured the frame of reference.*
   COMPASSION: *Well done.*

Daphne: That is me *failing*. Being emotional, struggling—basically anything
   where I'm not being applauded is, to my mother, deviating from the script.

· ·

We continued to talk about the impact Daphne's mother had on her life.
The more she spoke, the more the discussion became a balanced analysis.
I still had to pinch myself now and then. My own frame of reference still
wanted to marvel at this world-famous actor sitting in my office, but I kept
redirecting my focus because I was here for Daphne, the person behind
the persona.

Josh: It seems paradoxical. Do you think you could have achieved what you
   have if your mother was as nurturing and affectionate as you'd have
   liked?
Daphne: Who knows? It's impossible to imagine a parallel timeline, but I am
   certain I wouldn't have achieved as much as I have, if anything at all in
   my acting and stage career, if not for her. That said, I do wonder what my
   life would have been . . .

   ANALYTICAL: *Perhaps draw upon the Empty Chair from the Gestalt
   approach?*
   COMPASSION: *It can be very emotional but maybe it will help Daphne
   with these difficult emotions.*
   DETECTIVE: *It often reveals other things in our jug.*
   CRITIC: *She's not going to do the Empty Chair, Josh. You've watched too
   much TV, you're not Gabriel Byrne.*
   VOLITION: *Give it a go.*

Daphne was lost in contemplation and seemed to be staring at my peace lily.

Josh: Go with me on this—if you'd like. But imagine, hypothetically, if you could say something to your mother, talk to her face-to-face, but with a guarantee of nonjudgment, with empathy and care, what would you say?

She started to laugh.

Daphne: Are you going to dress up as my mother, Joshua? Suckle me into therapeutic growth?

IRREVERENCE: *LMAO. He's got the tits for it.*

I tried to silently convey the sincerity of inviting her into such a scenario. She looked back over at the peace lily.

Josh: You don't need to look at me if it helps. Choose anything in the room and say it to that. If Mum was the intimate, hugging type, what would you say?

I expected dismissal and a rebuke, but surprisingly Daphne continued to stare at the lily. I think she was considering the invitation. What happened next was simply remarkable.

Daphne: Hello, Mother. Oh my, you look different from the last time I saw you. Did you know you still have a price tag stuck to your pot? You were £4.99, apparently from Sainsbury's. I wonder what it's like living in this office all the time. I suppose it would give you a window into some levels of empathy and compassion. Are you being fed and watered appropriately?

She looked at me. I continued to listen attentively. She looked back at the lily.

Daphne: Oh, that's *new*, Mother. You'd usually respond with something abhorrent by now. A judgment, a snipe, an unfounded opinion projected as if Moses were etching it into the stone at your very command. Well, I thank you for allowing me the space to air my thoughts.

She looked at me for clarification.

Daphne: And you say this version of my mum is one that listens without judgment?

Josh: Mhm.

She sighed, took a deep breath, then resumed talking to the ever-patient peace lily.

Daphne: I've struggled with my mind all my life, Mum. It's different. It torments me. I've always wanted you to take it away for me, but I also appreciate that you wanted to make me strong. I'm afraid that if I ever told you the contents of my mind, you would leave me. Abandon me. That would break me. I'm sorry I was never enough for you, but you must realize that you also failed me in some ways. None of us are perfect, but I felt you held me hostage with your love. This . . . this has made me bury parts of myself that I am ashamed of.

The tears finally started to fall.

Daphne: I don't even know who I am when I'm not doing my job. The person I am offstage, offscreen, is such a complex mess, and I feel so, so alone. I lie to myself, my children, my family, and, most of all, I lie to you. I lie to you to feel safe. But I can't keep lying because it's killing me. It's unfair to my children and those close to me. It's . . . unfair to me too.

The professional veneer had totally disappeared. This was Daphne in a raw, emotional, and beautiful state. The tears streamed and her nose blocked up, but she continued.

Daphne: There are so many things I wish I could tell you. Or tell anyone, for that matter. I . . . I am not the woman you wished me to be. In fact, I have always questioned if I am a woman at all. I'm sorry I didn't settle with the charming man you wished for yourself. I've tried that. He turned out to be an asshole—an abusive one at that. I question whether I like men too. I don't know if I am a woman and I don't know if I am solely attracted to men. I cannot conform to your tradition, Mum. I am not the trophy you wish me to be. I am an identityless, genderless, queer middle-aged person still riding the wave of a skill you helped me to perfect. But I just wish you could see me for me. I wish you could see and love me. I . . . I wish *I* could see me and love me. I . . . wish you could help me with that. I'm sorry . . . I'm sorry that you can't.

COMPASSION: *Whoa.*
ANALYTICAL: *Congruence.*

Daphne looked up at me, her breathing labored from relief. She suddenly seemed struck by a pang of anxiety.

Daphne: This is all confidential, right? I mean, you could sell this stuff for so much money. Oh my God . . . what have I done? What have I done to my family?

EMPATHY: *Understandable to feel scared and vulnerable after that.*

Josh: Thank you for sharing that with me, Daphne. It was lovely to hear you open up. I reiterate that whatever you say in here stays strictly confidential. It stays in this room and can remain here forever if you wish it to.
Daphne: Thank you.

This time she took one of the tissues from the box between us.

Emotional Conservatism
Close to Home

Opening up can be very difficult for a lot of people. I present to you a scale: At one end you've got someone who is incredibly neurotic, attention seeking, and constantly vocalizes their emotions to anyone and everyone in the area. Basically, that's me every year on my birthday—or me at *your* birthday telling everyone about my childhood trauma when you're about to blow out your candles. At the other end of the scale, you have someone who is extremely emotionally conservative, a stiff upper lip, wouldn't cry at *Marley & Me,* cold, never shed a public tear in their life. They walk or shy away from any opportunity to talk about feelings, deeming it a weakness. Vulnerability to this person is nauseating: "Keep Calm and Carry On."

I invite you to consider where you might be on the scale. For context, you can use the people you know for comparison. Who is the strictest, most reserved person you know? Perhaps they would prefer to show anger instead of vulnerability? Which person wouldn't share a single tear of joy if a nuzzling baby otter was placed into their arms? Place them at one end of the scale. Now think of someone who is very open with their emotions, either tastefully or annoyingly. They could be confident with them or irritating, it's up to you. Place them at the other end. Now, where would you place yourself? Ideally, and whatever the context, my aim is to invite emotionally conservative people and the emotionally open to meet in the middle. It is here where I believe we can talk and work on tricky things that burden us.

The aim, for me, is not to encourage everyone to be a wailing neurotic, constantly at the mercy of their feelings (although you can be in my therapy room; it's more than welcome), but to see expressing vulnerability as a positive shift for our own well-being, not a fundamental change to who you are. Strength should not be defined by your ability to shut up but by your ability to shift across the scale of emotional conservatism when needed. For example, if I'm really struggling with anxious feelings and depressive thoughts and I'm contemplating self-harm, then I'm going to need to shift to a place where talking is going to help me. In contrast, there are times when it's completely okay to shut up, such as when a friend opens up about something traumatic. What they are saying may evoke negative feelings in me, but I'm going to stay quiet and listen to prioritize their feelings.

One of the major problems with emotional conservatism is that it is anchored by anxiety itself—the fear of feeling negative and often unknown emotions, or feeling awkward and helpless in response to someone needing help. I still see it in the people close to me in my life.

This is part of the emotionally conservative fear that listening to someone's problems automatically makes us responsible for that person. This isn't true. You don't have to become Florence Nightingale and someone's forever carer if you choose to take five minutes to listen to them. Instead, the emotionally conservative avoid difficult subjects because, quite frankly, it just isn't worth the fuss. The unknown is too scary. Placating our own feelings of helplessness often trumps the desire to be compassionate toward someone else. I've often found that I don't want my friends and family to feel that helplessness; this is why I have often lied in response to the question "How are you?"

"I'm fine. You?"

14
Harry:
Under the Floodlights

Steward: You lads look lost; do you need a hand?

I showed our tickets.

Steward: You're in the right place. Just go through this turnstile and up the stairs. Wait, hold on a sec . . .

He looked Harry up and down.

Steward: This says it's a child's ticket. You trying to swindle us here, young man?

Harry: I'm twelve!

Steward: Twelve my backside. You look older than him!

He gestured at me. We all laughed.

Steward: First time here?

Josh: Yeah, we're really excited. My brother is a huge fan.

Steward: Well, it's good to have you here. Enjoy the match, lads!

We climbed what seemed like a hundred flights of stairs. When we arrived at the top, I took a moment to lean over and catch my breath. My brother laughed at me.

Josh: Could have done with our *Portal* gun for that.

Harry: Or maybe just stop smoking?

Josh: Shut up.

The moment finally came when we walked from the gantry into the stadium. We were greeted by enormous floodlights that illuminated a perfect sea of green down below. It was remarkable and even better than I'd imagined. The stadium was enormous and filled with the chanting of excited fans.

Josh: Not bad for our first match this, is it?

Harry beamed and pointed toward the players warming up on the pitch below. Kickoff soon followed, and it took Harry's team only six minutes to find the back of the net. We screamed and jumped up simultaneously along with hundreds of people around us. The team went on to score two more and win the game comfortably. A wonderful buzz filtered around the stadium.

Harry: That was amazing! I'm losing my voice!
Josh: I can't wait to grass you up to Mum for all that shouting and swearing you've been doing.

As my little brother clapped the players off the pitch, I stared at the joy on his face. I'd not been making the best choices lately. I was wasting my money on stuff I shouldn't (whoever says cannabis isn't addictive is lying), and I'd gotten myself into debt. However, I'd used my last few pounds to take us to the football match. The look on Harry's face made me feel it was worth every penny. With the aperture shortening, the details of Harry's goofy grin, wonky glasses, and joy-filled eyes sharpened as I watched his gaze flit from player to player. I was vicariously experiencing his joy and became fully immersed within his frame of reference. Lately I had been feeling like a loser, but at least tonight suggested that I was a semidecent big brother.

Harry: I'm hungry. Let's get chips.
Josh: Well, you're buying. I'm broke as fuck.

Harry took out some pocket money Mum had given him and flicked the coins around in his palm.

Harry: Deal.

15
Levi

Five minutes earlier than the scheduled appointment time, my office door flew open like a saloon door that had just been kicked in.

Levi: You're not the only one who thinks this stuff is OCD.

> **ANXIETY:** *Jesus!*

I was halfway through a blueberry yogurt, and a spoonful of it splattered all over my jeans. Levi didn't seem to notice or care, but he sat down on the sofa ready to start.

> **ANALYTICAL:** *Remember your therapy boundaries. This includes time boundaries.*

Josh: Good morning, Levi. We're not due to start for a few minutes and I'm just finishing a snack. I'll go get us some hot drinks, if that's okay. Tea? Coffee?

Levi: Sure, I'll have a tea, please.

I headed to the communal kitchen, where I found Dr. Patel stirring a coffee. He greeted me warmly before spotting the white stains on my crotch, and he immediately returned back to his office. I patted myself down with some paper towel, made two cups of tea, and walked carefully back to the therapy room. I stepped in to see Levi fiddling with my window blinds.

Josh: There we go.

I placed the tea on a side table next to the sofa.

Levi: Cheers.

We both sat down. I was happy that he'd chosen to attend after his ominous exit at the end of the last session.

Josh: So, what's this about OCD?

Levi: After our last session I went to my doctor, like you said. Not the one Safia knows, but my one registered in Oldham. I said, "Doc, my shrink thinks I have OCD," and I showed him my back with all the cuts and bruises and things.

Levi bellowed a laugh.

Levi: You should have seen his face! Never been taken seriously by the doc before, but I had his attention on this occasion.

EMPATHY: *We know what that feels like.*

Josh: What happened then?

Levi: I was referred to a specialist on an "emergency" basis. I told the doc there was no need for drama and I wasn't in an emergency. I've *seen* emergencies, I told him. Lads and ladies with blood pouring out of their skulls over drunken disagreements. He was having none of it. The day after, I saw this psychologist and she asked me loads of weird questions, then started rambling on.

He took a loud, slurpy sip of his tea.

Levi: I started to zone out a bit when she went all science and stuff—could have been talking Japanese, for all I know. Then she mentioned about this obsessive disorder you were banging on about. "Oh See Dee." Started asking me about my intrusive thoughts and behaviors. I said to her that's what you said!

COMPASSION: *Well done for noticing it, Josh. It's also great that he went to his doctor like you suggested.*
CRITIC: *It only worked out because of your own OCD, charlatan. No empathetic skills here. "Oh look, there's someone like me." I'm not giving you a medal.*

Levi: Anyway, she prescribed me some wacky pills and said I should start OCD-specific therapy. Something called . . . what was it now . . . ? Exposure-prevention something whatever . . . ?

Josh: Exposure-response prevention? ERP for short?

Levi: Bingo! She offered to refer me to some people she knew, but I said I would see if I could do it with you.

Exposure-Response Prevention

Exposure-response prevention (ERP) is a type of therapy that encourages clients to face their fears and let obsessive and intrusive thoughts arise without trying to neutralize or banish them. ERP willingly invites the wrath of the amygdala, which can rewire itself when we expose ourselves to fear, but minus anxious compulsions. Interestingly, the amygdala can rewire itself only when it's active, so to me it makes sense to walk toward a specific fear as the first step in turning down the threat response.

Exposure-response prevention is the gold-standard treatment for obsessive-compulsive disorder (OCD) and is backed by worldwide empirical evidence. Full knowledge of OCD by a therapist is imperative in the treatment of OCD because research also shows that conventional open-talk therapy can, in the long term, make the disorder worse. This is because one of OCD's most common compulsions is to seek reassurance about the content of intrusive thoughts. Another common compulsion is rumination, which open-talk therapy can unknowingly facilitate. Compulsions arise from anxiety, and, as we know, if we act on what the anxiety tells us to do, we thank it (and the amygdala) and the cycle continues. Recovery from OCD, like any anxiety disorder, pivots on our willingness to lean in to uncertainty. I say this as someone who spent many years doing the opposite.

Levi (cont.)

Josh: Where are we starting, Levi?

Levi: What do you mean?

He shifted on the sofa and avoided my gaze.

Josh: Consider all the intrusive thoughts that trouble you: Which would you like to start with?

Levi: I can't . . .

Josh: I know it's scary, Levi. Facing your worst fears takes a particular kind of courage. Just know that this is a safe space and I'm with you during our first steps into it.

Levi: I can't do this. What if you're wrong? What if there is a demon and you have missed it? What if I turn into the horrible things the thoughts say I am? Why are you saying one thing and everyone else says something different?

DETECTIVE: *Perhaps look at the origins of this doubt, Captain.*

Josh: Everyone else?

Levi: My wife. People in our community. You know . . .

INTUITION: *Getting some red-flag vibes here.*

ANXIETY: *You could be wrong.*

Josh: Your "community"?

Levi: *(raising his voice)* Yes, my community! You some sort of therapy parrot? Just echoing my last sentence back to me?

I said nothing.

Levi: I apologize.

Josh: It's okay.

Levi: I am part of a faith community. We have a church. We conduct ceremonies and the like. They're kinda nutjobs to the outsider, but they're just devout to their faith. We . . . we are devout to our faith.

ANALYTICAL: *It's okay to lead if trying to explore red flags.*

Josh: Have you always been part of this community?

Levi: Nah, I've not always been religious. They accepted me at a difficult point in my life. I have Safia to thank for that. They saved me. *She* saved me. She's my guardian angel. She introduced me a couple of months after we met. Since then, I've been doing my best to pay penance for my . . . life choices. My sins. We got married in the chapel in front of the community. One of the happiest days of my life.

I smiled because it seemed like the polite thing to do. I didn't know what to feel at this point, so I just continued trying to immerse myself in Levi's world.

Levi: When I really started to struggle with my head, they wanted to help. Pastor Michael, Safia, and even some of the community really wanted to pitch in, you know? They think I'm a good man. They believe that a demon must have corrupted some of my mind. They're . . . a really caring community. I don't think they see things like some of you science lot do.

EMPATHY: *Sounds like there's a hint of doubt in his voice, as much as he clearly appreciates this support network.*

Josh: It feels like you're stuck between two contrasting modes of help for your intrusive thoughts: one narrative coming from home . . . the community . . . and the other from the health service?

He pondered for a moment.

Levi: Yeah. I suppose I am. It's weird, though. I haven't told Safia or Pastor Michael any of what we're doing. I haven't told them I went to see

the psychologist, or you, or that I went to see my doctor. The one I'm
registered with, that is.

Josh: Why do you feel the need to hide what you're doing here, Levi?

Out of what seemed like nowhere, he gave an enormous, full-body
shudder. He seemed to dissociate briefly. His giant arms curled in on
himself in what looked like an attempt to self-soothe.

Josh: Are you okay?

Levi: Yeah. I think . . .

He stood up and rotated one shoulder blade as if trying to ease out a
knot, gritting his teeth and exhaling with a forced effort. I wondered if the
shoulder pain was a welcome distraction from the question.

Levi: I just want to keep some things separate.

EMPATHY: *He feels scared. Trepidatious.*

COMPASSION: *Okay, let's not push this now.*

Josh: Okay.

He sat back down and, as he had in previous sessions, began to ceremo-
nially crack his knuckles. I know an anxious habit when I see one.

Josh: I can see this topic is making you feel uncomfortable, Levi. Remember
that this is a safe space and if you'd like to discuss it—or anything—with
me, then you can. It stays in here. I'm just aware that we should work
through tricky content at a manageable pace. Last time you hinted that
you might not come back to the sessions and, if I'm being honest, I'd be
sad if that happened.

COMPASSION: *Nice, you meant this.*

CRITIC: *Did he?*

ANXIETY: *Would save us some worry if he didn't come back.*

ESCAPIST: *Good point.*

Levi nodded. He ungripped his hands and placed them calmly on his knees.

Josh: If you don't mind me asking, who is this community doctor that you and Safia consult with?

He looked out the window for a moment, considering what I had asked.

Levi: An alternative doctor . . .

IRREVERENCE: *Don't say homeopathy.*
CRITIC: *Don't say homeopathy.*

I gently lifted my chin, gesturing for him to elaborate.

Levi: The community has an alternative, spiritual doctor. She migrated here a couple of decades ago and became part of our church. She is the antidote to the modern, normal medicine that pharmacies make huge profits from.

ANALYTICAL: *I think he meant pharmaceuticals. "Big Pharma."*

Levi: She has helped so many people in the community where normal treatment hasn't worked. She uses sacred spells and harnesses the power of the spirits to cleanse the mind, the body, and our souls and stuff. She has this ancient wisdom passed down through thousands of years. Generations after generations. That's why everyone was hopeful she could help me.

DETECTIVE: *Use of past tense.*
ANALYTICAL: *It appears he has lost trust in the help that's coming from his community.*
IRREVERENCE: *Of course he has! You can't go to a bloody witch doctor to cure your OCD. What planet are they on?! I really want to visit it. Mum, I'm home!*
CRITIC: *Absolutely bananas—the lot of them.*
VOLITION: *Go back to Levi's frame of reference and stop being so judgmental.*

Levi: But she couldn't. I mean . . . she has helped me a bit.

Josh: How so?

Levi: Paying penance.

Josh: The self-flagellation? I mean . . . the hitting yourself on your back?

Levi: Yes. I said penance.

Josh: What does Safia think of all this?

Levi: She's fully on board with it. She supports all the doctor's ideas and anything Pastor Michael says.

IRREVERENCE: *This is absolutely mental, Josh.*

VOLITION: *Frame of reference!*

Josh: Okay. Like what? Just so I can get an idea of what you have tried so far.

Levi: We've done a lot to try and make me better. Like . . . erm . . . I've starved myself to starve the demon. Given pints of my own blood as tribute. I've whipped myself, as you've so kindly pointed out. Vows of silence. I've even lent my sexual rites in these . . . ceremonies, which I'm not gonna talk about to you. I've always had Safia by my side encouraging me through it. She's like my rock.

TRIGGER: *Struggle.*

BIOLOGY: *Engaging.*

COMPASSION: *I could cry.*

VOLITION: *You're not going to.*

Josh: Wait . . . what . . . "ceremonies"?

Levi: All sorts of weird, spiritual stuff, Josh. Any stranger walking in, I think they'd lose their head if they saw it . . . what is it now . . . ? "Out of context"?

Josh: What could a stranger walk in on?

ANALYTICAL: *You've lost Levi and are now following your own intrigue. Your own needs.*

CRITIC: *You've made this session about yourself.*

ANXIETY: *You don't want to know this.*

Levi: I don't feel like sharing the specifics. Let's just say it's all in the name of "purification." Not that it has worked. Ha ha!

I noticed that my heart was racing, and my muscles felt tingly and restless. I was gripping the arms of my chair so tightly that when I let go there were sweaty imprints where my fingers had been. I reached over for the tea, trying to act calm and reassuring, but my hand shook and the brown liquid sloshed onto the table in front of Levi's now-attentive gaze.

Levi: Are you okay?

VOLITION: *Congruence. Authenticity. Professional honesty.*
ANALYTICAL: *Agreed.*

Josh: Yes. I'm just shocked at hearing about this, that's all. Not shocked at you. At all. I appreciate your sharing this with me. I'm shaken hearing what you've been through. That's a lot to go through, Levi. I'm really saddened to hear that you had to experience it.

He cocked his head slightly and studied my face for a moment, before suddenly seeming to shut down. Levi refused to say anything more on the subject. The knuckles began to crack again.

Josh: Would you like to try some ERP?
Levi: Running the nightclub doors around this city, I've been offered many things, but never that.

He smiled. I joined him. This was his take-it-or-leave-it offer of resuming the session on terms he could accept. Perhaps the nature of what he spoke about regarding his home life put the idea of doing ERP into a more positive context.

Levi: Okay. Let's do this.

..

Levi confided that he struggled with two forms of intrusive thoughts: violent and sexual. He experienced intrusive thoughts about physically and sexually harming his friends and family, which included his daughter and his infant granddaughter. The thoughts seemed to focus on his granddaughter, which is common for OCD and intrusive thoughts, as the threat response is more acute when the "stakes are high." This is why so many postnatal mothers experience intrusive thoughts toward their babies. I strongly reiterate that, after a risk assessment, I did not believe Levi to be a danger to his family. Levi was not his intrusive thoughts. Intrusive thoughts often thrive because they are the opposite of who we are. I did hold concerns about *his* well-being, though, especially given the number of potential ritualistic-abuse red flags I had heard about.

The beginning of our exposure-response prevention exercises started with Levi showing me pictures of his daughter and granddaughter. He found this incredibly difficult, but he persevered. I asked him to rate his anxiety at the start of the exposure and throughout it on a scale of one to ten. When we showed me a picture of his granddaughter in a wading pool, he immediately looked away and gritted his teeth in anguish.

Josh: It's okay to look at your granddaughter, Levi. Did you take this picture?

He started sobbing and turned away, looking disgusted with himself.

Levi: Yeah, I did.
Josh: Did you have the thoughts when you took this picture?
Levi: No! Of course not.
Josh: Well, isn't that an encouraging sign?

He said nothing.

ANALYTICAL: *Try to keep his attention on the exposure.*

Josh: Who else is in this picture?

Levi forced a turn of his head and looked at the picture.

Levi: That's my daughter. Over here is my ex-wife. And this . . . this is the fence I botched trying to construct.

He let out a stifled, sinus-blocked chuckle—temporarily forgetting the trigger in this image.

Josh: Tell me more about that day but keep looking at the picture. Try not to take your gaze away from it.

Levi proceeded to tell me about the day. It was his granddaughter's birthday, and most of his family was in the garden. They'd bought a paddling pool and enjoyed a barbecue together. He explained that he and his ex-wife had a good relationship and that both supported their daughter as much as they could. He said it was one of his favorite days that year.

Josh: That sounds lovely! Levi, you said you were a ten out of ten on the anxiety scale when you opened the picture. What is it now?

COMPASSION: *Come on . . . come on . . .*

Levi: It's . . . it's a six . . . I'm still scared and feel weird . . . but it's a six . . .

COMPASSION: *YES!*
EMPATHY: *YES!*

Josh: Notice how your anxiety came down without evading the picture? Some anxiety will still be there because the brain hasn't fully decided it is safe yet. But it will the more we work on it.

Levi sat with his mouth slightly agape. He was trying to process it all. I sensed an ounce of hope in his facial expression.

Levi: You really don't think I have a demon, do you?
Josh: No.

He nodded in acknowledgment.

Josh: We need to teach the threat response that these thoughts, despite their horrendous content, are not danger. They're just bizarre, weird thoughts that contrast with and antagonize our morals. Discomfort is not danger.
Levi: Do you think I can get better?

COMPASSION: *I don't think you're broken.*

Josh: Yes. In short. Yes, I do. But we're going to have to make more effort to look after ourselves.

Self-Care

I often ask clients, "What do you do to look after yourself?" and I'm frequently met with a confused expression. It's not surprising, as we're constantly bombarded, whether from the news or social media, with information about what we "should" be doing for our overall wellness. A vague platitude excreted from the popular sphere is the concept of "self-care." I'm a huge advocate of caring for the self—why wouldn't I be? I'm a therapist, I care about people, and it's important. Unfortunately, though, in my opinion this term has been hijacked, misused, and turned into a multimillion-dollar industry that often taps into our insecurities, fears, and perfectionism. If you type "self-care" into social media, you will be greeted by a montage of contemporary clichés, usually involving someone orgasmically swooning over a live bacteria yogurt, practicing meditation atop a mountain in front of a meticulously placed 4K camera, thrusting chiseled abs into your face while drinking a kale smoothie, or smugly hiking through nature behind a tenuously linked quote from the Dalai Lama. And let's not forget the ambiguous quotes about "boundaries" and "letting go" sketched upon a pastel meme.

It might be helpful to know that, in therapeutic terms, self-care is whatever you deem to be nurturing and wholesome for you. Everyone is different. We're not total beginners at caring for ourselves; we know that eating healthy, not drinking to excess, exercise, and sleep are important for day-to-day living. But self-care that is subjective to the individual is what really makes a difference to our overall well-being.

When I see clients who want some help with self-care for their anxieties, I find they're often coming from a *reactionary* place instead of a personal one. I have lost count of the number of times I have heard "I've tried mindfulness, yoga, tai chi, cutting out gluten, keeping a gratitude journal, breathwork, CBD oil, mantras, et cetera, and none of it works!" These methods can all be great ways to practice self-care and a great preventative approach for mental health, but none of them are instant medicine for a feeling we are trying to "fix." And they also don't work for everyone. If you're doing something to *simulate* self-care, rather than live it, then your self-care won't be effective. This is forcing self-care and not being yourself, like a person who forces themselves to run every morning but hates it. Full disclosure: I fell into this trap myself for many years.

Remember that self-care is not a skill to be perfected. This only leads to a self-depleting paradox in which the thing that is supposed to restore you just makes you feel bad instead. You can attend all the seminars and listen to all the podcasts about how to look after yourself, but ultimately you are the barometer of what works for you. Trust yourself when it comes to knowing what makes you feel good, rather than what works for anyone else. It saddens me when I see clients who struggle to absorb the core meaning of self-care and then use their supposed "failure" as a baton with which to beat themselves.

My own self-care presents itself in many ways. It can look conventional: I enjoy walks in nature, reading books, relaxing in a sauna, playing with the dog, lying in hot baths, and taking mindful moments throughout my day. However, my self-care can also look unconventional: sleeping in late, playing video games, drinking beers with my friends, staying up all night laughing, eating trash food on holidays. These things are nurturing for me too. I have learned to let go of trying to emulate perfectionism when it comes to stereotypical self-care and take time to listen to my mind and body and give them what they want. We are human: Sometimes we need rest, nutrition, and silence; on other occasions we want stimuli, hedonism, social time, and memorable experiences.

Don't be deflated if you feel you can't access a conventional mode of self-care. I'm happy that a lot of my friends can find peace through activities such as yoga or going to the gym. If this applies to you, then keep at it! I enjoy beginners' yoga now and then, but unfortunately I have the athletic constitution of a rubber ball, so sometimes I'll sit on my ass, enjoy a milkshake, and spend the evening insulting people through my headset while playing games online. Self-care is subjective and can shift according to what's going on in your life at any one time. You just have to find what works for you at the point you're at right now. Remember, self-care is less effective when it becomes something that you have to "do," as opposed to an expression of self-permission to unlock the shackles of rigid *productivity anxiety*.

In my practice, as well as personally, I've found that guilt can prevent us from taking time for self-care. It's such an annoying emotion. Try not to allow guilt to take the space that it doesn't deserve. It's okay to stop regularly and have time to yourself. If anything, when you're rested and recharged, you're more likely a fresher, better version of yourself. Much like *productivity anxiety*, when you hear an "I should . . ." from your mind during a time that is dedicated for you, consider telling it to get lost.

Self-care is a *skill*, and part of that skill is the ability to be flexible and compassionate to the self. This doesn't mean starving and neglecting your children, or refusing medication to the person for whom you're caring, or denying a spare life jacket to your sister because her drowning is interrupting your relaxing cigarette break. It *does* mean implementing a sacred, personal boundary that is mostly respected, by yourself and others. This is okay. It is healthy and needed. Self-care is a necessary skill for a balanced life and has nothing to do with doing stomach crunches in front of a camera while eating thrice-fermented kimchi. It's about doing what you know will be good for you, even if it means tolerating discomfort and being courageous about your boundaries from time to time.

16
Zahra

For the first time in our sessions, Zahra entered the office with a beaming smile.

Zahra: Josh, I drove here! Oh my God, I drove here!

She was almost visibly glowing with the triumph of it.

Zahra: Well, not exactly all the way. Nasrin, my friend, drove me to the top of your road and I drove the car about a kilometer to here. I haven't been behind the wheel of my own car for so long.

COMPASSION: *That's amazing.*
EMPATHY: *She feels some compassion for herself.*

Josh: That's incredible. Well done! What a way to face your anxiety. Such a great exposure and practice of willful tolerance.
Zahra: I know, right?!

She was suddenly blindsided by a thought, which materialized as a feeling, which then morphed into physical expression. All of a sudden she looked dejected. Her shoulders drooped, and she let out a sigh.

Zahra: I'll be honest. It was just one road. I've asked Nasrin to come back and drive me home later after she's been exploring. It still terrifies me. I was relieved to just get out of the car once I was here. I can't see myself ever being able to drive on the motorway again. I just . . .
Josh: For a moment there you were proud of yourself. One step at a time. Why allow the critic to decide the value of your success?

CRITIC: *Because I am amazing, powerful, and ruler of all things objective.*
VOLITION: *And full of yourself.*

Zahra: Just forget it. I'll moan about other stuff in my stress jug instead.

INTUITION: *Try to act before she sits down.*
ANALYTICAL: *Build on the exposure work she has already started.*
VOLITION: *Go grab your coat.*

Zahra: Where are you going?

I walked to the door and began to put my jacket on.

Josh: We can't do driving exposures sitting in here, can we?

Her eyes widened.

Driving Anxiety

Driving anxiety is one of the most common manifestations of panic disorder and agoraphobia. Most driving anxiety has nothing to do with the fear of driving itself but the fear of losing control in some way and ending up in a catastrophic accident. Most people with driving anxiety believe that their panic will make them lose control—causing them to veer into the central embankment and creating a thirty-two–car pileup. This is usually accompanied by graphic intrusive thoughts about crashing or suddenly steering off a bridge with the family screaming in the back. All of this is because we feel an adrenaline rush behind the wheel.

Anxiety and panic, in general, do not make you lose control. If anything, they make you hyperaware and extra cautious of your surroundings. Most accidents are caused by carelessness and a lack of attention. Anxiety turns your head the other way, and we overanalyze potential threats when on the road. However, it is that "just in case" that often convinces people to avoid driving their car. The threat response has convinced them that the stakes are far too high to attempt to drive again. What if you panic and lose control? What if you pass out? What if you have a heart attack behind the wheel? This is usually backed up by feelings of guilt, such as the desire to not risk the lives of family members, or being too irresponsible and a danger to other drivers.

There are varying levels of driving anxiety. Some people can drive wherever they like without giving it any thought. These people have a quiet amygdala when cruising in the fast lane of the motorway. Then you have people who will drive on the motorway but only in the slow lane. There are some people who avoid highways and motorways altogether and stick to local "safe" roads. It is common for people with agoraphobia to drive only within a certain geographical limit—perhaps a ten-mile zone surrounding their house. At the far end of the scale, you have people who avoid driving altogether, for whom the mere thought of driving triggers an adrenal dump that keeps them in the shadows of anxious avoidance.

Some people who have been involved in traffic accidents may be affected by post-traumatic stress disorder (PTSD). This requires more careful intervention when practicing exposure therapy, and it's likely they may require more trauma-specific treatment.

Zahra: Are you not scared that I'll kill you? What if I panic and lose control?

ANXIETY: *I'm terrified.*
BIOLOGY: *Really testing those ass muscles here.*

Josh: Why? You can drive, right? You've got a license?
Zahra: Yeah, but . . .

We sat in the front of Zahra's car in the car park behind my office building. She was shaking but preparing herself to drive, putting the key in the ignition and fastening her seat belt.

Zahra: Where are we even going? I'm really scared.
Josh: Let's start by going to the end of the road. Remember, one step at a time.

The car shuddered into movement and crept toward the main road. Zahra started to breathe more quickly. She blew away a loose strand of hair that kept dancing on her lips. Her hands were shaking. She gripped the wheel tightly.

Zahra: I can't do this . . . Look at me, my hands and legs are shaking. I am not in control.

Josh: Yes you are. You can still operate the vehicle safely. Look, this man here is letting you out.

I pointed to a man in a truck gesturing to Zahra that she could pull out in front of him. Zahra's foot slipped and she jammed it on the accelerator a bit too hard, causing a loud roar from the engine. The car remained stationary, however, because she did not engage the clutch. She became flustered and panicky.

Zahra: *(raising her voice)* Oh my God, see? I can't do it!

I turned to her. Smiled. Then turned on the radio.

Josh: Ah, yes, Shania Twain. What a belter.

In a fury, Zahra found the clutch and pulled out into the main road.

Josh: Well done! You nailed it. Where are you on your anxiety scale?

Zahra bit her bottom lip in concentration and scowled.

Josh: Zahra, anxiety out of ten?
Zahra: I'm too busy trying not to kill us or the public to fill in your audio questionnaire.
Josh: Okay, my bad.
Zahra: It's an eight. I'm scared but concentrating. Where are we even going?
Josh: Hmm . . . shall we go to the hospital?

Her eyes widened in horror.

Zahra: Oh my God, why? What's wrong with me? Is there something more than my anxiety happening? Do you believe we're going to die?!
Josh: Because it's where you work.

I started chuckling. I couldn't help it.

Zahra: Yes. That makes sense: practicing what nonanxious me would do. But what if someone sees me?
Josh: Why does it matter? They'll probably be happy to see you doing so well.

We approached a busy roundabout.

Zahra: Oh no. I'm terrified of roundabouts. What if I stall? Jesus, I really can't handle this.

ANXIETY: *You sure about this, Josh?*
ANALYTICAL: *Got to practice what you preach and be willing to go with the client.*
COMPASSION: *You're also conveying a belief in Zahra. That can be powerful.*

Josh: Just take your time. You've got this.

ANXIETY: *I hope she has!*

Zahra took her time and cautiously pulled out into the roundabout at an appropriate time. Hands still shaking, she navigated the circle and signaled to leave at her turning. She did it even more smoothly than I had expected.

Josh: Excellent. Let's keep going.

She managed a smile even though her eyes were still wide with fear. Suddenly a frightening screech emerged from behind us. An aggressive driver in a trades van weaved his way through the traffic and drove up right behind the car. The road started to narrow, leaving no room for the van to overtake us. He started sounding his horn and flashing his lights. I glanced in the rearview mirror.

CRITIC: *What a dickhead.*

Josh: What a dickhead.

Zahra became frightened. She couldn't pull over, as there was no room. We continued slowly down the narrow city road at a slow pace. Her shoulders were hunched forward and she was trembling. The man behind us continued to flash his lights and sound his horn.

Josh: You're doing a great job. All we can do is ignore him and concentrate on what we are doing.

Her arms started to tremble even more, and she wiped a tear away from her cheek with her sleeve.

VOLITION: *Perhaps we misjudged this one, Josh.*
ANXIETY: *Feeling the pressure here.*
BIOLOGY: *Would you like some sweat for your brow?*

The van drew even closer, almost bumper to bumper. The driver popped his creased, angry head out of the window and started shouting expletives. Pedestrians stopped and turned their heads to see what the noise was about. Zahra's shaking was even more intense, and the tears were freely flowing now. She was concerningly quiet. I was now worried about her. I also wanted to punch the man behind us.

COMPASSION: *She's doing so well.*
EMPATHY: *This must feel like hell. The exposure itself is hard enough.*
CRITIC: *The guy behind us is such a prick.*
DETECTIVE: *Take his plate number and the company name on the van.*
IRREVERENCE: *Then later we'll slash his tires when he sleeps cold and alone in the shadows of the memories of his family that left him.*
DETECTIVE: *No.*
SAVIOR: *You can drive her back shortly.*
CRITIC: *The White Knight of Manchester.*

We approached a zebra crossing, and Zahra stopped to allow a family to cross. Undiluted cries of disdain rang from the driver's seat of the van. There was a loud revving of his engine. The van crept up and, ever so slightly, bumped Zahra's car.

BIOLOGY: *Right, that's it. Fight response engaged.*

I unclipped my belt and opened the door. By the time I'd gotten out of the car and turned around to face the van driver, I saw Zahra already storming up to his window. She held her phone up—presumably recording this encounter. She approached the open driver's side window of the van with surprising authority.

Zahra: *(shouting)* I am TRYING to practice my exposure work. There is
absolutely NO reason for you to be recklessly driving and trying to
intimidate people.

The driver initially looked shocked but then started laughing. She
moved her phone to record the vehicles touching bumper to bumper.
Some passersby stopped to observe the scene. One kid got his phone out
to record.

Zahra: You should be ashamed of yourself. I will be reporting you to . . .

She looked at the company name emblazoned on the side of the van.

Zahra: . . . Shane Donahue Construction and providing this footage. You
awful man.

The driver smirked defensively.

Shane: Ha! I *am* Shane Donahue, so good luck, love. Now get the fuck out of
my face and move your shitty car. Or I'll move it for you, darling.

Unbelievably, he swiped an arm at Zahra's phone and batted it out of
her hand in the direction of her car. The phone flipped and clattered on the
tarmac. There were a couple of gasps from onlookers. My blood boiled and
I saw red; I was ready to confront the man myself, but Zahra steeled herself
and shot me a look as if to say "Don't." I remained next to the passenger
door. She slowly looked back at Mr. Donahue.

Zahra: Why would you do that?
Shane: MOVE! Do . . . you . . . understand . . . English?!

With ultrafast reflexes and stunning accuracy, Zahra's right hand shot
through Donahue's open window, reached behind the steering wheel,
turned the key in his ignition, and removed it, all before he could even
react to what was happening. The engine came to an immediate halt.
Zahra stood with the car key aloft in her hand, while Donahue stared at it,
and her, in utter bewilderment.

Zahra: I do understand English, thank you. Now understand this: It feels
frightening to have an aggressive person close behind you, beeping
away and flashing his lights, never mind the swearing.

Shane: Give me my fucking key . . .

He reached out, but Zahra moved her arm away tauntingly.

Shane: How fucking dare you!

He shifted in his seat, clambering for the door handle. He opened the door in a rage.

ANXIETY: *Oh no!*
VOLITION: *Stop him.*

Zahra calmly stepped back and shot me another look. She was shaking but seemed in control. She held up the key.

Zahra: You take another step toward me, Mr. Donahue, and I swear on my doctor's oath that this key, the one required to operate your vehicle, goes into the canal over there.

She gestured at the water nearby. It was easily within throwing distance.

Zahra: Do you understand me? Do you comprehend the English that I am speaking, Mr. Donahue?

He went to move forward. Zahra bent her elbow to throw.

Zahra: Ah—I wouldn't . . .

He froze.

Shane: Okay . . . okay, just leave it.

The macho veneer evaporated as he realized this could be costly to him. He glanced over at me, then at the surrounding onlookers, now perhaps realizing the magnitude of the situation.

Shane: I just . . . I'm sorry, I'm just late to a job. It's . . . important . . .
Zahra: Important enough to endanger people's lives on the roads?!

There were several cars waiting behind the van. They all seemed to be engrossed enough in what was happening to be tolerant of the delay. Donahue continued to look flustered. He was becoming desperate. I leaned on the roof of Zahra's car and watched.

Shane: I . . . I was being selfish. Please don't throw my key into the canal. I'd be screwed. I have a family to feed at home, you know?

Zahra: A family? I truly hope your children haven't learned this kind of behavior from you. But then again, that's how it works, doesn't it? Blindly absorbing ideals from our fathers, including their flaws.

IRREVERENCE: *Oof.*

Zahra turned the key in her hands behind her back.

Shane: Listen, lady. I'm sorry. Can I just please have my key back?

Zahra: Thanks for apologizing, Mr. Donahue. Now let's get on with our equally important days.

She threw the key to him, which he fumblingly caught. The moment he had it in his hands his demeanor changed.

Shane: You're a stupid bitch, aren't you? I thought doctors were supposed to be smart. You that gullible? I'm going to ram your shitheap of a fucking car off this road if I have to. If you were a guy, I'd have socked you one by now. Now fucking move your car. You've got three seconds before this accelerator pedal hits the floor.

ANXIETY: *Oh no.*

Zahra calmly smiled and said nothing. She got into her car at a leisurely pace and I followed suit. She strapped herself in, smiling to herself, then we pulled away. There was a calm confidence in her manner now. Her posture had changed and she allowed one hand to rest on top of the steering wheel, cool as you like.

Zahra: To the hospital!

Bemused, I looked behind us through the rear window. Surprisingly, the van had not moved. It started to shrink into the distance. Then, just as we began to turn a corner, I saw Donahue get out of the van, wildly waving both arms in the air. He then kicked the front fender of his van hard in front of the surrounding public. As we completed the corner, both Donahue and his van disappeared from view. I looked at Zahra for an explanation. She threw a van key into my lap.

IRREVERENCE: *This is so brilliant.*
CRITIC: *He had it coming.*

Josh: Wait, if this is Donahue's key, then what did you throw him?

Zahra smirked, not a hint of regret in her face.

Zahra: I have a heavy-duty bicycle lock, and the key for it looks similar to some car keys. I gambled it would be enough alike for that prick not to notice.

I was dumbfounded but couldn't help laughing. What a play.

Zahra: I've technically broken the law: I stole his key. Are you legally obliged to report me to the police?
Josh: No. I don't think they'll care, especially as you're going to mail it back to Shane Donahue Construction later today, aren't you?
Zahra: Yes, I will. With an apology letter?
Josh: Nah.

..

We arrived at the hospital car park. Zahra seemed to have navigated there on autopilot. She stopped the car, applied the handbrake, and, after a huge sigh, started to cry. It was awkward. I was sitting alongside and not in the home comfort of my office therapy chair. That said, the principles of compassion and empathy still applied, I just felt a bit weird. Then she really started to sob. A deep, sternum-squeezing bawl—an understandable catharsis given the events of earlier.

EMPATHY: *So much emotion to process today.*
COMPASSION: *She's done so well.*

She leaned over the steering wheel and used her arms as a temporary rest. She sobbed into them, her body convulsing in waves of emotion. I saw this as therapeutic and emotional growth, but in the context of sitting in a hospital car park next to someone shaking with tears, I found it a slightly difficult situation.

COMPASSION: *If this was a friend, I'd put a supportive hand on their back. I really want to do that. She's struggling.*
ANALYTICAL: *She isn't a friend, though, is she? She's a client.*
VOLITION: *Don't. It's not professional. Do not touch your client.*
EMPATHY: *Imagine, as a currently vulnerable woman, who has recently engaged in verbal conflict with an aggressive man, having another man place their hand on her without permission.*
COMPASSION: *I know some female therapy colleagues who have done it on the rare occasion when they felt it applied. Surely this applies now?*
INTUITION: *You're not female, though, Josh. You're in the real world, now.*
ANALYTICAL: *You're a six-foot-two man in a therapeutic relationship with a clear power dynamic that puts you at an influential advantage. Consider this, please. It's not worth it.*

Josh: Fine.
Zahra: What?
Josh: Oh, sorry, I was disputing with my thoughts. Are you okay?
Zahra: I'm okay. Thank you for . . . giving me the time and space. This was all a lot. You're right, though, about exposures. I feel so much more confident driving.

She leaned back and recomposed herself.

Zahra: *(smiling)* You probably set this whole thing up, didn't you? Shane is your friend or something?
Josh: Oh, Shane and I go way back . . .

She smiled.

Zahra: Do you mind if I go into the hospital alone? I suppose this is a great time to face the music.

ANALYTICAL: *That's even better.*
COMPASSION: *Yes!*

Josh: Of course. Go ahead. I'll loiter out here. Come and find me when you're done.

Zahra went through the front doors of the Manchester Royal Infirmary. I felt proud of her. I left her to it and instead went for a stroll down a road I hadn't visited for many years. The same familiar bustle was here: a mixture of the Rusholme through traffic and the laughter of university students outside bars. I walked through the local park and took in the sights. The whistling of the wind through the branches of the trees. The faint smell of weed from a group of friends having fun on the grass. A dog walker was recalling his Staffordshire terrier, who was chasing a ball. It was another sunny day. It felt nice to be here.

I closed the park gate behind me and walked down the road adjacent to the hospital. I was thirsty so I was searching for a newsagent to buy a Fanta. I turned onto a very familiar street, remembering there was a shop that I used to frequent here. I was suddenly overcome with a chill and a nasty bite of nostalgia that felt like a corkscrew had jabbed me in the intestines. I carried on walking. My stomach began to fold. It suddenly felt like I was trekking through custard.

TRIGGER: *Manchester Children's Hospital.*
BIOLOGY: *I don't know what these buttons mean but I'm definitely pressing them all.*
ANXIETY: *Whoa, where's all this come from?*

I dissociated. Everything felt close and far away at the same time. The new entrance to Manchester Children's Hospital greeted me like the sliding of a curtain. I felt uneasy on my feet and light-headed. My heart pounded and my tongue went numb. I stumbled slightly but rested my hand against a nearby shop window. I took some mindful breaths. A middle-aged woman walked by and removed a cigarette from her mouth.

Woman: Are you okay, love? You don't look so great.

Her eyes scanned me warily for signs that I was a crackhead.

Josh: I'm okay. Have . . . have you got a spare cigarette? I could do with one right now.

17
Harry:
The Boathouse

March 2010

I sank my sixth discounted coffee courtesy of my good friend Michael,
who worked behind the bar. I was attempting to work, but I'd consumed
enough caffeine to start my own electricity grid. When my phone rang I
jumped on it, grateful for the excuse to stop writing.

Josh: Hi, Mum. I hope you know you're distracting your hardworking son.
I'm doing my dissertation!
Mum: I just saw on your Facebook that you were out last night, don't give
me that.
Josh: It was my friend's birthday!
Mum: Yeah . . . yeah . . . Are you okay? How's it going?
Josh: It's going all right, yeah. You know me, leaving things to the last
minute as usual. How's it going there?
Mum: I'm okay. Will you have a word with your brother? He's been upset the
last week or so. He's here now.
Josh: Of course! Just give me a sec—I'll go outside; it's a better signal. And
I can walk along the riverbank to stretch my legs.

I signaled to Michael to keep an eye on my stuff as Mum handed the
phone to Harry.

Josh: Hey, man, you all right?
Harry: Yeah.
Josh: You sound glum. What's up?
Harry: Nothing.
Josh: Come on . . . don't give me that . . .

There was a silence before he spoke.

Harry: I hate how I look. I'm fat.

Josh: You look great, mate. It doesn't matter what you look like—it shouldn't matter for anyone, man. You're a beanpole, though. What's brought this on?

Harry: There's just things about my body I'm really embarrassed about. I'm afraid to get changed for PE. My stomach is bloated all the time and I always feel sick.

Harry had been struggling recently with quite severe bloating, which sometimes caused him to vomit. Mum had taken him to the doctor several times, and he was prescribed medication for acid reflux.

Josh: Your belly still playing up then? The meds not working?

Harry: The doctor said it takes some time. I'm just scared the other boys will laugh at me if they see how massive my stomach is. I keep telling lies to get out of PE.

I could hear the hesitation in his words, even talking to his own brother. Harry was a shy lad, and the quiver in his voice told me that talking about this was difficult. It broke my heart to hear his sadness, but I also felt privileged that he trusted me to share his vulnerabilities and insecurities.

Josh: Oh, I remember that feeling being in those changing rooms. It used to fill me with dread. When I was there we had a joke about Mr. Scholes, the gym teacher. "Let's hit the showers, boys!" "But we haven't done gym yet, sir!"

Harry broke into a laugh.

Harry: That's so wrong.

Josh: I know. We were grim. Anyway, you look great, mate. Handsome bastard. If you're ever in doubt, go downstairs and look at my Year 11 picture. I look like I've been dragged from Cell Block C and there's a slit through my eyebrow.

Harry: I know, Mum hated it when you shaved your head. You have a massive egg head.

Josh: Thanks.

We both chuckled.

Josh: When are you coming down to see me?

Harry: Mum and I are coming down at half-term.

Josh: Make sure you bring that handsome face of yours. There's some really hot people at this uni who I'll have to protect you from—cradle snatchers.

I could imagine Harry rolling his eyes at the other end of the line.

Josh: Oh, and bring an extra controller so we can play some games. My housemate Mike says he's never played *Portal*.

Harry: Okay. I'm gonna go now. Thanks for the chat.

He didn't like long phone conversations.

Josh: No worries. Drop me a message if you ever need me! Your stomach will sort itself out soon, I'm sure of it. Love you, man!

Harry: Love you too.

I felt happier knowing *he* sounded happier. However much I doubted myself in some ways, I was always good at making Harry laugh and conveying my unconditional love for him. Helping him feel seen made me feel good. I couldn't decide if that feeling was selfless, selfish, or both—or even if it mattered—as long as it made him feel better.

I returned inside the Boathouse to my open laptop and yet another coffee from Michael. I gave him a thumbs-up.

Josh: Cheers, mate. I was just chatting to my brother.

Michael: That handsome guy? What was up with him?

I told Michael about Harry's problems with acid reflux, and we laughed about the bloating being from his love of KFC and confectionery. I wished that was the reason he was bloating and throwing up. I'd have given anything for that to be true.

18
Noah

Therapists are not immune to getting entangled in the web of existential dread, as well as the anxiety and panic that accompany it. Self-awareness does not save us from experiencing the full range of human emotions; it just provides knowledge as the tool to understand it. That knowledge, however, didn't seem able to prevent me from pacing around my office, focusing on the futility of my own existence, until a sudden clatter of falling magazines snapped me off the hamster wheel of existential thoughts. Four years' worth of unread *Therapy Today* magazines had crumbled under their own weight and fallen to the floor. I had always believed that I would sit and read through them one day—an optimistic delusion of my projected, ideal self. I think I just enjoy collecting them. If I'd used even half the time reading that I'd spent on *Candy Crush*, YouTube, Reddit, or just ruminating about existential anxiety, I'd have finished all the magazines ages ago. I regret nothing. There was a quiet knock on the door. It was time for Noah's session.

Josh: How are you, Noah?
Noah: I'm okay, thanks, Josh. How are you?
Josh: All good here.

We took our usual seats. I poured us some water and we both took a moment to settle into the room. Rain patted against the window and clotted into deltas spread by the strong wind. It felt to me that Noah had brought with him a sadness today.

Noah: I'm not that good, actually. Sorry, the pleasantries just seem to be automatic, don't they? Like I was talking with the grocery store owner. Anyway, I lied.
Josh: Okay. Do you want to tell me more about how you've been feeling?
Noah: It's more the opposite of "feeling," really. I've mostly not been feeling anything at all. Like a numbness. I get bouts of teariness now and then,

just to break the monotony of absent feeling, but it's mostly . . . nothing I
feel.

He looked at me as if hoping for reassurance.

ANALYTICAL: *Depression.*

Josh: Feeling numb, dissociated, and teary is often associated with
   depression. I know you've lived with depression in the past: Is this
   feeling, or lack of feeling, familiar?
Noah: Yes, I've had this before.
Josh: Okay. So you've come through an episode like this before? Do you find
   that encouraging? Knowing that you've come out the other side?
Noah: Rationally, yes. It's just difficult.

I nodded.

EMPATHY: *Feeling nothing in the clutches of depression is such an
isolating experience.*

Noah: I have had very little motivation over the last four days. I've managed
   to go through the motions at work and drag myself here today. But my
   limbs feel like they're made of lead. My brain isn't functioning as I'd like
   it to. It's hard to focus. It's hard to recall and retain things.

ANALYTICAL: *Brain fog.*
EMPATHY: *Can be hindersome.*

Josh: Brain fog can be hindersome. Especially alongside the other
   symptoms of depression. Would you like to explore some potential
   reasons why you may be depressed?
Noah: I've heard depression can just be a chemical imbalance. Is just
   talking about it going to help?
Josh: I believe talking about you, your experiences, what's in the stress
   jug, and your beliefs about yourself can be really helpful for depression.
   Whether there's a chemical imbalance or not, I think it would be great
   to talk in here and also with your doctor or psychiatrist regarding the
   medication side of things.

Noah: How is talking about it helpful?

Josh: It's been theorized, and in many aspects scientifically proven, that open-talk therapy for depression can help. It can help us contextualize our thoughts and feelings, notice things that perhaps have been hiding in the periphery of our awareness; and I'm a believer that it is a good way to lighten the load and get things off our chest. We can also look at how our beliefs inform our behavior too, as I believe our behavior can keep us in sticky cycles.

Noah: Did you ever experience depression?

Josh: Yes, I did.

ANALYTICAL: *Be wary.*

INTUITION: *I think a tasteful amount of self-disclosure may help here.*

DETECTIVE: *Hmm.*

Noah: How did you deal with it?

Josh: Everyone is different, Noah. What helped me might not be applicable to you. Depression can have different factors.

Noah: I acknowledge that. I would just like to hear a story of hope.

Josh: Keeping it short, I realized one of the main components of my depression was my compulsion to ruminate. Going round and round with the same thoughts and worries and playing every possible scenario out in my mind to try to be okay with it. I was a chief ruminator and I realized I had to work a lot on rumination as a behavior, as well as challenge self-limiting beliefs about myself and the world. This was accompanied by more nurturing life choices too.

VOLITION: *Reverse it back to Noah's frame of reference.*

Josh: Would you say you struggle with rumination?

He grinned unexpectedly.

Noah: I was never any good at sports, but if rumination was an event I'd be going to the Olympics.

He sat back in his chair.

Noah: It's interesting. Yes, when I am depressed I *do* spend a lot of time in my head. Yesterday, for example, I sat in my office chair just staring at nothing and overthinking. I'd have looked quite peculiar to any outsider looking in. All of my focus was in my head. The same happened in the shower. I was in there for forty minutes completely captivated by the internal workings of my awful mind. The same when I lie in bed too. It's like I stew for an hour in my thoughts before I get out of bed. So you're saying that rumination is a behavior that's part of the depression? Not just me working stuff out? Or processing things?

ANALYTICAL: *It depends.*

Josh: Rumination is a behavior, yes. You know it's rumination—as opposed to critical or analytical thinking—when you're going round and round in circles playing out catastrophes in your mind and living out worst-case scenarios. This applies to both depression and anxiety. With depression, we are often drawn to the worst-case scenario, or we're convinced that our existence has presented itself in its truest, bleakest form, when we're actually seeing it through the lens of depression.

Noah: A lens?

Josh: Yeah. Depression and anxiety affect how we perceive the world by providing their own lenses. It's a bit like someone who is smitten after a successful first date . . .

CRITIC: *No one has felt like that after a date with you, Josh.*

IRREVERENCE: *Ha ha.*

Josh: They see the world through *rose-tinted glasses*. There's a spring in their step and they feel light and full of joy. Like Ebenezer Scrooge on Christmas morning when he realizes he's alive and not weeping at his own grave. The lens we see the world through can change depending on the state of our mind. If we're depressed—

Noah: Then we may see the world through shit-tinted glasses.

DETECTIVE: *Quite unusual language for Noah.*

Josh: Yeah . . . depression and anxiety can make us see the world through shit-tinted glasses. I agree.

Noah: But it's just a lens. The wrong prescription, perhaps? I suppose it's helpful to remind myself of that: that what I see, and feel, is not absolute. It is not the objective truth.

Josh: Mhm.

Noah: But the experience is so . . . strong. So convincing. I was going to say that it feels so real. The sadness is real, then the numbness is so consuming it feels like I'm in an unreality.

A strong gust of wind rattled the windowpane, briefly startling us both.

Noah: So, I went to the staff night out I was telling you about.

Josh: Okay. How'd that go?

Noah: If I'm being honest, I think it is what started this wave of depression off.

I tried not to show that I was instantly intrigued.

Noah: We met up at the restaurant, and even before I got there I could feel the pressure of wanting to impress everyone. I sat at one end of the dinner table with a group of colleagues, and they were all fine . . . kind and attentive. But it was my head, Josh. My head was giving me so much trouble. I was having all these weird thoughts, and it was like I was just simulating being sociable. A complete act. My thoughts were brutal.

Josh: How so?

Noah: It was like a voice sniping at me saying, "Once they get to know you, they'll hate you. You're a bad person, you're an impostor." And it just carried on and on. "You are not worthy, you are unlovable." It was interminable. Relentless. I just felt myself withdrawing; then, when I was involved in conversation, I just nodded along. Agreed. Of course, the internal critic loved that: "You can't even stick up for yourself, you're a coward."

Josh: It's like you were hounded by a bully trying to spoil your good time. That sounds horrible and exhausting.

Noah began to tear up. He wiped his eyes briskly.

Noah: I deserve it.
Josh: What makes you think that?

He gazed into a corner of the office and seemed to ignore the question.

Noah: What can I do to turn it off? The critic, the depression, the thoughts:
How do I make them stop? I feel hopeless. Then on top of it I've got
the anxiety—the social anxiety. Ever since the staff night out I've been
sucked into this depression. Everything feels like a horrible, murky
cloud.
Josh: I don't think you deserve an internal bully, Noah. No one does. Why do
you think it's there? Does it sound like anyone?
Noah: Childhood 101. The critic does sound a bit like my father. But that
would be easy to pin it to, wouldn't it? Also, I'm terrified that I *am* my
father. The voice is my voice, but it feels influenced by him. It also
feels devoid of any compassion. Which . . . would be my mother. A lack
of protection, a lack of someone being in my corner. I appear to have
amalgamated both of their dispositions. Cowardly in their own ways.
My mother is still a victim, though. I must remind myself of that from
time to time.

He went with his train of thought.

Noah: Then add dissipating friendships and my journey through education.
My lack of intimacy in relationships. All my mistakes. So . . . many . . .
mistakes.

COMPASSION: *He doesn't have much compassion for himself.*

Noah: It's like this voice has been cultivated from birth. Like it was meant to
happen to me in some twisted, fatalistic way. You can't have the rough
without the smooth, can you? Yin and yang? I am the rough. I am the ugly
weed that makes a wisteria look so beautiful in comparison. You can't
have beauty as a concept without knowing its contrasting opposite. I am
that opposite. I make other people look good.

CRITIC: *Wow, he's good.*

He scratched at his arm.

ANALYTICAL: *Self-harm? Due diligence.*
VOLITION: *Ask.*

Josh: It's painful to hear you describe yourself like this, Noah. I noticed that you're touching your arm a lot. I have to ask this, but are you self-harming again?

He looked at me as if I'd caught him out.

ANXIETY: *I hope he's okay. We worry about him.*

Noah: Don't worry. I am not cutting myself. I am . . . picking at my skin a lot, though.

ANALYTICAL: *Excoriation and dermatillomania [skin-picking disorder].*

Noah: Just around the old wounds.
Josh: Okay.

After a discussion about his medication and the importance of keeping in frequent contact with his doctor and psychiatrist, we continued to talk about some of the beliefs that Noah had about himself, particularly those around value and worthiness. I drew upon the person-centered model of allowing a space for Noah to direct the exploration and noted down some of the introjected beliefs, as well as negative self-schemas—frameworks through which we interpret information about ourselves—he had developed since childhood. Then I drew upon the CBT model to help us construct an informal assessment of what was happening.

We began to note down *core beliefs*. I obviously used the whiteboard. A core belief is something that at some point we assume to be true—a deeply held belief about ourselves or the world around us that often goes unchallenged. Some examples of Noah's core beliefs are: "I am unlovable"; "I'm a bad person"; "I'm an impostor"; "I do not deserve good things." I invited Noah to take part in a revisiting technique, a return to his turbulent childhood to explore why these core beliefs may have been established. I also challenged his absolutism by suggesting that no single behavior is an indicator of who he is as a person. Abusive behavior from a parent is not a sign that you are unlovable; instead, it's more likely the parent's failure to fulfill a protective role. You can see *why* parental abuse could cause you to come to the conclusion that you are unlovable, but it does not mean it is true.

Looking at these core beliefs in the present, we began to explore how our behavior may be reinforcing these unhelpful core beliefs. Noah believed he had proof he was unlovable: He'd never had a serious relationship. But when we looked at this belief, we saw that he often shied away from intimacy as an anxious safety behavior. This was completely understandable, given his traumatic upbringing and how a stable, safe relationship probably felt alien to him. He also realized it was no surprise he hadn't had a close, authentic relationship because he had hardly ever experienced one or even witnessed one modeled to him. He pinpointed more safety behaviors, such as people pleasing and placation. Again, we pinpointed the behavioral similarities between the present and the past and how these *core beliefs* were being reinforced by such behaviors.

Noah: I get it. I see how my rationale is flawed and skewed by the lens of my past and my core beliefs. I *am* a bad person, though.

He looked forlorn, tired, and hollow.

DETECTIVE: *This is that secret again.*
ANXIETY: *I have a strange feeling about this.*
BIOLOGY: *Butterflies in your belly really get the anticipation going.*

Josh: I recall from our first session that you said you wanted to have the confidence to share the secret that you've been holding on to. Do you think it would be helpful to share what seems to be burdening you? We could look at it in relation to your core beliefs, challenge it, and perhaps it would be nice to empty something weighty out of the jug?

His arms began to tremble. Followed by his legs.

Noah: I'm a bad person . . .

COMPASSION: *You're not.*
SAVIOR: *It's okay.*

Josh: It's okay, Noah . . .

CRITIC: *You can't say that.*
ANALYTICAL: *Don't provide empty reassurance.*
SAVIOR: *But he's really struggling.*

Noah: It's not okay, Josh. There are some things that are not okay.

DETECTIVE: *Remember, if he declares something serious, you've got to pick up that phone and tell the authorities.*
ANXIETY: *I know. It's terrifying.*

I tried my best to remain calm and reassuring, but I was anxious—and not in an excited way. The rain battering the window was the only noise that filled the silence. I sat and waited.

Noah: I . . .

His shaking grew more intense. He rocked back and forth to self-soothe. His jaw was clenched tight, and his neck pulsed from tension.

Noah: I . . . can't now. I don't deserve your compassion. I don't deserve love. I don't deserve to be here.

He immediately stood up and walked to the door, opened it, and left.

Josh: Noah!

I leaped to my feet and caught the door before it closed. I looked down the corridor and saw the door to the stairway swinging shut. I called for the elevator and took it to the ground floor in the hope that I could meet him in time at the reception. The doors opened and, frustratingly, the foyer was extremely busy—there was a networking event happening in the conference hall and it had spilled out into the reception area. I arched on tiptoes and rotated on the spot like a periscope, peering over the heads of people chatting and eating buffet food, but Noah was gone.

ANXIETY: *I hope he's okay and doesn't do anything rash.*
INTUITION: *This isn't good.*
ANALYTICAL: *He's high risk.*

I returned to my office and picked up the phone to call his doctor. It is my duty to let them know if I feel a client is at risk of self-harm or suicide.

Depression

Depression is a common but debilitating mental illness that negatively affects how we feel. Feeling depressed differs slightly from clinical depression: We can all feel down and have low moods from time to time, particularly in response to sad news or traumatic events, but clinical depression can be described as having a low mood that lasts for a prolonged time. Depression, like anxiety, can often be seen as a scale: At one end you may experience a mild form of depression, which can mean you feel down, in low spirits, or a bit empty. At the other end, you can feel endlessly despondent, feel numb both physically and emotionally, have an unwavering, negativistic view of yourself and the world, and experience a raging and callous internal critic. Severe depression can make you feel suicidal. It can feel like existence in a horrible, sticky underworld containing a tumult of psychological and physical indications.

Psychological symptoms of depression can come in the form of self-criticizing thoughts, such as a harsh voice in your own head. Clients often tell me these voices say things like: "What's the point of you?"; "You're bringing people down"; "You're a burden"; "You're unlovable." Our perception of our own existence is also altered by depression and can feel very convincing in the moment. Some examples of depressive thoughts are: "What's the point in anything?"; "The world is a sad place"; "I am destined to be lonely here." These are often accompanied by a strong urge to self-isolate, which takes us away from the soothing context of other opinions, which might balance out these negative thoughts.

On top of this, we can experience depression in the form of physical symptoms. The most common of these are tiredness and exhaustion, chest and shoulder pain, a depleted posture, a general heaviness, nausea, and headaches. Our sleep can be affected too, either by not sleeping at all or sleeping far too much. Depression often changes our appetite, with many sufferers not eating at all, while others overeat on a continuous basis. If you are experiencing any of these physical symptoms, try not to beat yourself up for being "lazy" or "unmotivated" or "greedy." Instead, consider if this may be depression, and seek help from friends, family, or a professional. Judging yourself at a time when you are low is never helpful.

There are many reasons why we may feel depressed. Depression can be due to personal issues such as heartbreak or bereavement, it can be a consequence of our environment, and it can even be genetic. As a therapist, I feel it is my job to help clients navigate any potential origins of their depression, as well as enable them to challenge hindering beliefs about themselves and the world around them.

Depression will seek to isolate you, and I believe that working with a good therapist can help bring you back into the world.

19
Lidl

I had ambled over to the supermarket after discovering that my cupboards were bare. I was almost broke. There had been seven client no-shows that week, and I was questioning whether counseling was for me. It didn't feel like I was making any progress with any of my clients lately, and I was annoyed at myself for borrowing so much money from the government to pay for this career. Altruism and empathy are for losers. I felt like I was failing my clients, and this sense of despair was exacerbated by the screaming feral children who were blocking the aisle and preventing me from buying my cans of budget vegetable soup.

I loaded my trolley with basic, easy-to-cook food like pasta, soups, vegetables, bread, and an unnerving amount of cheese. It felt like nearly everything I'd eaten over the last few months was either beige or yellow, and the sight of the trolley depressed me. The Four Tops started playing through the supermarket speakers: "Loco in Acapulco." It's a song I love, but in that moment it made me feel sad, lonely, and disconnected. I quickly threw some semiskimmed milk into the trolley and made my way to the checkout before I ended up bursting into tears in the middle of Lidl.

The cashier started scanning my items at anxiety-inducing speed. I tried to pack everything away at a pace to match, but some things fell out of the bags, while some dropped on the floor and the cashier glared. I collected myself and packed the rest of my things into my shopping bags. Under the cashier's stern and unwavering gaze, I removed my bank card to pay for the groceries.

Card declined.

The stony face of the cashier did not soften. The line of people behind me seemed to hum with annoyance. I tried again.

Card declined.

I shifted my hands to my pocket to pick out another card. In doing so, I clipped a shopping bag and the contents spilled out and clattered to the floor. It sounded like there was a groan from the queue, but mostly I think the chorus was in my mind. The lead feeling in my chest intensified, my tear ducts quivered, and now my arms felt heavy as well as my legs. I was about to pour tears in front of everyone in Lidl. I don't believe in adhering to emotional conservatism, but I'm not immune to embarrassment.

I also don't believe in divine intervention because I don't consider solipsism to be realistic or healthy. I am no more special or worthy of God's personal attention than the next person. But today, on this overcast afternoon in Salford, a guardian angel decided to visit me in a time of need. A stocky man, ornamented with facial piercings, had finished packing his shopping on the next checkout and noticed me hesitating over my fallen cheese.

Declan: Hey! Here . . . you . . . is your name Josh?

I was kneeling next to my shopping bags on the floor, quickly wiping away a tear that had sneaked down my cheek.

Josh: Yeah. That's me.

I didn't recognize him.

Declan: You all right there? Card not working? It's a bastard when that happens.

He swayed over with admirable confidence. He winked at the cashier, pulled out his credit card, then pressed it against the card reader. It was followed by a beep as the transaction went through.

Declan: This contactless stuff is dangerous. You can make all sorts of impulsive purchases.

I was stunned.

Josh: I . . . I . . . thank you. I think there's an ATM around the corner. I'll pay you back in cash. Sorry my card wasn't working. Why did you do that?
Declan: Don't worry about it, lad. Pack your cheese away.

He folded his wallet and put it back into his shorts.

Declan: You're Josh. The man who helped my sister. She was all sorts of
messed up, man. Couldn't leave the house and stuff. Was scared she'd
have my nieces and nephews taken off her. You really helped her, man.
We, as a family, appreciate it. She's doing all right now. Not quite where
she wants to be, but all right. A lot better than where she was.

Josh: I . . .

He smiled.

Declan: It's on me. It's not much. Take it as a tip and as a thank-you. From us.

He walked out without looking back.

I finally gathered my shopping bags and headed for home. There were
tears streaming down my face as I left Lidl, but they weren't sad tears. My
love for my job is not paper-thin—it almost defines me—but in a difficult
period of my life, this man reminded me that I love my job even when in
the clutches of doubt.

20
Daphne

I'd made an effort with my appearance today, splashing out on some new clothes and looking like I'd just been kicked through Uniqlo. The clothes were so new that one of the labels on my sweater was still attached; I'd had to remove it when I felt it digging into my back just before Daphne arrived.

Daphne: Good morning, Joshua. Do you mind if we get a coffee? I'm exhausted.

Josh: Sure, I'll make us some. How do you like it? There's a semidecent coffee machine in the communal area if you don't mind me nipping out for a moment?

Daphne: I'll come with you. Let me make the coffee. No offense, but the one you made in the past was . . . subpar. Awful, in fact.

CRITIC: *Ha ha.*
SAVIOR: *The communal area is usually busy. You sure it's a good idea to walk in with a Hollywood actor?! It might draw unwanted attention.*
ANALYTICAL: *Confidentiality is important.*

Josh: Are you sure? Remember, these sessions are protected by the sanctity of confidentiality. That communal room is often busy, teeming with rambunctious yahoos. I wouldn't want you to receive unwanted attention or risk your confidentiality. Everyone here knows I'm a therapist.

She raised a critical eyebrow.

Daphne: Do you think I rolled into this building in disguise, Joshua? Dressed as your mail? People have seen me walk in and out of this building on several occasions. I have had a lifetime of acute attention from the public, and I don't think the kitchen area of your office building will be the most challenging of scenarios.

Josh: Fair enough. After you . . .

••

Daphne nonchalantly walked into the communal area and headed for the coffee machine. About twenty people were scattered around the room in different areas: some reading, staring at their phones, drinking coffee, or taking an early lunch. This all felt very surreal. My brain had become desensitized to Daphne within the walls of the therapy room, but being here, mingling with the public, put the whole situation into another perspective.

> **ANXIETY:** *I hope no one notices her.*
> **SAVIOR:** *I don't want her to feel uncomfortable.*
> **CRITIC:** *She's an intelligent, grown adult. Let her whip up the coffees.*
> **ANXIETY:** *I just don't want to feel awkward.*

Daphne: Americano, wasn't it?

She glanced over at me. A few people lifted their heads to see who was talking. I could see multiple double takes in my peripheral vision.

Josh: Yes. Thank you.

The crunching of the coffee beans was followed by a loud steaming as the sounds of the machine filled the room. I glanced around, and a few people had noticed who was in the room. A man had let his magazine fall flat on his table. A young woman sat with her jaw agape as her thumb hovered idly over the screen of her phone. Another woman typed frantically while gazing up at Daphne, as if she was texting an urgent message while driving. Daphne took no notice. She walked over to me with two mugs of coffee and presented me with mine. I gestured for us to return to the office. Suddenly, we were interrupted by a voice. We turned, and I saw Jemima from the building company down the corridor. Shit.

Jemima: Uh . . . Uh . . . excuse me . . . I . . . Are you . . . ?

My eyes widened and I silently signaled with my face a "No! Fuck off!" expression. Of course, Jemima wasn't paying attention to anything I was doing. She was transfixed by Daphne. I didn't blame her. A bona fide megastar was mincing about in the staff room of our unassuming office building. Not an everyday occurrence. Daphne turned to her. Jemima blushed at being acknowledged.

Jemima: I'm so sorry to disturb you. I just wanted to say I'm such a huge fan of your work. I'm Jemima.

IRREVERENCE: *Shut up, Jemima. I'm the megafan here. Jog on.*
VOLITION: *No, you're the therapist.*
CRITIC: *Grow up, Josh.*

Daphne: Hi, Jemima. It's lovely to meet you. I appreciate this consideration and I thank you for your warm words. I presume you work here?
Jemima: Yes . . . yes, I work down the corridor doing comms for a building maintenance company. It's not riveting, but it . . .
Daphne: Pays the bills?
Jemima: Yes, it does. I work with some lovely people too. It's a nice job.

Daphne smiled at her.

Daphne: What I'd give to come to work every day and work with lovely, compassionate people. I am envious, genuinely.

Jemima found herself looking at me. It appeared the dots had finally connected: She had worked out the reason Daphne was here. She began to fidget awkwardly.

Jemima: Thank you for being so nice. Once again, I am so sorry for disturbing you. Josh is really good at what he does. My friend Tasha says he's excellent at working with anxiety. I mean, I don't mean to assume . . . I . . . I'm sorry . . . I'm just going to go . . .
Daphne: Thank you, Jemima. My name is Daphne. You know me by my stage name. But today I am Daphne, and you are absolutely right: Josh seems to be a very helpful professional.

She looked at me and smiled.

COMPASSION: *Aw. That's so lovely.*
BIOLOGY: *Let's thud that heart and release the butterflies. Fancy some blusher on that face?*

I smiled awkwardly at the space between them, not sure where to look.

CRITIC: *Bullshit. You've been a sounding board. Nothing more. Any therapist would have done the same. Daphne was ready to spill the beans in any therapeutic environment. You're a swindler impersonating someone special when all you do is ignore your own control issues and deficiencies by living vicariously through the achievements of others.*
COMPASSION: *Enough. You're talking nonsense.*
VOLITION: *I agree, shut up.*
BIOLOGY: *This caffeine is making us shake.*

Daphne: We've got to head off, Jemima. Thank you for your kind words, and have a lovely rest of your day.

■ ■

Back in the therapy room, we were sitting in our usual seats. Daphne had a relaxed demeanor and an air of confidence.

Daphne: I have been thinking and reflecting a lot this week.

I nodded.

Daphne: Everything about identity. Reflecting on who I am. Asking myself: What is authenticity? What is congruence? And reflecting on what it looks like to live a life fulfilled. All of this in the space between shows. I've been busy! Helps that I've had some boundaries with my mother too. Apologies for the neurotic whinge about her last week.

Her eyes were locked on mine today, and it seemed to me that I could see respect there, and trust. This made me feel content, and I allowed myself a self-acknowledgment that I had made Daphne feel safe to be herself. The feeling was an antidote to the interminable self-doubt that a lot of therapists feel, no matter how experienced they are.

Josh: You've put some healthy boundaries in place?

Daphne: Yes. My mother usually texts or rings me every day, but I have requested that she only text in the evenings. She complained and started lecturing me, so I just bought a new phone and SIM card and hid my old phone until the evenings. All my close friends and family have my new number. It's cruel, but I don't want to cut my mother off. This way I can have a healthy interaction with her that doesn't overshadow my day.

EMPATHY: *That's understandable.*

Josh: That's understandable.

Daphne: What I really wanted to tell you is that I went on a date the other night.

She smiled sheepishly. The mannerisms of the fifty-three-year-old woman suddenly emulated what I imagined the nineteen-year-old version of herself to be, albeit briefly.

Josh: Oh, wow. Firstly, I'm envious you're managing to fit all of this into your schedule . . .

CRITIC: *You took a whole hour in the bathroom this morning because you were playing that dumb tennis game on your phone. Lazy bastard.*

Josh: How did it go?

Daphne: It went well, thank you. I don't think it's going to develop into anything serious, but it was . . . wonderful . . . Freeing, even . . .

ANALYTICAL: *Daphne briefly mentioned about her sexuality and questioned her identity in the previous session when doing the Empty Chair technique.*

INTUITION: *I'd leave those details for Daphne to fill in. If she wants to.*

Josh: Oh yeah? How so?

Daphne bent forward over her folded leg and fiddled with her elbow. A giddy smile spread across her face and her tongue pressed out her cheek.

Daphne: I think it was one of the first dates that I've ever been on where I felt myself. It was just me and the other person. I was in the moment. Not considering what outside influences thought of me—my work, the public, my family. There was a present connection.

She leaned back in her chair.

Daphne: Apparently Manchester has some wonderful, quiet bars. We went to this lovely speakeasy hidden in the center. We were tucked away in a dark corner and hardly anyone noticed we were there. It was such a charming escape from the busy schedule.

EMPATHY: *I can imagine this being a luxury when you're as famous as Daphne.*

Daphne: You're not intrigued to know who it was?

DETECTIVE: *It should be intuitively obvious that I want to know!*
ANALYTICAL: *We're staying in your frame of reference.*

Josh: I'd be lying if I said I wasn't a bit intrigued, but the details are only necessary if you want to share them.

It was clear that she did.

Daphne: It was with a person from our theater group. I have known them for years. They're significantly younger than me, but in many ways more . . . mature. Knowledgeable. Self-assured. I find it outrageously attractive. They made me feel human.

Daphne recalled something from our last session.

Daphne: I remember us talking about the notion of conditionality and unconditional love. What was that again?
Josh: Unconditional positive regard is a term Carl Rogers coined to describe the unconditionality that therapists and other people can use when helping others who are in emotional need. It's listening without hasty judgment, using empathy instead of dismissal, and caring about

the person holistically, regardless of whether their opinions may contrast with our own. I think Rogers recognized that it's superannoying when people play "back to me" and make tough conversations all about their need to prioritize their own emotions.

Daphne: Well, Jordan was all of that. They were so attentive. It was in the way they disagreed with me too, but held that positive regard. They weren't looking to attack or make it about themselves. I also got lost in their words and in their world.

Josh: Sounds like a great date. You sure you're closing the door on the possibility of anything more serious?

She contemplated the question, leaning forward and placing her chin on her palm. Her leg bounced energetically.

Daphne: I don't think so. For various reasons. Like I said, I've been reflecting of late, and I feel like I have a lot to discover to be comfortable in myself. There are several emotional hurdles that I feel would be best achieved alone. Like you say in one of your Instagram videos, when you face your anxieties alone, you're the one who ends up with all the credit for standing up to it. You grow past it. The credit doesn't become shared to support any unhealthy codependency issues.

BIOLOGY: *More butterflies.*

Josh: That doesn't mean that you must make difficult decisions and go through life alone, though. I see it as healthy if someone is with you, guiding you, through certain transitions in life. Especially from a place of unconditional love and care.

Daphne: I understand. It just feels very much like a deep intuition, you know?

INTUITION: *Aye.*

Daphne: My inner critic tells me all of this . . . identity exploring at my age is needless and dramatic. As if I should cash in my chips and cut my losses. But a lot of that voice isn't me. It's . . . it's an accumulation of everything that I have been influenced by, which has partly shaped me.

And I don't just mean my mother—I know you therapists get a hard-on for the matriarch stuff. She's only a piece of the puzzle. And I don't blame her, either. She hasn't been great, admittedly, but it's me who should take responsibility for how I measure and judge myself.

She looked out the window and continued.

Daphne: It's everything, isn't it? The conditions we try to adhere to when growing up? They have such a colossal impact. Gender conditioning, patriarchal norms, ideals of what womanhood or manhood should be. It's the constructionism that messes people up. I have never understood the sum of my parts, Joshua. So all I have done is try to present the parts as best I could. Fortunately for me, I did it extremely well. I imagine others haven't had the opportunities to be so fortunate.

I nodded in acknowledgment.

Daphne: When my daughter was a child we bought her a Lego set.

IRREVERENCE: *It's dear that stuff nowadays. All right, moneybags.*

Daphne: She would attempt to construct houses and little Lego people and named them after us. Herself, her mother and her father. They were . . . different. Beautifully expressive. At the time I thought they were terrible, but I tried not to convey this to her. She didn't need putting down—her father did enough of that. I did acknowledge, however, that my judgment derived from the sum of my own imperfect construction. If that makes sense.

Josh: Yes. You're seeing symbolism from your own life, the Lego representing a reflection of your own identity construction.

Daphne: I suppose I am.

There was a long, steady pause.

Daphne: I think doing more things where I feel more like my authentic self, without freezing and fawning, is the way forward for me. It's as if my mind and body are telling me that doing the opposite makes my life unsustainable. It's . . . heavy . . .

EMPATHY: *Living up on a pedestal all your life must be lonely and exhausting to maintain.*

Josh: Pedestals are usually heavy.

She looked at me and grinned in agreement.

Daphne: It does feel very much like I am living on a pedestal. One that I am constantly propping up.

She gazed down at her lap and I could see that, instead of performing, she was allowing herself to feel the sadness.

Josh: It's okay to come off the pedestal, you know. It's all right down here. Plus the tops of people's heads can be unflattering.

Daphne forced a smile. She lifted her head and looked at me with utter genuineness.

Daphne: I wish I could, Joshua. But I'm scared . . .

I met her gaze. It was a beautifully intense therapeutic moment.

SAVIOR: *It's okay.*
COMPASSION: *It's okay.*
EMPATHY: *It's okay.*
IRREVERENCE: *You're not telepathic, Josh.*

Daphne: I am scared to be seen for who I really am. I am scared of criticism of me as a person, of rejection. I'm scared of losing everything I have worked for. I fear losing my daughter, my work. The . . . the pedestal is . . . too high, Joshua. I understand the principle, but for some people it's just not possible to come down.

Two tears trickled down her face.

ANALYTICAL: *A binary view of thinking about it.*
VOLITION: *Perhaps challenge or bring attention to it?*

Josh: Hmm . . . do you not think this sounds very "one or the other," though? As if coming off the pedestal means abandoning it altogether? No one is suggesting that you have to do that. You said that your public persona is someone exceptional, who has been conditioned by many things in your life: May I first ask if you enjoy being that person?

Daphne: Why, yes, of course. Not all the time, but yes, I do love being an artist. I do love acting, directing, and being immersed in admiration and adoration. It's otherworldly, and I'm so fortunate to have access to it. I must admit that I do revel in the idea that people think I am "strong," that my independence as a woman is inspiring.

She dabbed at her cheeks with a tissue.

Daphne: However, fame can be a deserted place. Isolating. People become excited to wear masks at Halloween or to a masquerade ball, all in the knowledge that it's something quite different, something temporary and out of the ordinary. When the day finishes, they can remove their masks . . . and the next time they can buy a different one and the fun starts all over again. I am so scared to remove my mask, or climb down from the pillar, because I am so, so different from the person atop it, Joshua.

A shared silence surrounded us while I thought how to respond.

Josh: Have you considered that you . . . could do both? Jump off and onto the pedestal when needed? Perhaps consider that your public face is just one configuration of yourself? We all have many configurations—there's nothing rigid about personality, identity, or being human.

IRREVERENCE: *That's why those "I am who I am . . ." people are so irritating.*

Josh: But I'd be very interested to speak more to the person who's here, at eye and ground level with me. It's safe here.

More silent tears streamed down her face. I felt she was almost ready to seize an opportunity that might be open only for a limited time before she climbed back up the pedestal and pulled the ladder up behind her. Daphne was vulnerable.

INTUITION: *Introduce yourself.*
CRITIC: *Don't infantilize her!*
INTUITION: *Something tells me we should.*

Josh: Hi, my name is Josh. What's your name?

She looked at me and could acknowledge the sincerity in my question. It was asked in all seriousness.

Daphne: Hello, Josh. My name is . . . I . . . don't know . . . Daphne feels so distant from me. I feel like . . . I feel like I don't know who I am . . .

．．

We spoke about the delicate subjects of identity, gender, pedestals, sexuality, and the impact they could have on Daphne's personal life should she choose to live a more congruent, authentic existence. A part of me felt it inappropriate to refer to Daphne as "she" now, but this was a difficulty I had to navigate while respecting Daphne's explicit wishes. I asked her if she would like to be referred to by a different pronoun, but she said she wasn't ready for that yet. Until she told me otherwise or declared her preferred pronoun, I would continue referring to Daphne as "she." I felt scared of being presumptive. It wasn't my declaration to make.

Daphne explained about living uncomfortably with her gender defined as a woman, but she never felt safe enough to challenge it, especially with the pressures and skin-deep prejudices that come with fame. The overarching theme was that Daphne was tired of being what she had been conditioned to be but still appreciated and wanted to keep the version of herself that had become a successful professional. I think she wished to be able to step on and off the pedestal when needed—and not be confined by rigid expectations of what a woman should be. I suggested that stepping on and off the pedestal was always an option, and this seemed to ease an enormous pressure on her.

The longer the session went on, the more I was experiencing this deeply pure form of a wonderful human being. I genuinely forgot about the movie star and marveled at meeting this rare person that I doubt many people had seen before.

Daphne decided, willingly, to become her famous self again. It was the practice of gently switching configurations of self so that it became a natural flow. A skill at jumping off and on the pedestal—something I believed to be very beneficial for her. It was something she would become very good at doing.

Daphne: Which is your favorite movie of mine?

The question stunned me.

Daphne: Don't tell me it was the detective noir one? I cringe at that so hard. The nineties were a peculiar time. Ah, yes, I recall your impression of me with the lighter.

Josh: I love that movie. I also love that lighter. When I smoked, my friends would groan every time I asked them if they "got a boon for my light?" Basically, it was me sponging cigarettes off people when I was poor. Do you still have the lighter? I tried to get one, but the replicas are pretty poor.

We laughed.

ANALYTICAL: *Be careful—too much in your frame of reference here.*

Daphne: I'm not in the habit of keeping lighters, never mind ones from twenty-plus years ago. I appreciate the sentiment.

She zipped up her bag.

Daphne: I'd like to thank you, Joshua. I know our session is ending, but I wanted to express my sincere gratitude. You listen to me, without judgment, as a human, and you have helped me to feel some semblance of myself—whatever that even means. I thank you so much. I have a lot of reflecting to do, but it feels positive, like a fun puzzle to assemble while relaxing in the evening. I have a path forward . . .

She smiled, and my whole body trembled in gratitude. I could have cried, but I kept my composure and smiled back.

Daphne: I would love it if you could attend one of our shows. *Lyrebird* is in its final week, and it would mean so much if you would come.

ANXIETY: *OMG.*

Josh: I . . . er . . .

Daphne: I understand. Confidentiality and things. Therapeutic boundaries, professionalism, and the like. Well, I'd like to let you know that it is me who is making a conscious decision to invite you to watch a play. We don't need to speak, and I assure you that your professional integrity will not be called into question.

Josh: That is a very kind gesture. Unfortunately, I don't think it would be right. Professional boundaries are rigid for a reason—sometimes at the expense of my own wants! I'd like to let you know that I massively appreciate the invitation, though. Thank you. I'll be pinching myself for years to come that the star of the show gave me a personal invite!

A beautiful smile grew across her face: an ear-to-ear beam that revealed the pearl-white teeth of someone who seemed—in the moment, anyway—to be very happy.

21
Harry:
Daytime Quiz Show

April 2012

Harry was watching a daytime quiz show in Ward 84 of Manchester Children's Hospital as we sat with the oncology consultant that nobody had known my brother needed until two weeks ago. The consultant stared at my mum with a rehearsed gaze. I imagine that she must have had to give this news many times, but it didn't look like it got any easier. Just more practiced.

Dr. Finnan: During the exploratory biopsy, I'm afraid we found multiple tumors that have metastasized across the liver and into the perineum, which has caused a large buildup of ascites. This would explain the recent bloating and Harry's inability to keep food down.

My mum was frozen. Petrified. Seeing the look on her face was heartbreaking, worse even than the pang of horror I felt. I was going to have to support my mum, as well as my brother, through what was going to be a difficult time ahead.

Dr. Finnan: We recommend starting a course of chemotherapy immediately. We have decided that a mixture of cisplatin and oxaliplatin should be administered for six rounds, starting today. I'm sure you have many questions, so . . .

Her voice trailed off into an incomprehensible blur as my tinnitus screeched. Mum sat with her mouth agape, struggling to process everything. The doctor continued to talk about the intricacies of treatment, side effects, and what we would need to do practically for the next week or so.

Mum: Sorry, I can't hear all of this now, it's too much.

She walked out of the room, and the sound of her sobbing echoed down the corridor. It would haunt me for a long time afterward.

Josh: I'm sure you can understand . . . this is all just . . . shocking and awful for us to hear.

Dr. Finnan: I understand. I'm so sorry for your mum and you. Do you have any questions for me? I can answer them now, or whenever you feel ready. You can ask anything you need now and share it with your mum later.

My brain whirled in a soup of panic and confusion. I just wanted re-assurance. Anything.

Josh: Is it . . . is it . . . curable?

I think I already knew the answer to this, but part of me hoped I had misunderstood.

Dr. Finnan: People react differently to chemotherapy, so it's difficult to say. It'll be very tricky, given the number of metastasized tumors, but we'll give it a go. If we can shrink the smaller tumors—zap them, even—then we can look at surgery on the liver. It's a long shot, but like I said, we'll do our best and give it a go.

Josh: What's the prognosis?

Dr. Finnan: I don't think it's helpful to be putting time predictions on this for now. We'll take it stage by stage.

Josh: Just be honest with me: How many people get better from a presentation like this?

Dr. Finnan looked over at the nurse who was taking the minutes. The nurse nodded at her, as if to signal that it was okay to declare it. Dr. Finnan then returned her gaze to me.

Dr. Finnan: Not many, I'm afraid. It's . . . difficult odds.

I couldn't hold it in anymore. I wailed with my head in my hands, deeply and irreversibly desolate. It felt like something had broken inside of me—physically and mentally. It was as if they were trying to dress up a death sentence with their talk of odds.

The nurse came and placed his hand on my back. He said nothing but communicated a warm compassion with his touch.

Dr. Finnan: One thing at a time, Joshua. We'll get there. One at a time. Just think about what we need to do next.

I wiped away some tears and blew my nose with a tissue the nurse had given to me.

Josh: But how do I tell him?! How do I tell a fourteen-year-old boy that he's fucking riddled with cancer? How do I tell my own brother? Oh God, I love him so much . . . I'm older than him . . . I've abused my body . . . why has he got it?!

The wails came again. My ribs hurt. My mouth was dry. I felt so nauseous.

Dr. Finnan: I'm so sorry. I will tell Harry, if that makes it easier. Sometimes families like to break the news to the children themselves, but I completely understand if you and your mum would find this difficult today. I do advise that we start treatment today, though. Just let me know your wishes.

..

I left the oncologist's office, steadying myself on the wall a couple of times to prevent myself falling over. What was I going to do? Poor Harry. My poor Harry. My little brother. I couldn't see him yet. I had no plan. I couldn't go find him without a plan! I couldn't see him yet because I was a coward. It would be too painful. Oh, and my mum! Where was she? I hoped she was okay. *Man, I'm so selfish.*

CRITIC: *You are.*

I stumbled outside into the hospital gardens. My eyes were bloodshot, and my hands trembled. I pulled out a cigarette, lit it, and slumped my back against the cold stone of a statue plinth. Some people moved away from me, afraid that they'd get sucked into the event horizon of whatever the hell was happening to me. I stubbed out the butt and instantly lit another. I needed to make a plan.

Josh: Think, Josh. Think.

..

I walked out of the elevator to Ward 84—the children's oncology ward of Manchester Children's Hospital. I was slightly more composed, but I still trembled. The sick feeling in my sternum was there to stay. I pressed the buzzer, and the receptionist came to the door to greet me. It was obvious that she was experienced in greeting newly shocked families to this ward. She took my arm gently and guided me down the corridor.

Shaneya: Are you here to see Harry? Is he your brother?

Josh: Yes. I'm his big brother. Here to pick on him, which is my job. I . . . I . . . need to tell him some bad news. He doesn't know yet, does he? Has the doctor told him? We need to tell him! Have you seen my mum?

Shaneya: It's okay. He's over here in Room 8. Your mum is here too. Go in when you're ready.

Through the long, vertical door window of Room 8 I could see a small TV playing a daytime quiz show. My mum was sitting next to the hospital bed, holding Harry's hand. She wore an expression of calm encouragement—something I believe the strongest of parents can conjure when they know they're needed by their children in the most difficult of situations. She had told him. I could tell. I knew my mum and Harry well. They were both smiling. They were amazing. They were stronger than I could ever be.

I gently sidestepped across the window and saw a nurse hooking up some strange, colored liquid to an IV-drip stand. I couldn't hear what she was saying, but I could tell Mum was trying to normalize everything for Harry. I stared, too scared to go in. Frozen, gazing at my beautiful family. A hapless observer encased like a trapped fly in a sap of shock and grief. I clenched my fists and shook. Harry was talking to the nurse—being lovely and polite as usual.

SAVIOR: *We will save him. We will go to the ends of the earth to do it. We're going to contact all the best consultants in the world who specialize in fibrolamellar hepatocellular carcinoma. We'll get them to liaise together and nail the cure. Mum and I will make sure you're in the best physical shape for the chemo to work. We're going to zap the small tumors, then operate on the large liver tumor. If this chemo* *doesn't work, then we'll find one that does. I'll raise the money. I'll find a hospital or a doctor that can do it. I'll work three jobs. Maybe there are trials—experimental trials for a new wonder drug. We hear about them every day! This will work one way or another. Every time I've put my mind to something it has come out great. This is no different. We will save him. I promise it. I know it.*

I turned the handle and opened the door.

Josh: Hey . . .

22
Levi

Not for the first time, the door to my office was burst open by the head of security of Seneka nightclub. The mug of soup I was sipping flew skyward and sprayed red liquid over my chin and top. Levi's face was lit up with delight, like that of a child who had walked into their own surprise birthday party.

ANXIETY: *Jesus.*
BIOLOGY: *Let's get that heart rate up and those bowels loosened, Joshy boy.*
VOLITION: *Perhaps have the door locked in future.*
CRITIC: *Captain Hindsight is right.*

Levi: Josh! You're not gonna believe this . . . I . . .

He glimpsed at my chin and shirt.

Levi: Whoa, what's gone on there? Has someone chinned you? You all right? Spicy previous client?

IRREVERENCE: *You're killing me, man.*

Josh: It's soup.
Levi: Oh . . . ha! I'll bring you a straw next time. It's supposed to go in your mouth, mate.

CRITIC: *Damn you, Levi.*
COMPASSION: *Lovely to see him beaming, though.*

Josh: It makes me happy to see you're smiling, Levi. Not that it's how we measure progress in here. I'm looking forward to hearing what you bring today.
Levi: You make it sound like I'm entertainment.

I smiled. He took a seat, blowing a small raspberry through his lips.

Josh: You mentioned that there was something I wouldn't believe?
Levi: Yes! You're gonna love this. So I . . .

We were interrupted by his Nokia blasting out the sounds of Don Henley's "The Boys of Summer." I couldn't help but find it amusing, despite the interruption.

Levi: Sorry, Josh. Do you mind if I take this? There was an incident last night at the club that I need to provide a short verbal statement for.
Josh: Sure. Go for it.

Levi stood up and walked to the window to continue his conversation. His self-awareness of his voice volume was nonexistent and I could hear every word. I sat and twiddled my fingers.

BIOLOGY: *Thought you were being healthy eating all that fruit at dinner? I reward you with a gallon of gastric acid. You're welcome.*

I walked over to my desk to fetch some antacids. I washed them down with some cold tea and faffed around with some papers on my desk, because if I were being honest, I felt a little awkward and wanted to feel like I was doing something. I was aware that there was a particular dynamic between Levi and me, and I mostly felt okay with it, because there are some situations where an unusual dynamic that's kept within professional boundaries is the best you believe you can achieve. My intuition told me that Levi's presence in therapy, as well as his eagerness to engage in our therapeutic relationship, was something I had to treat delicately. Within reason.

ANALYTICAL: *Perhaps make the boundaries clear. Remember your training.*
COMPASSION: *You're good at what you do. You can make this work without threatening the relationship.*

Levi sat back down. The sofa squeaked under his weight and the fibers of his denim jeans changed color as they stretched over his muscular thighs.

Levi: Right, sorry about that. What was I saying . . . ?

I sat back down, slightly annoyed at what I perceived to be Levi's dictating of the structure of the session but remembering that he wanted to share this enthusiasm for progress, which is something that all therapists love to hear about.

CRITIC: *You don't have the balls to tell him you're irritated by his taking over the running of the session.*
VOLITION: *"The balls"? Really? A bit asinine that phrase, nowadays.*

Josh: Please, go ahead. You seemed excited to share something.
Levi: Ha, yes! Sorry about that phone call. I had to help a friend out with their statement. My colleague Sandra got into a scuffle last night trying to remove this airhead from the dance floor. This man was so off his face on sniff that we could see the powder making a trail down his face onto his shirt. His eyes were wider than dinner plates . . . He starts bouncing off people like a pinball, knocking drinks, starting fights. He was causing a right ruckus. Anyway, a group of young women approached Sandra and reported him to us.

Levi sneezed. Loudly. Then he pulled a tissue from the box, blew his nose—still more loudly—and continued.

Levi: Sandra approached the guy. She politely requested that he come with her so she can escort him out for his disorderly behavior. Obviously, this man has had enough sniff to think he's He-Man, and through his dumb eyes he saw Sandra as Skeletor. So he takes a swing at Skeletor . . .

Levi unleashed a loud bellow as he got into character in the story.

Levi: I'll tell you this now: Sandra would crush Skeletor with a look, never mind a punch. She is one scary woman who takes no nonsense from anyone, especially if you push her too far. She gives the sniffhead's lame punch the slip, Cassius Clay–style, then cracks him one right in the nose. His face exploded. Usually you'd get horrified reactions from the punters, but they applauded! He was a complete tool. We then lobbed him out onto the street.

His convulsing stomach settled, and he let out a post-laugh sigh.

Levi: Anyway, that phone call was talking to one of the team to make sure Sandra's self-defense story was all in line. The police were making their routine inquiries.

Josh: Sounds like an eventful evening.

Levi: I wish I could say it was out of the ordinary.

He returned his phone to his pocket.

Levi: So . . . that ERP stuff you taught me about, the stuff that was my homework . . . I did it. Exposure-response prevention. That's the one.

Don Henley suddenly started screaming again from Levi's pocket. He leaned back and pulled the phone out.

CRITIC: *FFS.*

Levi: Ah, it's Gary wanting to iron things out; no one gave him the pep talk . . .

Josh: If you would like to rearrange this session because of more pressing matters then we can do that. I don't mind.

CRITIC: *Liar.*

He must have noticed a slight unintentional frustration in my tone because he shot me an intimidating glance. Don Henley stopped, then started again.

ANXIETY: *Explain yourself.*

ANALYTICAL: *Boundaries. Congruence.*

COMPASSION: *You can do it.*

Don Henley finally gave up singing, leaving us looking at each other.

Josh: Therapy is a commitment from both of us, Levi. I'm just concerned that these phone calls may obstruct what can be achieved today. Whatever that may be. Actually, I believe they *are* obstructing us already. I also feel a bit silly just sitting here waiting for us to start. If now isn't the right time, I am happy to rearrange to a less busy and more suitable time.

ANXIETY: *Thud . . . thud . . . thud . . .*
COMPASSION: *That was okay.*
ANXIETY: *He's going to drop the "I'm paying you so you'll do what I like" line and rinse the hell out of you.*

He squinted his eyes. I hoped he could see my sincerity.

Levi: You're right. Apologies. I'm . . . I'm not used to this. It was disrespectful.

He clicked his phone to silent and put it away.

Josh: Thank you. I appreciate it. Now, you left me on tenterhooks. How was your ERP homework?

His face lit up again.

Levi: So, I was having horrible thoughts about my daughter and granddaughter, and we set some homework around that, didn't we? Those challenges were so against my instincts, but you're on to something there, my friend. Safia and the book bashers in the community think it's the work of the divine, but, man . . . I want the credit for it . . .

COMPASSION: *You deserve any credit for trying.*
EMPATHY: *ERP is tough.*

Levi: Homework number one was to hang out with my granddaughter on my own. This was so hard! I've done it so many times around when she was born, but since the thoughts started, I had put it off for so long. Chantale—that's my daughter—came round and was sewing something with Safia in the back room. I would usually make an excuse and go out for fear of the thoughts and feelings. That threat response you talk about. This time . . . though . . . I said, "Sewing is boring. Bimpe can hang with her grandad." Then my heart started pounding. The thoughts flickered in my head . . .

EMPATHY: *And you are filled with doubt, fear, and guilt. Your instinct tells you to do everything to run and avoid.*

Levi: I was getting guilty thoughts and the "just in case" things that we were chatting about. Then I thought, "No, Levi. This is the threat response. This is like that time those machete guys jumped out of that car. But this time it is safe!"

BIOLOGY: *Would you like some watery eye secretion?*
VOLITION: *No. Not now.*
COMPASSION: *We're proud of this guy.*
CRITIC: *For hanging out with a kid?*

Levi: I bounced her on my lap. We played. Listened to music. We laughed . . .

I'd never seen Levi as happy as he was in this moment: reliving this memory. He mimed playing with an invisible Bimpe in the therapy room.

Levi: I was still scared. But the more I committed to playing with Bimpe, the more I . . . the less the fear got, you know?
Josh: That's incredible, Levi. That took outstanding courage.

COMPASSION: *I'm proud of you.*

Levi: Cheers, mate! Anyway, it doesn't stop there. The horrid thoughts kept coming but my feelings were getting less intense the more I played with her. I kept reminding myself of what you said about the threat response and stuff. And you'll never guess what . . .

He began to bellow again. I couldn't help but mirror his infectious joy.

Levi: This vile smell filled the room. I thought I'd soiled myself at first, but then I realized I was holding a toddler.

DETECTIVE: *Let's get this man a desk!*
IRREVERENCE: *Ha ha.*

Levi: Who would have thought something so small could create such a deadly stench? I picked her up, ready to dump her with Chantale to

do the dirty work, but then . . . then I thought . . . this would be a good
exposure. An exposure without my threat response dictating what I
do . . . "No, I want to change my granddaughter's nappy!" I said aloud.

I smiled. I find listening to courage enthralling.

Levi: So I changed her. The thoughts came . . . the demon thoughts . . .
the devil himself . . . but I carried on. There was so much poo it was
like Bimpe had dropped a sewage grenade down there. I did it. I did it,
Josh. I . . .

He started to cry but stopped himself.

Levi: I did it! A terrible job, like. Safia and Chantale came through and redid
the nappy because I'd put it on backward. But they seemed happy. I'm
going to keep practicing, though. Not going to be one of those guys that
shies away from changing nappies. I regretted not doing it much with
Chantale. I felt good . . .

Josh: Outstanding. How was the anxiety by the end?

Levi: Barely there. The thoughts calmed down too. I was able to focus on my
family.

COMPASSION: *Get in! Well done!*
ANALYTICAL: *A successful exposure.*
IRREVERENCE: *Demon slaying at its best.*

Josh: No demon slaying required?

Levi: Not today. Thank you. Got a long way to go, but thank you. I get your . . .
theories now. I did some more! Listen to this . . .

. .

Levi spoke about his other exposures that involved both sexual and violent
intrusive thoughts about his family. He struggled with graphic thoughts
about Safia and Chantale, particularly involving knives, so as an exposure
he chose to carve a roast chicken in the same room as his family. The threat
response once again alarmed him and made him feel highly anxious and

doubtful, but like his exposure with Bimpe, the anxiety abated toward the end and he was able to enjoy his Sunday roast. We'd also set a challenge to go to the spa with his daughter. She had invited him several times and, despite wanting to go, Levi always declined because he was afraid that his intrusive sexual thoughts about his daughter might be prompted by seeing her in swimwear. He went to the spa anyway and encouraged himself to do some exposure work. He was understandably very proud of himself.

Josh: Your willingness to tolerate discomfort without avoiding it, or ritually hitting yourself, is brilliant, Levi. How is the self-flagellation?

He looked at me with a sudden worried expression. He then painted on a fake smile.

Levi: Well, I assure you that I have done none of that.

ANALYTICAL: *That's impressive. Ritualistic compulsions can take such a long time to conquer.*
DETECTIVE: *Something isn't right here.*
INTUITION: *Agreed.*

Levi: But, er . . .

Levi's phone sounded again. This time it wasn't Don Henley but a standard ringtone.

DETECTIVE: *Hmm. He'd definitely put that phone on silent.*

The worried expression on Levi's face became more prominent. He briefly froze in fear. Then he pulled out a different phone from his top jacket pocket.

Levi: I'm sorry. I have to take this. This is my emergency phone.
Josh: Sure, I understand.
Levi: I wish you did . . .

He answered the phone trembling. He was reacting physically as though he was explaining about his intrusive thoughts or recalling difficult memories.

Levi: Hey, darling, how are you? . . . I'm . . . I'm out at work at the
moment . . . Yes? . . . No . . . I don't see the shrink anymore . . . It's a work
meeting . . . Well, of course Gary isn't going to tell you, he isn't at this
work meeting . . . Yes, I'm sorry . . . I said I'm sorry . . . I will . . . Okay . . .
Bye, darling . . .

DETECTIVE: (lights a mind cigar) *What's going on here then?*
COMPASSION: *That was concerning. I hope he's okay.*

Levi put the phone back in his jacket pocket. He did not put it on silent.
He was stunned out of his recent feelings of positivity, having chosen instead to withdraw into a forlorn, worried version of himself.

Josh: Are you okay, Levi? That phone call seems to have shaken you.
Levi: It was Safia. You're right . . . my . . . threat response went off when my
phone rang. It almost always does these days.
Josh: What's going on, Levi?
Levi: I shouldn't be here . . .
Josh: Why?
Levi: She said I wasn't allowed to come in the first place. Said it was
blasphemy and would get in the way of my healing.
Josh: What? Therapy? Safia said you shouldn't come to therapy?

He continued to look frightened.

Levi: Josh, there's a lot I've not told you about my marriage. It's
complicated. I'm confused. Is it the therapy stuff that's helping, or is it
what we're doing at home?

ANXIETY: *Got a bad feeling about this.*
DETECTIVE: *We need more details.*

Josh: What are you doing at home? Let's look at it together.
Levi: Josh, Safia is a special person. She's unique. She possesses this
unique ability to channel the voices of spirits and the holiness. It's not
always her that speaks truth. She's like a vessel that passes judgment
from above. I know how crazy it sounds . . .

ANXIETY: *Oh no . . .*
IRREVERENCE: *Back to crazy town we go . . .*
COMPASSION: *What's happening to him?*
INTUITION: *There are a lot of red flags here, Josh.*

Levi: Since she became anointed, it changed our marriage. She changed. We both changed. Then our lives became the community.

He looked at me with sad, childlike eyes.

Levi: Penance must be paid. I owe so much for my sins.

ANXIETY: *I'm really worried here.*
DETECTIVE: *Find out!*

Josh: Okay. Levi, can you tell me how penance is paid in the community? What are they making you do? What is Safia doing to you?
Levi: I can't, Josh. I shouldn't be here.
Josh: Levi, are you in danger?
Levi: No . . . I must go. I'll see you next time. I'll keep doing the ERP stuff. Thank you.

He rushed out, leaving me feeling concerned for his well-being. I hoped that he would return.

Domestic Abuse

A quarter of domestic abuse crimes reported are against men. Yet most male survivors don't seek follow-up help for their situation. There are undoubtedly reasons for this that are subjective to each individual, but don't disregard the societal shame associated with being a male victim of domestic abuse. It goes against the historical conditioning in which men should be seen to be "strong" or "macho."

When a therapist suspects domestic abuse, it isn't always the case that we will immediately report the incident to the authorities (unless there's an imminent threat to life). We have to work with the client where they are, rather than abide by rigid rules, and a more positive outcome can arise when taking the time to understand the situation from the client's point of view. An insistence on reporting the abuse immediately can sometimes serve to make complex domestic situations worse. As a therapist in the UK, I must abide by my counseling body's ethical framework, which states that I will carefully consider how I manage situations when protecting clients or others from serious harm. This particularly applies to complex cases. If I broke Levi's confidentiality, I would lose his trust. My intuition was telling me that, if confronted by the authorities, Levi would deny that anything was wrong and go back to his life, minus the safety of the therapy room.

It takes a lot of bravery for a client to open up about potentially abusive relationships. Levi had been courageous to share this with me. Often therapists are the first person to whom survivors of abuse open up. I feel a precedent of distrust would arise if every therapist broke confidentiality and reported domestic abuse to the authorities as a matter of course. In the case of Levi, I was in the stage of understanding and formulating the whole picture. I felt my connection with Levi was strong but balanced on a brittle foundation—at any moment I believed I would lose him and, as a result, suspected that he might lose faith in therapy altogether. My intuition told me that reporting the fragments of information he had shared with me so far wouldn't help him in the long run. It was a risk I was willing to take, and one with which some may not agree. However, as a therapist, I also have to comply with the law, so if I felt or discovered that the threat to life was explicit, I wouldn't hesitate to report domestic abuse to the police.

There are different types of abuse, the most common being *emotional*. According to the National Centre for Domestic Violence and the charity ManKind, emotional abuse accounts for 95 percent of the calls they receive from men; 68 percent of male callers also reported physical violence, 41 percent psychological, 23 percent financial, 13 percent coercive control, and 3 percent sexual abuse. ManKind has highlighted research into why men stay in abusive relationships: 89 percent of men from the study claimed the main reason for staying was concern for their children; 81 percent strongly believed in marriage for life; and staying for love was 71 percent. Other reasons included a belief that their partner will change, fear of losing the children, lack of money, having nowhere to go, embarrassment, and fear for their partner's health. Remarkably, 24 percent stayed for fear they would be killed otherwise.

Coercive control is a form of abuse in which the perpetrator uses forms of emotional abuse to manipulate the other person. This can include punishing, demanding, name-calling, emotional blackmail, attempting to question one's own sanity (gaslighting), invading someone's privacy, and assault. The survivor is often conditioned to behave out of fear of receiving a negative consequence from their partner, as opposed to going with what they would prefer.

Whatever was happening within Levi's relationship—and in all similar cases—as a therapist it's my job to find the delicate balance between what is ethical, what is in the client's best interests, and what safeguarding might be necessary.

23
Speakeasy

We got out of an Uber in a seedy-looking side street, already quite merry from an afternoon bar crawl of Manchester's cocktail bars.

Josh: You sure this is the right place?
Amos: Yes, this is it.

Amos knocked on what looked like a rusted fire exit. The door swung open and an austere doorman peered out at us.

Doorman: Amos! How are you doing? Not seen you for ages!
Amos: I'm good, Stevie. You know me, I'm always great. You're looking well! Don't let *him* in, though: He's a prick.

He pointed to Sean, who responded with an awkward, pleading expression.

Doorman: Would explain why he's friends with you, then.

They clasped hands in an affirmative shake, then he stood aside to let us in.

We walked into a dimly lit bar strewn with groups of people sitting around candlelit tables. There were sounds of syncopated, propulsive jazz from a trio on the small stage. A respectful, quiet chatter filled the air. The bar oozed class and exclusivity. Two mixologists were busy behind the mirrored bar, one finishing with a shaker and the other adding toppings to a foamy drink.

Amos: Let's get this table.

We sat down, and a young woman with a green apron came to take our drinks orders. I asked for a bourbon old-fashioned. My friends' orders blurred into obscurity as I focused on the music. The drinks came, we quietly toasted, then sat in awe as we listened to the deliberate distortions of timbre and breathtaking improvisation.

BIOLOGY: *Bladder full. Empty me.*

Josh: Going to nip to the restroom.
Sean: Me too.
Kyla: Aww.

Sean and I shifted out of the booth and navigated our way through the labyrinth of tables to a dark corner where the restrooms were located. I approached two tables where it looked like it would be a particularly tight squeeze, but the hollow confidence induced by the alcohol persuaded me I could do it. I was pressing through two chairs with an apologetic gesture when something caught my eye.

BIOLOGY: *Thud . . . thud . . . thud . . .*
DETECTIVE: *What do we have here?!*

I looked up to see a woman with long black hair sitting at a table near the stage. She was with a group of friends.

ANXIETY: *Well, this is a surprise.*
DETECTIVE: *Is that . . . Zahra?*
ANALYTICAL: *Hmmm . . . A person with crippling agoraphobia sitting at the front of a music gig? What are the odds?*
CRITIC: *You're pissed, Josh. Calm down.*

I returned from the restroom and tried to glance over at her table. Every member of that party had their backs to us. I sat down and swirled the remainder of my drink.

Amos: You all right, Columbo?
Josh: What?
Amos: I asked if you're all right.
Josh: Yeah. Just think I recognize someone at the front.
Kyla: Has our presence become too tame for you?
Josh: Always.

The trio finished a passage of their music to warm applause. The silhouette of the woman with the dark hair clapped in the backdrop of the candlelight.

Memories of the last session with Zahra came flooding back. The outrageous exposure session driving through Manchester. The altercation with the van driver, the bravery of her continuing despite her anxiety, the insistence that she wanted to return to the hospital where she worked, the awe in which she left me. I'd forgotten a lot of it because of the panic I'd felt afterward when I realized I was close to the children's hospital.

DETECTIVE: *She's a cool customer, Josh.*
BIOLOGY: *Let's warp the perspective for a moment. Thank you, bourbon.*
ESCAPIST: *Candlelight, city vigilantes. What a fantastic fantasy.*
VOLITION: *Shut up. Shut up.*

The double-bass player of the trio stepped forward and announced an intermission. The hum of voices grew louder and there was a scraping of chairs. I squinted at the group in front and still couldn't work out if it was Zahra.

ANXIETY: *It is.*
INTUITION: *No it isn't. You want it to be.*

The woman stood up and moved over to another bar at the end of the room. Two of the party sat on stools and turned around to face the other group members. There was laughter among them all.

DETECTIVE: *I need to find out.*
ANALYTICAL: *No you don't.*
BIOLOGY: *If you want to rid yourself of this feeling, you will.*

Josh: Shall I get us some more drinks?
Sean: It's table service, you know.
Josh: I need to know if the person over there is someone I recognize. It's doing my head in.
Kyla: Who do you think it is?

ANXIETY: *Lie.*
VOLITION: *Don't lie to your friends.*

ANALYTICAL: *Confidentiality.*
CRITIC: *Why are you purposefully going out of your way to go near a client outside the confines of the therapeutic hour? To satiate your own selfish desires?*
ANALYTICAL: *They have a point.*

Josh: It's no one you know.

I started to make my way toward the bar before an outstretched arm obstructed my progress.

Amos: I know you. It's a client, isn't it?

I felt like a child who had just been caught stealing. I couldn't lie to my friends.

Josh: Yes. I just . . . just need to know . . . if it's them . . .
Amos: But what if they see you? That surely has implications, right?

He didn't bring up that time we went out raving and I projectile vomited on an ex-client. He wasn't like that. Amos was considerate, unconditional, and—what I feel to be one of his most underrated traits—tasteful. He knew that evening had more context than just me being off my face. I wasn't in a good place back then.

Josh: I won't speak to them. I just want to see if it's who I think it is.
Amos: Curiosity killed the bourbon-filled cat, my friend.

He studied me.

Amos: Wait . . . you *want* to be seen. Look at you: You've brushed your hair and adjusted your collar. You're wearing that expression you make when you're trying to look . . . imperturbable. As if you're cool in some way.

He started smiling.

BIOLOGY: *Your face needs blood right now. Lots of blood in your cheeks and head.*

Josh: I . . .
Amos: Come on then . . . let's go find out.

Amos took me to the bar. We walked past the group that included the woman with long dark hair. Frustratingly, it was as if she was tidally locked to our position; no matter where we moved across the room, our angle of view never seemed to change. She constantly had her back to us. Amos placed his hands on the bar. I stood to his right, trying to act nonchalant.

CRITIC: *What are you doing, man?*

Mixologist: Hey, Amos. What can I get you?
Amos: Hemingway Daiquiri for me and . . .

He stood back, straightened up, and slapped me on the back, shouting so everyone could hear.

Amos: . . . a bourbon old-fashioned for my extremely handsome and famous friend here!

ANXIETY: *Kill me.*
IRREVERENCE: *I love it. Bathe me in the cringe.*
BIOLOGY: *You're not getting butterflies. I prescribe you moths!*

Several people around us looked out of interest. I stood there awkwardly, shifting from one foot to another. The group to our left glanced over and I couldn't help but look back. The fascination and need to know was too strong. The woman with the long dark hair locked eyes with me, studying my face. My heart started to pound.

DETECTIVE: *It's not her, Columbo.*
ANXIETY: *Phew.*

A wave of relief washed over me. Amos and I returned to our table after ordering Kyla and Sean their drinks. The red velvet curtain at the back of the room rippled and the jazz trio returned to the stage to resounding applause. The silhouette of impostor Zahra took her seat at the front.

Amos: So . . . was it who you thought it was?

Josh: No. Thankfully.

The trio burst into an outgrowth of fusion, and that familiar, warm feeling filled the insides of the audience once more. Amos leaned in closer.

Amos: Then why do you keep looking at her?

He was right. I was. I didn't know why. I should have been glad that I didn't have to be in the predicament of being in the same room as a client in a coincidental and potentially awkward overlapping of our personal lives. But I recognized that there was a part of me, one temporarily pulling the strings, that wished it had been Zahra.

24
Zahra

Zahra was due to arrive in a few minutes. Meanwhile, I had been in intense training for the overthinking championships and was putting in a good session. I had brushed my hair, then messed it up again, because why would I brush my hair ahead of a client appointment? To impress Zahra? For my professionalism? I'd worn a nice shirt, then ruminated on whether this was what I'd usually do. Then I decided it wasn't what I'd usually do, so I put a T-shirt back on. This was all getting a bit silly; it was an anxious reaction to the strange situation that had happened the other night. There was no need to make it bigger than it was. I took a long, deep breath, then calmed myself with a reminder of the purpose of my role as a therapist. A few more deep breaths and my mind became clearer.

There was a knock at the door and I was relieved to notice that I didn't react like an excited teenager. My professional head was back on. I was back in the room.

Josh: Hey, Zahra, come on in!

Zahra: I have a date to return to work! I'm so happy. I never thought I'd get to this point.

COMPASSION: *Yes!*

EMPATHY: *When hopelessness abates it's such an amazing feeling.*

Zahra: Thank you for doing the exposure work with me. It has helped so much, especially with the driving.

Josh: You were very courageous and you applied what we spoke about. Well done.

Zahra: I honestly couldn't imagine myself back there, returning to the hospital. I still have that niggling inner critic saying I'm pathetic, but I've realized listening to it hasn't helped me with all this anxiety.

ANALYTICAL: *Inner critic is always a good point of discussion.*

Josh: Is the inner critic something that you'd like to talk about today?

Zahra pondered for a moment.

Zahra: I think I'd like to, yes. Hmm . . . "like" is an overstatement. I think I
should. I think I know where it comes from.
Josh: Yeah?
Zahra: Do you know when you said that disordered anxiety can come
from an overflowing stress jug? I think my fear of panic and the social
consequences was a big part of what was filling it up. I feel like I'm on
my way to dealing with that now. Which . . . which is a big thing, isn't it?

COMPASSION: *It is.*

I smiled.

Zahra: It won't surprise you that a big part of my stress jug is grief. My father.
The nature in which he passed away.

DETECTIVE: *Stabbed multiple times by his mentally unwell son.*

Zahra: I think . . . I think I should talk about that . . . maybe . . .

SAVIOR: *We'll be here for you should you decide to.*

It was one of those moments as a therapist when you yearn for the client
to delve into the difficult place—and to jump in with them. Admittedly,
some of that yearning stemmed from my own interest, which is a human
part of me that can't be shut off, but most of it came from a place of
compassion and the belief that exploring difficult topics allows therapeutic growth. The simple act of talking about difficult subjects, in a safe
environment where we feel listened to and cared for, helps us to start
emptying the stress jug.

Josh: Just know that I'm ready to hear anything you have to say. Doesn't
have to be in order. Just go where your mind takes you—it usually shows
you the relevant stuff.

Zahra folded one leg over one knee. It was clear she felt like she had to talk about difficult things at some point. It seemed she had decided today was the day she would lean in to the difficult feelings to give her future self a chance at contentment. It was a considered decision after reflection in between therapy sessions.

Zahra: How do you begin to even unpick your father being murdered?

I nodded, encouraging her to go on.

Josh: I remember you saying that you were close to your father.
Zahra: Yes. In many ways. He was a very accomplished man. He was the main reason I became a doctor.

IRREVERENCE: *And also Operation was a great battery-operated game for ages six and up.*

Zahra: And no, it wasn't one of those relationships where I was starved of love if I didn't get straight *A*'s. I wasn't coerced into being a doctor. My dad inspired me through his own hard work and dedication. He is . . . *was* outstanding in his field. His work in neurology is still heavily cited in modern medicine. Ironic, really . . .
Josh: How so?
Zahra: Because it upset him how he couldn't really connect with my brother. My dad spent his life studying and trying to understand the brain, but the more he tried, the more it split an ever-widening chasm between him and my brother. My brother is very unwell. He has struggled most of his life with paranoid delusions, bouts of rage and confusion, as well as anxiety and crippling depression. We all struggled with his behavior, despite loving him with all our hearts. But my father tried to go the extra mile.

I nodded slightly again.

Zahra: He tried to fix him. I know you believe in this fairy-tale notion that none of us is broken, that it's a matter of perspective, but my brother has severe needs, Josh.
Josh: I understand.

EMPATHY: *Let's try to understand what witnessing all of this was like from Zahra's perspective.*

Josh: I'm trying to understand what it was like to witness all of this from your point of view.

Zahra: It's not an attentional issue. I've always been mature for my age. I wasn't pining for Daddy's attention because he was too busy playing Dr. House with my brother. He made time for me, and it was wonderful. He just struggled. I understand and love him for it.

She seemed utterly committed to telling this story. The lid was off, Pandora's box was opened. There was no going back.

Josh: I'm hearing a lot of admiration for him.

Zahra: I worshipped the ground he walked on. I can understand his struggles and his flaws.

ANALYTICAL: *Idealization? Pedestal?*

Josh: Flaws?

Zahra: Yes. Flaws, Joshua. We all have them. I'm sure you'll come round to admitting yours one day.

ANXIETY: *Ouch.*

Zahra: I'm sorry. I didn't mean to react like that.

Josh: It's okay. I can see that you're very protective of your dad.

Zahra: Obviously not protective enough. He was stabbed to death.

She said the line with almost total apathy. This kind of flat reaction can happen when people try to repress painful life events.

EMPATHY: *Her feelings toward her brother must be complicated.*

Josh: I imagine that your feelings toward your brother must be complicated. I'm hearing empathy and an understanding of his state of mental health. I haven't heard any feelings about his actions, though.

Her posture tightened.

Zahra: It's because he's a fucking psycho, Josh! An oxygen-starved piece of shit who killed our father! Broke our hearts. Broke our mother's heart. None of us will be the same again!

She allowed a croak of a cry that wanted to be let out ten minutes ago.

ANALYTICAL: *Expressing anger in this circumstance is healthy and needed.*

Zahra: I hate him . . . I hate him . . . I hate him . . .

Her chin fell to her chest and she began to weep. I remained quiet so she could process her emotions. After a minute, she raised her head again.

Zahra: The night it happened my brother had locked himself in the garage and boarded up the windows. I was out with my parents having dinner—a rare time when we were all free. My brother had refused to come with us, unsurprisingly. Mum was worried about leaving him alone, but Dad insisted we show trust in him. We all had to trust in his ability to be independent and autonomous. I get that on the surface it sounds wholesome and admirable, but it turned out not to be the wisest of decisions.

Zahra squinted, completely enveloped in the memory.

Zahra: My father got a call from our neighbors, Frank and Shirley, when we were at the restaurant. They said they could hear banging and shouting from the garage. They were concerned because they knew of my brother's difficulties. They said he was screaming: "They're coming to get me!" or something along those lines. So my father immediately got to his feet to go save the day . . . yet again . . . Dr. Hosseini to the rescue . . .

Her face was now streaming with tears. She stuttered slightly as she struggled to continue.

Zahra: Mum was also worried and wanted to get back. I was upset that my brother had spoiled yet another family get-together. So you know what I said? The last thing I said to my father?

ANALYTICAL: *This is going to be a linchpin for some serious guilt.*

Zahra: I shouted at him, embarrassed him in front of a busy restaurant. "There you go again, with your savior complex. Dad, do you really need to be a hero more than you need to spend time with me?"

She took several tissues and dabbed at her face.

Zahra: I was so pathetic. Like a child whining for attention. Of course, my brother needed his time; he was drastically unwell. I just . . . I . . .

Josh: You were disappointed that you couldn't savor what sounds like a rare opportunity to spend time alone with your parents?

She nodded while blowing her nose into a tissue.

Zahra: They . . . returned home. I stayed in the city, sulking. Apparently, Dad tried to get into the garage to get to my brother. I think my parents were worried he'd kill himself or something. My brother wouldn't open the garage door or engage with Dad at all; instead, he was living these paranoid delusions, trying to lock himself away from a world he was petrified of. My mum pleaded with my dad to ring the police, but he was having none of it. Dr. Hosseini can save anyone. It was on *his* terms. It was *his* son.

Zahra started to tremble but was determined to go on.

COMPASSION: *Come on, you can do it.*
SAVIOR: *I can help you!*

Zahra: Dad . . . he . . . managed to fetch a crowbar from the side of the garage. He pryed the door open and . . . well . . . Babak was there with a carving knife. He warned Dad not to come closer . . . but Dad had de-escalated these episodes in the past. He was good at calming Babak, but today my brother was particularly . . . unwell. Then he . . . he stabbed Dad in the neck multiple times, severing an artery, then continued in a frenzy . . . He wouldn't stop . . .

Zahra's body froze, but she continued talking as if in a trance.

Zahra: The neighbors heard all the commotion and came running. Frank managed to tackle Babak to the floor while Shirley pulled my mum away

before she had time to see what was happening. She took Mum to her
house and pretty much locked her inside. I appreciate that gesture so
much, as I don't think Mum would ever have gotten over the vision of her
husband lying in a pool of his own blood. The police arrived and seized
my brother. Mum could tell by the speed of the paramedics attending
at the garage that Dad had no chance of being alive. My . . . poor mum.
And my dad . . . I . . . it's horrible . . . And even Babak . . . he's been
committed . . . his life ended that day too . . .

BIOLOGY: *Tried my best but one tear slipped away.*

I dabbed my eye discreetly.

Josh: What a horrendously traumatic time you've been through. An
unthinkably tragic event. I'm so sorry, Zahra.

She looked at me teary-eyed.

Josh: That must have been difficult for you to tell me . . . I appreciate it
a lot.
Zahra: It feels good to talk about it . . . not good . . . but . . . like I feel less
encumbered . . . lighter in a way.
Josh: Can you feel where it's lighter? In your body?

She pondered a moment.

Zahra: Yes. My shoulders and chest. They feel . . . freer?
Josh: Our bodies often hold on to unprocessed emotions, particularly those
that are in response to traumatic events. I believe talking and allowing
emotions to rise and be expressed is a good way of releasing the
heaviness our bodies can endure.
Zahra: Like an exorcism?

We both smiled.

Josh: If you like.

Zahra's mind was tugged by a memory.

Zahra: I remember wanting to see my dad before the funeral. I . . . don't
know why . . .

Josh: For a sense of closure, perhaps?

Zahra: Yes. That's it. So I went to see his body at the funeral home.

> **TRIGGER:** *Funeral home.*
> **BIOLOGY:** *Sympathetic nervous system engaged. Epinephrine and norepinephrine released. Let's see how tight these muscles can really go!*
> **ANXIETY:** *Whoa!*

Zahra: You okay?

Josh: I'm fine, please continue. Mild heartburn.

> **VOLITION:** *Attention stations back to Zahra's frame of reference.*
> **COMPASSION:** *False alarm, this doesn't need our attention right now. It'll pass soon.*

Zahra: I think I needed to see him there. They'd washed and cleaned his body, and he was wrapped in a white cloth. I can't imagine it is ever pleasant to see a loved one's dead body, but I felt like it was an antidote to the versions of my dad that my imagination was throwing at me—all mauled and cut open. He looked . . . peaceful.

∙∙

Zahra continued to reminisce about her father. How he was an inspiration for her work. How she admired his standing in the field of medicine and neuroscience. How other people venerated him and how she hoped to earn the same respect from her peers one day. She also spoke about her brother being committed to a psychiatric unit and the grief she was experiencing around the collapse of what had once been, for all its complications, a close family unit.

Zahra: Josh, is it possible to go crazy from anxiety? As in, if it gets too much, can my mind snap?

ANALYTICAL: *A fear influenced by observing her brother's mental illness?*
DETECTIVE: *I was thinking the same.*

Josh: From anxiety on its own? No. It's a common question I hear from people who experience panic attacks, though. I promise that panic attacks cannot make you "go crazy."
Zahra: But can anxiety be the trigger for, say . . . hidden underlying mental conditions?

VOLITION: *Provide assurance here.*

Josh: You're not your brother, Zahra. Anxiety will try to convince you that you will lose control, often by drawing upon things around you and the environment.
Zahra: Okay. But . . . is it possible?
Josh: Yes. Pretty much anything is possible, even our greatest fears, but you must play the odds when it comes to the scary things in life. I believe the odds in this situation to be heavily in your favor. And it's okay to live like that. The biggest mistake people with anxiety make is to live in trepidation that their fears are around the corner and about to come true, despite the unlikelihood. The fear comes from the belief that we won't be able to cope if the bad things do happen, which is almost always untrue. Humans have a remarkable ability to adapt. My motto is "The bad thing almost certainly isn't going to happen, but even if it did, I will be able to cope with it."

Zahra thought about what I had said. It seemed she took comfort from it.

Zahra: I think I've got to stop seeing being anxious as failure. It's like I hate myself every time I get anxious, like it's my fault. Not only is it an alarm that makes me feel scared, but it also feels like a siren going off, letting me know that I have failed in some way.
Josh: I see. It's common for people who hold themselves to high standards

to misinterpret anxiety as failure. It sounds like you'd like to change your relationship with your anxiety.

Zahra: Yes. I think it would help.

ANALYTICAL: *Cognitive reframe?*
INTUITION: *That's a good idea.*

Zahra and I spent the rest of the session drafting a letter to her anxiety, as if it was a conscious entity living inside of her. The aim was to draw upon self-compassion and gain a more balanced understanding of what was happening. We laughed as Zahra tried to reframe anxiety from something that she despised into something about which she could feel more ambivalent. We eventually produced a rough draft of a letter of which she seemed proud. She folded the letter and placed it in her bag, then she looked up at me.

Zahra: I read in that article that bad things have happened to you too. How can you play the odds like this when you know that awful things can and do happen?

TRIGGER: *Traumatic memories.*
COMPASSION: *You've got this.*
VOLITION: *We have.*

Josh: Because I'm still here now and I live a content and comfortable life. We're not here to discuss me, though.

Zahra looked me in the eyes: a deep and compassionate look that felt to me like it conveyed sincerity and respect. Time slowed slightly. The light caught her chestnut eyes.

BIOLOGY: *She's beautiful.*
VOLITION: *Stop.*

Zahra: I think it's amazing what you have achieved, Joshua. I . . . deeply respect who you are, and I don't think I could have made this progress without you. Thank you.

BIOLOGY: *Flutter, flutter, toil and butter.*

Josh: . . . er . . .

I began to feel overwhelmed, and my cheeks began to flush.

CRITIC: *Wake up, you idiot. Have you not been listening?*
ANALYTICAL: *The whole session has been about her admiration for her father, an authority figure who inspires her. This is emotional projection.*
CRITIC: *Not in a Hugh Grant movie, pal.*

Josh: I appreciate the compliment. I'm just aware of the time, Zahra . . .

It was three minutes before the end. I was flustered.

Josh: Shall we . . . er . . . catch up next week?

She smiled.

Zahra: Sure.

∙∙

From my office window I watched Zahra walk to her car and drive away.

COMPASSION: *She's come a long way. She's brave.*
IRREVERENCE: *And funny.*
BIOLOGY: *And attractive.*
VOLITION: *Stop it.*
CRITIC: *Aw, he's a teenager again! Told you he's a charlatan. Can't handle anyone attractive smiling at him.*
VOLITION: *Please stop it.*
CRITIC: *Never!*
COMPASSION: *We'll work around it. These things can happen in the therapy room.*

25
A Letter to My Anxiety

Later that evening I sat down and wrote a letter to my own anxiety after being inspired by the exercise in Zahra's session. Once the pen hit the paper, I let the words flow:

Dear Anxiety,

I know at times we've had our difficulties. We've maybe not always seen eye to eye and we've struggled to get along. Clearing the air and putting it all behind us so we can work together is the best way to go, so I've been meaning to have this conversation with you for a while. Given that you do not have ears and can't listen when I speak, I thought maybe the experience of writing this letter would help you understand how I feel.

I must come clean. There was a time when I wished you gone. I just wanted you to be quiet, to go away and leave me alone. I'm embarrassed to say this, and I hope you can forgive me, but at one point while in the depths of a disordered relationship with you, I even asked my therapist if I could have my amygdala removed to stop the suffering. I'm not proud of that and I won't blame you if you're cross with me now, but you have to understand that it was a dark time and neither of us was thinking clearly in those days. I'm sorry for hating you the way I did back then. I understand now that you were just trying to keep me safe and making mistakes like we all do.

I'm grateful that I've come to a point in my life where I am appreciative of you and thankful for having you in my life. You are a part of me that I could not live without, and I know now that I would be incomplete without you. Maybe this is just me feeling guilty for wanting to (literally) cut you out of my life years ago, but I want to thank you for a few things.

Thank you for keeping me alive. Without you, I would be dead. I might have spent years running into traffic, jumping from rooftop to rooftop high above my city and mouthing off to bullies much larger and stronger than me. You make me aware of real danger, and have undoubtedly saved me from cuts, scrapes, bruises, black eyes, broken bones, and even worse. I was enough of a reckless problem child. Without you, I cannot even imagine what my poor mum would have had to endure.

Thank you for helping me consider options and make rational choices when they need to be made. You sit at the table next to the other guys, like Analytical, Intuition, and Volition, providing valuable insight that I can take into account before making decisions.

Thank you for making life more fun. Without you, I would never be able to truly enjoy the thrill of roller coasters and scary movies. Without you, I would not experience the delicious nervous anticipation of a public speaking engagement or an important football match. Without you, I would miss out on the exhilarating frustration of my favorite player banging a shot off the bar in a close match. You can be a bit of a pain sometimes, but you really do make things more interesting.

Thank you for letting me know when I need to worry about my loved ones. You help me understand when it's time to tend to them, make time for them, help them, and show them how much I care about them. You motivate me to give my special people the attention they deserve.

Thank you for my panic attacks. I know this sounds somewhat mad, but really, thank you. Without having experienced the grim depths of panic attacks and disordered anxiety, I would not be able to put day-to-day life issues into proper context. As much as I struggled when you were overenthusiastic about my safety, in some ways you taught me how to know what is truly worth worrying about, and what is not. You've helped me learn how to enjoy even the mundane, ordinary, lovely moments in life. I really appreciate that lesson.

I know now why you're here. I understand your purpose. I'm grateful for the work you do on my behalf. You do make me a better person in many ways. But since we are putting all the old issues

behind us now, I do need to ask you for a few small favors that I
think will help keep us on the same page.

Please. Going forward, please work with me.

You do not need to fire off while I'm at Sunday dinner with my
family. I don't need you guarding me while I'm in a theater trying to
enjoy a well-written drama. I don't need you when I'm just walking
through the woods, trying to enjoy the quiet and beauty of nature.
I don't need you to fire off when I'm trying to slog through a boring
speech without putting my audience to sleep. I can do without the
intrusive thoughts that you randomly suggest could be cause for
concern when I'm just hanging out with my friends. Speaking of
my friends, I'd prefer it if you would just relax while I'm at birthday
parties and weddings. Those things are about people I care about;
don't make them about me.

This is a big one: I'm going to respectfully request that you stop
messing with my bowels, my muscles, and the rest of my body for no
good reason. I just want to relax on my days off rather than run to
the bathroom every twenty minutes, wondering why my legs won't
stop shaking. That's really not necessary.

Look, I understand that you're just trying to do a job. I know
that you're working with the best of intentions, trying to take care of
me. But sometimes you get a little too loud, and you overstay your
welcome. I'd like you to consider that you do not always have to be in
charge of everything. There are lots of useful voices in my head that
are all trying to work together. Sometimes it's better to just be part
of the team. Chime in if you think you must, then let the rest of the
team weigh in, and we'll all make good choices together that way.
I know you can do that. I see you do it all the time.

So, going forward, let's work together. You give me some time.
I'll give you some time. I promise that we'll take care of everything
that needs to be taken care of. You have my word. Sometimes I
will have to dismiss you when you get a little overzealous and riled
up for no reason. Please don't take it personally. I'm only doing it
because I respect you. I value you. I want you to be around to work
with me because I know that you are probably going to save my life
many times before I take my last breath. But that being said, I want
you to be around as the best version of yourself. The version that

makes things better. No more extended, unhinged, unprovoked rants, okay?

Well, Anxiety, it seems I've prattled on long enough. I do hope that you accept my apologies for the times when I hated you, and that we can move on from here in a spirit of mutual admiration, respect, and trust.

Thank you for your attention and have a nice day.

Warm regards,
Josh

26
Harry:
Big-Ring Doughnut

June 2012

Josh: Am I allowed to go in with him?

I had to shout over the noises of the machine.

Radiologist: Of course. You must wear one of these, though.

He offered me a choice of two lead aprons.

Radiologist: You can have the blue one, or the one with fluffy little farm animals on.

Naturally, I grasped the animal apron and placed it over my head. It was heavy and pulled down on my shoulders.

Josh: Whoa, this is weighty.
Radiologist: Yeah, lead is heavy. It's to stop the radiation from the CT scanner.
Josh: Then how do I morph into a superhero afterward?

We walked through a set of reinforced double doors, and I saw Harry sitting on the end of a table. He looked up and smiled, but I could tell he was anxious.

Josh: Hey, man!
Harry: Hey.
Josh: You all right?
Harry: I don't want to lie down. The pressure in my stomach pushes too hard against my ribs.

His distended abdomen was swollen to the size of a beach ball. I turned to the radiologist, who was now on the other side of a pane of glass in the control office.

Josh: Is there any way we can do this without him lying down? Harry's perineum has a buildup of ascites, and it hurts him to lie down flat. He also struggles to breathe.

She smiled.

Radiologist: Someone's polished up on their medical lingo.
Josh: These past weeks I've done enough studying at the University of Google.
Radiologist: I'm so sorry, but this machine requires you to lie as flat as possible. We'll try to get you on as much of an angle as we can, Harry. I know you've done this once before, but I always remind people to imagine they're flying through a big-ring doughnut.
Josh: Or a portal!

I walked around the other side of the machine and waved at Harry through the ring of the CT scanner. He didn't engage with my goofing around. He was suffering too much. A nurse came through and provided pillows and padding to make Harry less uncomfortable.

Harry: It's okay. I'm ready. I can do it.
Josh: I'll hold your hand till the doughnut starts moving. We don't want my hand to appear on the scan—the doctors will lose their minds. They'll think you're growing extra limbs or something.

The lights dimmed and Harry was passed through the giant slip rings of the CT scanner. I could see the discomfort in his gritted teeth and labored breathing, but he didn't complain once, and it nearly broke me. If I could have done it for him, I would have. The CT scan, the tumors, everything.

Radiologist: Okay, all done. I think we have the images we need. I'll send them through to Dr. Finnan straightaway.

I helped Harry to sit up on the end of the table.

Josh: Nailed it, lad. Let me get your wheelchair.

We shuffled him into the seat, and I guided him out of the room.

Josh: Well done, mate. I'll get us pizza and a DVD tonight and we can watch it on the ward.
Harry: Okay. Sounds good.
Josh: For now, though, we venture to the fifth floor to see Dr. Finnan and discuss the results of the CT scan. We'll kick the door in, smoking cigars and—
Harry: Josh . . .
Josh: Sorry.

．．

We met my mum at the office. There was a silent acknowledgment of a shared fear that hung in the air more heavily than the lead apron. Dr. Finnan invited us in, and we sat across from her on the other side of a sad-looking coffee table. A box of tissues sat in the middle. I wondered how many people took a tissue after hearing news about loved ones in this room.

Dr. Finnan studied her screen alongside another doctor whom I hadn't met before. They seemed to silently confer, then Dr. Finnan swung her chair around, and my stomach felt like it was swinging with it. The moment of truth was coming.

Dr. Finnan: Well, as you know, Harry, you have a lot of tumors in your belly and a large one on your liver. You have been exceptionally courageous these last three weeks, and I understand you've had some awful complications with the chemotherapy. I know you even had to spend a few days in intensive care.
Harry: My brother said I was "tripping balls" on morphine.

We all shared a nervous laugh.

CRITIC: *Hurry the fuck up, Finnan, this isn't the* Strictly Come Dancing *results . . .*
ANXIETY: *I am so, so scared.*

Dr. Finnan: Well, the scans show us that there has been a significant reduction in all the tumors that we can see. The big one has halved in size, and the little ones seem a lot smaller. You are doing incredibly well . . .

My mum squeezed my brother tightly.

Harry: Mum! That hurts . . .

They both started laughing.

Mum: I don't care. I'm allowed to beat you up.

Meanwhile, I had jumped up and left the room to do an enormous and prolonged knee slide down the corridor. I startled an auxiliary nurse as he saw a massive man screaming "Yeeessss!!" flying past him on the floor.

Josh: He's gonna do it! He's gonna fucking do it!

Some nearby nurses looked up from a monitoring station. They looked shocked. A few of them recognized me and smiled. They could see what was happening.

Josh: I'm so sorry for my language. Oh my God. I need to get pizza!

I ran outside the hospital toward Oxford Road, feeling the most relieved I had felt in a long, long time.

· ·

I emerged from the elevator and buzzed myself into Ward 84. Harry had been moved to a private room where he sat up in his bed. He was surrounded by Mum, his dad and stepmum, and a nurse who was loading up his next batch of chemotherapy. The grind never stops when you're battling cancer.

Josh: I couldn't wait! I got pizza now. Pizza is good. We all love pizza!
Mum: It's eleven in the morning!
Josh: When in Rome!
Nurse: That doesn't make any sense.

I placed the pizza boxes on the side and leaned over the bed to hug my brother. Despite his discomfort, he sat up and hugged me back. It was the tightest hug I have ever received from him.

Harry: I'm not letting you go!
Josh: But . . . pizza?
Harry: Nope! I'm not letting you go. Ever!

I squeezed him with every ounce of love I had.

Josh: Fine. If we're playing "hug chicken," I'm here for the long haul. First one who lets go loses. Just wait until you need a shit or a shower, then things will get dicey. It'll get beyond weird.
Mum: Josh!

We started laughing, my brother's happy convulsions shaking against my sternum.

Josh: Sorry . . .

That hug was one of the happiest moments of my life.

27

Noah

I felt guilty as I closed the door after my last client. Even though I had stayed professional and the session had gone well, inside I knew that I'd struggled to give them as much attention as I would have liked. While I had put in the effort, my mind just wanted to wander to anxious thoughts. Anxious thoughts about my next client, Noah, who was due to arrive in ten minutes.

ANXIETY: *What if he doesn't show up? I hope he's okay.*
DETECTIVE: *We've not heard from him. You check your emails?*
ANXIETY: *What if something bad has happened?*
ANALYTICAL: *It's likely you would have been contacted by now if something had happened.*

I walked over to my desk and loaded up my inbox. Nothing. I had been nervous since this morning when I looked at my schedule. It's unsettling how anxiety spreads and morphs quietly in the vacuum of silence. After the previous session, when Noah made a quick exit after declaring that he didn't deserve love and hinted that he didn't deserve to live, I had called his doctor to share my concerns. In these situations, the doctor should then liaise with the appropriate mental health team or get in contact with the client themselves. I hadn't heard back from the doctor so I had no idea what might have happened.

CRITIC: *You should've called the doctor to follow up.*

Ten minutes had now passed since the start time of Noah's appointment and there was no sign of him. I did laps pacing the office and monitoring my sentry checkpoints: Out the window down at the entrance to the building; no sign. To the office door peering down the corridor; nope. To my desk to check my work phone and computer; still no contact.

After twenty minutes I picked up my phone and dialed Noah's number.

Straight to voicemail. I tried again, hoping it was because he was engaged or in an area with no signal, but the same happened. Then I rang his doctor. Unsurprisingly, the doctor was busy, but the receptionist told me that she'd get back to me as soon as she was free. Thirty minutes passed and I resigned myself to the assumption that Noah wasn't coming.

Lunchtime arrived. I stared at my Tupperware box filled with last night's Indian takeaway and couldn't muster any hunger. There was an uneasy feeling in the pit of my stomach, and my anxiety tried its best to auction its thoughts for my attention. It was winning. The gavel could come down only when I had some closure about what was happening with Noah. I looked at my calendar and saw I had three more clients today.

ANALYTICAL: *I don't think it's wise to see more clients given your state of mind.*
CRITIC: *Don't be so pathetic. Do your job.*
COMPASSION: *Life can get in the way sometimes, and you're doing right by your clients to acknowledge your limitations.*
EMPATHY: *It's not fair to provide counseling if you're not fully in the client's frame of reference.*

Once Noah's session time had passed, I called my other clients and rearranged our sessions. Then I headed home.

.   .

My house was a pigsty, so as a distraction from my worries about Noah, I attempted to do something about it, keeping my phone on loud just in case his doctor called with an update. I carried a mountain of cardboard recycling and stomped it into an already full recycling bin. I popped on some latex gloves and cleaned the kitchen and bathroom, then vacuumed the floors. I got carried away with the vacuuming and even did the stairs—a job I always find painfully tedious. As I reached the final step, the vacuum cleaner sputtered, made a clunking noise, then cut out. A smoky, burning metallic smell filled the landing.

ANALYTICAL: *I think this is the last time you'll be using this machine.*

I carried the remnants of my vacuum to the outside bin, closed the lid, and walked into the kitchen to wash my hands. As I got close to the sink, I saw my mobile phone screen light up. Two missed calls from a Manchester-based number.

Josh: Shit.

I hadn't heard the phone over the sound of the vacuum cleaner. I dialed back and got the receptionist from Noah's doctor's practice.

Josh: I'm so sorry, I think I've just missed a call from Dr. Davies. My name is Joshua Fletcher.
Receptionist: You're in luck, Dr. Davies hasn't gone on her break yet. I'll put you through now.

There was a short burst of music before Dr. Davies picked up.

Dr. Davies: Hello, is that Joshua?
Josh: It is. Hi, Doctor. Do we have any news on Noah? I called last week to pass on my concerns and I haven't heard from anyone, including him. He didn't turn up to his session today.

There was a pause.

Dr. Davies: Joshua, I'm sorry to tell you that Noah attempted to take his own life over the weekend. He took an overdose of painkillers. Thankfully he is alive and recovering at the hospital. He's working closely with the crisis team. I'm very sorry I didn't inform you earlier. I meant to.

I was stunned. I couldn't bring myself to say anything.

Dr. Davies: I appreciated you informing me of your concerns. I immediately passed them on to the crisis team. They visited Noah on Friday evening and reported that they thought he wasn't a severe risk to life. Unfortunately, he attempted the overdose the morning after. As you know, that can happen. Especially if the suicide attempt was premeditated.
Josh: Okay. Thank you for letting me know.

Dr. Davies: I have a note here saying the crisis team would like to get in touch with you. Is it okay to pass on your details?

Josh: Sure.

ANXIETY: *I told you something awful was going to happen.*
INTUITION: *I didn't think it would result in this, but you did your due diligence.*
CRITIC: *How can you say that? You didn't even chase up the doctor.*

..

An hour later I spoke to Diane from the crisis team. She informed me that Noah was up and talking at the Parsonage Hospital. However, he was reluctant to disclose the reasons behind his suicide attempt.

Diane: Noah keeps asking to talk to you, Joshua. But please don't feel under any pressure to do so. He's officially under our care now and has been committed. That said, we're all in agreement that it may be helpful—from a preventative perspective—if he could speak to someone to whom he's willing to open up. Just in the short term. We're aware of the professional boundaries, and please don't feel under any obligation if this feels uncomfortable. I'm sure we'll get through to him at some point.

ESCAPIST: *You can leave it. He's in the right place now. He's safe.*
COMPASSION: *Why on earth would such a gentle soul do such a thing?*
DETECTIVE: *There's something he didn't tell you. I wouldn't rush into tarring him with the gentle brush.*
ANALYTICAL: *It's your call. It's quite an unusual situation.*
ANXIETY: *I need to know. I need closure.*
CRITIC: *Course you do. It's about you, isn't it, mate?*

Josh: I can come over today.
Diane: Okay, great! When you arrive, someone will meet you and talk you through the safeguarding protocols.
Josh: Okay, see you soon.

We ended the call and I took a deep, lung-filling breath. I looked up at my ceiling and was enveloped by a sense of doubt and confusion.

INTUITION: *Just go with it. It feels right.*
COMPASSION: *If there's something we can do to help, then let's do it.*

I poured myself a glass of water and downed it. Then I fetched my coat.

．．

The hospital was an old Victorian building just outside one of the suburbs of Greater Manchester. The road leading to the reception building was lined with firs, spruces, and pines, and the grounds were a refreshing mix of country greens. Despite my bleak reasons for visiting, the sight was a welcome break from the gray hues of city life.

Once inside, I was escorted to a room dominated by a large bay window with a view out over a rock garden. Next to the window Noah was in a hospital bed, receiving some form of intravenous medication. He looked up and smiled as he saw me enter. I was relieved to see he was still a recognizable version of himself. He'd had a close call.

Noah: Hey . . .
Josh: Hi, Noah. I, er . . .

I wasn't sure what to say.

IRREVERENCE: *He's having a great time, Josh. Party time here.*

Josh: You partying it up in here?

ANXIETY: *Why on earth did you say that?*
CRITIC: *Seriously . . .*

Noah: Having a brilliant time, Josh.

He smiled, presumably thankful for some normality.

ANXIETY: *Phew.*

I pulled up a chair next to his bed. It felt awkward because this conversation wasn't protected by the usual confines of the therapy room, and I wasn't sure what the precise boundaries were, given that we were in a hospital.

VOLITION: *Remember the principles of therapy: confidentiality, unconditional positive regard, and contractual expectations.*

Josh: I thought I'd pop in and just see how you were doing. This isn't necessarily a therapy session as such, but obviously I'll keep what you say confidential. How are you feeling?

There was a mechanical noise as Noah adjusted his bed, using a remote that tilted him into more of a sitting-up position.

Noah: Feeling better than I was. I'm so sorry, Josh. I'm so selfish. I didn't tell you I wasn't coming to the session. I . . . I was all over the place in my head . . . I . . .

Josh: It's okay. Honestly.

Noah: I did something stupid. No surprise, really—I was being self-centered as usual.

Josh: You must have felt like you were in a very desperate place to do that.

Noah: I was. That horrid internal critic had clasped its claws around me and wouldn't stop shaking. I was sucked into a darkness that I was genuinely convinced I couldn't crawl out of. I . . . I'm so sorry . . . I'm so embarrassed. What a waste of everyone's time. I'm such a burden.

Josh: Sounds like the internal critic is still trying to run the show. Even now.

Noah: Perhaps.

He reached over for a drink of water. I pushed the glass closer to him. He took a sip, then closed his eyes, as if he was enduring a pain of some sort.

Noah: What does self-forgiveness look like?

Josh: Hmm . . . I suppose it's when we accept that we have responsibility for our behavior. Perhaps our behavior has resulted in undesirable things happening. Self-forgiveness is when we choose to lean in to the belief that we are measured by our ability to change, grow, and learn from our shortfalls, while also choosing to give our focus to the more admirable parts of ourselves.

Noah rolled his head across the pillow to look at me. He had lost weight in the week that I hadn't see him.

Noah: Can you teach me how?

EMPATHY: *He wants some guidance. There's a scarcity of self-compassion.*
DETECTIVE: *What are we forgiving?*

Josh: What would you like to forgive?
Noah: That I've become my father.
Josh: You are not your father, Noah.

Two tears made their way from one eye and trickled down his gaunt face.

Noah: I'm ready to tell you now.
Josh: The secret you mentioned?

He nodded.

Noah: This is confidential, isn't it?

ANXIETY: *Hmm . . . this isn't good.*

Josh: Yes. Within the confines of what I laid out in the first session. Do you remember?
Noah: Yes.

He wiped his eyes with a seam of his hospital gown before he spoke again.

Noah: In April . . . I . . . attended a meetup for people to try to make friends in the city. It was specifically an LGBTQI+ meet and we all gathered at a pub in the Gay Village. It was a nice evening, and everyone was warm and welcoming. I tried to speak to everyone, but I was naturally drawn to Jacob, one of the quieter people in the group, as we were both quite nervous. He is still a teenager—nineteen, I think—so younger than me. Maybe that's why I felt empowered to take him under my wing.

Noah closed his eyes, presumably because it felt easier to continue without looking at me directly.

Noah: The night carried on and got lively. We went barhopping, but Jacob and I mostly stuck together. A lot of alcohol was consumed, as well as other things. We didn't partake in the drug-taking until later. Jacqui, who was the naturally anointed group leader, suggested we could have an after-party at their place, so that's where we all headed. Jacqui's place was just outside of town, so we all got cabs. Jacob and I shared one separate from the rest of the group. We . . .

More tears came.

Noah: We kissed in the back of the cab. Well, only briefly. I think the cab driver was a homophobe as he began to drive recklessly as soon as we did. Either that or we were just being obnoxious and he'd had enough of us. Who knows? Anyway, we arrived at Jacqui's place. It was enormous. Like one of those fraternity houses you see in American movies. Apparently, Jacqui used to own a construction company when they were called Solomon. They sold the business and chose to live a life of luxury. The drugs came out. I wasn't very experienced in them. But I tried several. Jacob was kindly telling me what each one was, how much to take, what "buzz" or effects it would have.

DETECTIVE: *I wonder where this is going.*

Noah: After a while, Jacob grabbed me by the arm, and we explored the house together like two giddy teenagers. Well, he *is* a teenager, so . . . Upstairs there were several bedrooms. We found one and sat on the edge of the bed together and kissed for a while. Then Jacob pulled out a vial and explained it was something called GHB. He explained it's something you can pop into your drink to feel euphoric, but we shouldn't do much because of the amount of alcohol we had consumed. I obliged, because when someone offers you euphoria in a lonely, miserable life, Joshua, it's difficult to turn it down.

He stopped talking.

Noah: I can't, Josh . . .

I sat patiently. I didn't pressure him to disclose. Some people when pressured will recoil and close up. I desperately wanted to know, though.

IRREVERENCE: *Spill the beans, man. What happened?!*
VOLITION: *Don't press.*
INTUITION: *Seems the best idea.*

Josh: It's okay. I'm not going to pressure you to continue. I'd invite you to reflect on how you may feel talking to someone about it, though. It may lighten the load.

There was a respectful knock on the door before a nurse walked in.

Nurse: Just here to do your obs, Noah.
Noah: Do you mind if we do it in ten minutes? I just need to tell my therapist something.
Nurse: Of course. I'll be back later.

The nurse closed the door carefully behind him.

Noah: We mixed the GHB into some lemonade and downed it. Jacob was right: It did start with euphoria. We both interlocked, our hands wandered, and we became incredibly frolicsome. Apparently GHB is a powerful aphrodisiac. Then . . . things became a blur . . . for us both . . .

He went pale.

Noah: . . . more for Jacob. I think the effects of the alcohol, or a miscalculated dose, hit him harder and he became limp and drowsy. I was also reacting to it, but the high was intense. We . . . we were naked . . . the door was locked . . .

I nodded gently, indicating that it was okay for him to go on.

Noah: Then it was . . . just images . . . a blur . . .

He began to sob violently. The heart-rate monitor illuminated his increased heartbeat and blood pressure. An alarm sounded, and the nurse walked in.

Nurse: Everything okay?

Josh: He was talking about something difficult. If it's too risky to his health, we can leave it.

Noah: No . . . I need to say it. I'm fine. I'm just crying.

The nurse walked over and silenced the alarms on the monitors. He looked over Noah, who nodded that he was fine. The nurse left again and Noah collected himself.

Noah: It wasn't just images and a blur, Joshua. I'm trying to delude myself. I remember some of it. I . . . I was on top of him . . . I was inside him. He . . . was unconscious . . . he was unconscious, Josh . . .

ANXIETY: *OMG.*

VOLITION: *Keep listening.*

Noah: I was inebriated, and the drugs were new to me and overwhelming, but . . . I was inside him and he was not conscious . . . not conscious . . .

He looked horrified. His entire body had curled into a seated fetal position.

Noah: I continued . . . I just carried on . . . I . . . I . . .

CRITIC: *Raped him.*

He was wailing now.

DETECTIVE: *Damn.*

Noah: Then he woke up and . . . the horror in his eyes, Josh. He knew what had happened. I knew what had happened . . .

My heart was pounding and tinnitus pierced through my ears. I was reduced to a shocked, one-word question that was burning on the end of my tongue.

Josh: I appreciate you disclosing this to me. I have to ask, Noah . . . why?

Noah wiped his eyes down and blew his nose.

Noah: I don't know. Impulse, I suppose. It all happened so quickly. The . . . power of it. Part of me felt empowered. Not the rational, kind part of me, but the animalistic, evil part of me I didn't realize I had. I want to blame an evil part of me because it's easier to separate from it and lay blame on something external. But it was me that did it, Josh. I did it . . . And this is why I can't live with myself.

Josh: I'm hearing a lot of regret, Noah. I'm not condoning what you have done, but I don't think attempting to take your life is the solution here. The regret and crippling guilt points to a side of you that's worth nurturing. That's worth your time and attention.

Noah: Do you think I have inherited an evil from my father?

CRITIC: *You're a grown-ass adult who is responsible for your own actions. You raped a young man. Take responsibility!*
ANALYTICAL: *You are still Noah's therapist.*
COMPASSION: *This young man tried to kill himself. He is still high risk.*
VOLITION: *I'm struggling to see him unconditionally at the moment.*

Josh: I think we are responsible for our own actions and behaviors. What I can see is a crippling remorse for your behavior. I'm worried about you, Noah. I think this was a secret of yours that has allowed guilt and depression to thrive. I appreciate you telling me this, and admittedly it's difficult to hear . . .

ANXIETY: *I hate this, but we're going to have to say it.*

Josh: What happened after the event? Did . . . Jacob inform the police?

Noah pulled his covers up to his face. He became infantile.

Noah: No. Nothing ever happened. I tried to call him and make amends. But nothing. I think he confided in some people because my friends from the meetup all seemed to blank me afterward. They cut me off.

DETECTIVE: *Ah, man . . . We got to report this.*
BIOLOGY: *I feel sick.*

Josh: This is a serious crime, Noah . . .

Noah: Please . . . no! Don't! Don't get me arrested!

Josh: Noah, there are certain contractual obligations I'm bound by . . .

INTUITION: *Stop! This man is on suicide watch.*

The alarms on the monitors awoke from their sleep. Noah started to writhe and thrash around on his bed, screaming. He began pulling the cannula out of his arm and pushed his IV trolley to the floor with a crash. Within seconds, three nurses burst into the room and began to restrain him to the bed.

Nurse: You need to leave, sir.

Horrified, I stood up and traced the wall all the way to the door, where I stepped out. The three nurses were on top of Noah and managed to muffle his screams.

ANXIETY: *Fuck. This is messed up.*

I walked down the corridor and pushed open a fire exit to the outdoors. My heart was pounding. I closed my eyes and tried to compose myself.

..

Part of a therapist's ethical framework is to report serious crime should it arise in the therapy room, especially if it is a perpetrator's confession. I've worked with many clients who have broken the law, and on most occasions it's what could be deemed "mild" crime; I use my judgment, and the mild crimes often remain unreported at my discretion. There's no therapeutic benefit to snitching on a guy who littered in a park three years ago or bought peach schnapps for and at the request of his sixteen-year-old younger brother. Noah, however, had sexually assaulted someone, a serious crime that cannot remain unreported. This would explain the sickly feeling spreading through my abdomen. I felt so conflicted: There was a visceral repulsion toward Noah that erupted within seconds of the confession, but also the latent effects of seeing him holistically, as a flawed, remorseful, and suicidal young man. The confusion made my head pound.

I returned inside and requested an emergency meeting with Noah's crisis team. I found it depressing to be put in a situation where I must break confidentiality. You mourn and grieve the sacrosanctity of the therapeutic relationship, which would dissolve the moment I explained the news to his care team. The manager would then inform the police, and together they would work out the safest plan of action for Noah. I felt like I was handing over something cursed—a horrible feeling of guilt and responsibility, even though rationally I knew this to be untrue. I felt an illogical guilt for unearthing Noah's secret, although I still held hope for him to be able to process his troubles and work toward a fulfilling life after his confession—to personally atone and seek his own redemption without the weight of his crime.

His actions meant he would lose everything: his job, his new roots, and, temporarily, his independence, whether he went to jail or was committed. Even though I was angry and bitterly disappointed in Noah, I took no joy from knowing this was what awaited him. I also hoped that Jacob had managed to seek the appropriate support for the trauma through which he had gone.

When Therapy Isn't Working

One of the saddest things I hear—and I hear it often—is "I tried therapy. It didn't work for me."

Before I say another word here, I need to make a clear statement: When therapy doesn't work, the failure is not yours. Therapy is a process, and it can involve several false starts before you find the therapist or the modality that is right for you.

Hollywood has a lot to answer for in the way we imagine what therapy will be like. Forget the onscreen image of a perfectly linear process where you sit for months or years getting sage advice from a wise therapist who plumbs the deepest recesses of your soul so you can achieve wisdom and enlightenment. Therapy does not always culminate in dramatic revelations and epiphanies that solve your problems and free you from your demons. Real therapy can be messy and confrontational, and uncomfortable, and it often feels like it's going nowhere.

If therapy is bumpy and ugly and complicated, that's okay. You're still not failing. Many people work with a number of therapists before finding one with whom they really click. That's normal and to be expected. That's also not failure. That's just how this often works. Also, remember that even if you do leave your therapist and find another, you are still learning and benefiting from it, even if this is the fifth time you've had to do so. You might learn one thing from one therapist, three things from another, then ten things from a third. Those lessons all count. Just because you did not find—or have not yet found—someone to work with consistently does not mean you are failing or wasting your time. Therapy is a process that can and often does involve different helpers at different times.

Why is it that sometimes therapy doesn't work? In most instances, it comes down to a mismatch between you and a therapist, or a mismatch between the problem you're addressing and the theoretical orientation of the therapist in question. In thankfully rare instances, failure of a given therapy relationship comes down to a poorly trained, incompetent, or unethical therapist. Sadly, that can happen, just as it can in any other profession. But I'd like to think that bad therapists are the exception, not the rule.

If you find yourself working with a therapist who treats you in a disinterested fashion, seems ill prepared or misinformed when it comes to your particular concern, acts in an unprofessional manner when it comes to things like scheduling and bookkeeping, or makes therapy more about them than you, then you deserve better. In those situations, the best advice is to cleanly end the relationship and move on. Nobody is required to stick with a bad therapist any more than they should stick with a bad gardener or a bad auto mechanic.

But even with a well-trained, engaged, caring, professional therapist, things might not work out. Therapy is a passionate profession. Therapists believe in the work they do. They believe in the modalities they embrace and the theories beneath them. They embrace them, sometimes emotionally. That's great, but that doesn't automatically mean that the treatment a therapist believes in will be a good fit for your situation. I made progress with my own therapy only when I found a therapist trained in and passionate about the treatment of panic attacks and OCD. That doesn't mean the other therapists with whom I worked were necessarily bad. They were just not a good match for me.

All therapy is not the same. Some treatment modalities are more passive in nature, where the therapist acts as a mostly silent reflective guide while you find your own way. Others require that the therapist be more insistent or directive in setting the pace or agenda. On top of that we need to factor in personality. If you prefer to be independent and autonomous, a therapist who is more inclined to be prescriptive and directive may not work for you. That same therapist may be a great fit for someone who responds better to clear direction and requires more of an active guiding hand. Personal preference, personality type, and behavioral style all matter here, and there is no right or wrong.

We also have to acknowledge that therapists are humans, and humans have flaws. It's okay to recognize those flaws. You don't have to put up with them. Sometimes we have to act if those flaws are impacting our therapy experience and outcomes. I'm not saying that your therapist is a raging, abusive narcissist, but they might just rub you the wrong way. That can happen. Don't feel like you are failing or doing something wrong if it does. In fact, when you run into a situation like this, you can learn what you don't want in a therapist in terms of personality. That can be valuable information too.

Sometimes the therapeutic relationship between two people just doesn't work out, and it's nobody's fault. There's no need to point fingers and spend time and energy on blame. Some of my friends like Turkish delight. I think it's okay, but I don't love it the way they do. We can part ways on some things without it being anyone's fault or anyone's failure. This can happen with your therapist too. What happens then? You can find yourself in a situation where therapy is not working for you, but you are finding it difficult to make a change. You may be thinking about leaving and finding a new therapist. You might want to say something to your therapist about what's not working for you. You may have questions about why your therapist is doing what they're doing. You can wind up in a situation in which you feel that you are not making progress, which starts to feel frustrating. You know something should change, yet you remain silent and try to soldier on.

You may feel responsible for your therapist's feelings and are therefore afraid to speak up or make any change because you do not want to risk hurting them or insulting them. This is a common error. Naturally, therapists are human and should be treated kindly and respectfully like anyone else, but you are never responsible for your therapist's feelings. Not ever. Your therapist is trained to handle their feelings in session and to remain focused on *you*, not themselves. If you say that you feel disconnected, or that things are not working for you, or that you are getting frustrated by your lack of progress, you will not be hurting anyone's feelings. If you want to end the relationship and find a new therapist, nobody will be insulted. You are not responsible for managing the feelings and reactions of your therapist, so do not worry about this.

People change lawyers, accountants, doctors, and dentists all the time. You are allowed to change therapists if you think that is in your best interests. It's perfectly okay. Frankly, if your therapist does experience an emotional reaction to that, the onus is on them to manage that outside of your relationship. A failure to do so is their failure, not yours. As long as you do not go on an insult-laden tirade in which you call into question the character of your therapist or their ancestors, you're fine.

Another reason why people find themselves stuck in therapy that isn't working for them is that one of the problems they need help with is people pleasing or seeking the approval of authority figures. By definition, your therapist is automatically in a position of power in your relationship. They are the authority. You are going to them for help. If you struggle with people pleasing or you find yourself in need of approval from "important" people in your life, you may find it very difficult to question your therapist or leave them. You may fear that you will lose their approval if you appear "rebellious" or "ungrateful."

Speaking openly to your therapist about your well-being and the effectiveness of the help they are providing is not rebellious, ungrateful, or disloyal. You are allowed to advocate for yourself. A good therapist wants you to do that and will welcome and encourage it. Your therapist is trained to recognize the power dynamic in the therapeutic relationship and should not allow it to become a problem. They do not want you to adore them, idolize them, or be loyal to them. That's what cult leaders want. Therapists are not cult leaders, or at least they shouldn't be. Your therapist may recognize that you are seeking their approval because that's not terribly uncommon, but they are not there to approve of you, only to accept and encourage you. If you find yourself in a situation where therapy is not working for you because you're just not meshing with your therapist or they are not being effective in addressing your specific problem, it is not a problem to make a change.

If you're engaged with a therapist and you feel that things are veering off course or that you are not getting the help you want or need, it's important to speak up.

When therapy doesn't work, it can be frustrating and upsetting. You may feel like you are hitting a huge roadblock or that the work you've been doing has been for nothing. I understand all those feelings. It's okay to have them and express them. Just remember that there is no failure here and that the process can be a bit bumpy at times. Remember also that even the experiences that don't work out often teach us something about the process, our specific problems, or about ourselves in general.

If you've had an experience of therapy that didn't work out, take some time to lick your wounds and express your emotions to someone you trust. You may feel the need to take a break from therapy for a while. That's fine. Take the time you need. Then, when and if you are ready, get back on that horse and ride again. Just the act of seeking out help is courageous and should be recognized for what it is: you doing a good thing for you, which is never bad, even when it isn't perfect or pretty.

28
Daphne

There was an unusual sound at my office door. Rather than a knock, it sounded like the muffled thump of a light kick. I opened the door to reveal a multiple award-winning actor holding two mugs of coffee.

COMPASSION: *What a beautifully considerate gesture.*
VOLITION: *I'm going to take a mental picture of this moment.*

Daphne: I came prepared!

I noticed she had a fresh new short haircut.

Josh: Thank you. That's very considerate. Come on in. Have you had your ears lowered?
Daphne: I thought that painful dad joke died in the last century. Yes, I have changed my hair.

She set the mugs down on the table. As well as the haircut, she was dressed differently—more casual than usual. Even so, it would be impossible for her to fail to look impressive.

Josh: How are you doing?
Daphne: I'm doing okay. My mind is whirling with many questions but . . . I'm surprisingly doing okay.
Josh: It felt like we explored several important topics in our last session.
Daphne: Yes. I appreciate your listening and encouraging me to explore these things. Talking about it has eased a weight I have been carrying, and strangely, I haven't thought about it much since. I've been so busy that I haven't had the time for rubber-stamping my rapid-onset metamorphosis.
Josh: That's understandable. Metamorphosis as opposed to . . . evolution?
Daphne: I wouldn't deny any definition that you wish to use, Joshua. After all, you have helped me so much this last month. But if it were up to me,

I would stay clear of any terminology that describes me as a . . . oh, what is it called . . . ? My daughter watched it when growing up and my youngest still does . . .

IRREVERENCE: *Pokémon.*

Josh: A Pokémon?

Daphne: Yes! That's the ticket. The annoying things that scream and torture each other and transform into different beings. Probably right up your street. I am not a Pokémon. Although I appreciate the sentiment and the acknowledgment of my . . . growth.

She took a long sip of her coffee.

Daphne: I'm sorry that I can't stay long today. It's the last performance of the show tonight. Are you sure you don't want to come? I can get you wonderful seats near the front. You may have to wear something more respectable, mind you.

CRITIC: *Ha ha. I knew I should've changed these trousers.*

Josh: Hey!

We both laughed.

Josh: How are you feeling about the show closing? I'm sad that I can't come tonight. But without the rigid boundaries, these sessions wouldn't exist in the way that they do. There's got to be a professional line. As annoying as it is. I'd have loved to come.

She rolled her eyes.

Daphne: I get it . . . really, I do.

Josh: Your invitation makes me feel appreciated as a therapist. I would like to make that clear. And that . . . that appreciation is better than any gift, or free ticket, you could give me.

CRITIC: *I tried my best to prove you're a liar, but you're right on this one. You genuinely care about your role as a therapist. You absolute loser.*

Daphne looked at me with a sense of deep understanding. I hoped I had conveyed how much I meant what I said. It was impossible not to mirror the wonderful smile I saw on her face.

Daphne: Doing the show has been brilliant in many ways. I've found that I have approached my character from all of these different mindsets since coming to these sessions. It's also been so exciting to give my latest stage ideas a go. I have thoroughly enjoyed my time in Manchester.

I grinned and finished my coffee.

Daphne: I'm so sorry our sessions have to end so abruptly. I must go soon. I've got my usual media commitments to attend to. The final night is always demanding. Could you do me a favor and move to London? And always be my therapist?

BIOLOGY: *The grand opening of the butterfly house is happening in Josh's stomach right now! Don't miss it!*

Josh: That's very flattering. But I enjoy living in Manchester. It's my home. I know many great therapists I could recommend in London. I strongly advocate having a safe space near to where you live with someone you feel comfortable with. It'll be confidential. I wouldn't recommend someone who wasn't professional.

ANALYTICAL: *It may be beneficial to get different perspectives and skills deriving from alternative modalities.*

I could see that Daphne was hit with the sudden realization that our therapeutic relationship was about to end. Her eyes widened, and I sensed an anxious unease. She looked at me, as if given the last chance to say something before boarding a plane.

Daphne: You . . . made me feel safe. You made me feel heard . . . and seen . . . and made me feel like I exist without the mask of my public persona. You taught me that the pedestal I believe I've been placed on isn't too high, and that I can climb down from it whenever I want. You made me feel . . . human. Less trapped. You helped me to see hope. Thank you for your unconditionality. It has been more powerful than you'll ever realize.

She began to shed a tear. Then immediately began to laugh. That beautiful cocktail of a human's two most powerful emotions striving for dominance in an emotionally conflicting situation. The sight reassured almost every doubt that I had felt about myself as a therapist leading up to that moment. Daphne's reaction was the magnificence of therapy in its purest form.

Daphne: I haven't had any night panics for the last week. I've been sleeping fairly well . . . I . . . I will miss you, Joshua.

INTUITION: *It's okay to say it.*

Josh: I will miss you too.

29
Vacuum Cleaner

I walked through Manchester City Centre wielding my new vacuum cleaner. Part of me was genuinely excited to plug it in and try it out when I got home. Another part of me acknowledged that feeling this level of excitement about a domestic appliance meant I was now firmly entrenched in adulthood. There was a noticeable buzz emanating throughout the city, the mingling of sounds and smells transforming as I walked through wide streets, alleyways, and across public plazas. I walked down Oxford Road and popped into one of my favorite pubs for a pint, navigating the cumbersome vacuum around the tables.

ESCAPIST: *We deserve a pint!*

The bartender eyed what I was carrying.

Bartender: Who's your friend?
Josh: Oh, ignore him. He sucks.
Bartender: *(eyes rolling)* Wow.

She poured a pint of some pretentiously named IPA and placed it in front of me. We chewed the fat for a while, and I dialed in some songs on the jukebox: a mixture of Manchester bands such as the Stone Roses and Doves, then added a side order of John Coltrane for a jazz twist. It was pleasant to have a conversation in which the expectation of me being a therapist was nonexistent. Although I imagine many a bartender has inadvertently adopted the therapist role in their time, along with hair-dressers, massage therapists, or any trade that requires the customer to be in a relaxed state of mind within an intimate space.

I was halfway through my third pint when Justin Bieber started playing on the jukebox. The bartender raised her head and one eyebrow while she was chopping limes. The autoplay feature engaged, as I had run out of credits.

Bartender: Not this song again. A few months back, there was a clown who would come in and drop a fiver into the jukebox and request Bieber ten times, then walk out.

IRREVERENCE: *LOL.*

Josh: Ah . . . the *Bieber Bandit*!

She smiled thoughtfully.

Bartender: Yeah, that's what we called them.

I finished my pint and stood up, ready to head for home. Justin Bieber was finishing his song and I gestured to the bartender a grateful "thank you" and "goodbye" in one waving hand signal.

Bartender: Catch you soon.

The vacuum and I trundled over to the door, where Manchester awaited us on the other side.

Josh: Not any time soon!

Justin Bieber started to play again. The same song. Song two of five. The bartender dropped her fruit knife, stood to attention, and sighed.

Josh: For it is I that is the *Bieber Bandit*!
Bartender: Noooo!

I walked outside laughing to myself. The bartender shook her head, but I swear I caught her smiling as I slipped out.

▪▪

My walk to the bus stop took me past the Exchange Theatre. Outside, displayed on an enormous poster, was an image of Daphne along with her cast. The poster was festooned with lights around the border. "Lyrebird," it said, with an adjoining poster stating, "Last Performance This Evening." There was a murmuring from a crowd of well-dressed people queuing outside and loitering in the theater bar.

Josh: I hope it goes well for you, Daphne. Make sure you break a leg when jumping from that pedestal.

The sun dipped behind a high-rise office building, bouncing a dazzling orange light across the street. The curtain was calling on Daphne's temporary stay here. I felt a mixture of emotions, but the most prominent one was an unusual form of pride. I made my way with my cumbersome box past the crowd outside the theater. I reached the corner and was hailed by a shady-looking guy in a leather jacket.

Ticket tout: Need a ticket for tonight's show, my man?
Josh: Yeah, one that's handwritten and going to cost me several appendages?
Ticket tout: I'm being serious, my man. Can't get one for your friend, though.

He eyeballed the vacuum box.

Josh: Sorry, man. Not interested.

I started toward the bus stop and glanced over my shoulder. My bus was turning the corner, so I'd have to hotfoot it if I wanted to make it to the bus stop in time. The contents of the box rumbled rhythmically as I jogged down the street. The bus was getting closer, but I was going to make it. Suddenly my foot caught on one of the pavement slabs; I tripped slightly and was forced to regain my balance, but in doing so I lost hold of my box, which skidded across the pavement and landed on its side. The double-decker hissed past me, leaving me staring at the floor. I placed my hands on my hips and made an audible sigh. I looked over my other shoulder in the direction from which I had just walked. I don't know whether it was intuition, or the beers, or frustration with the bus, but I found myself walking back toward the ticket tout, dragging my sorry vacuum with me.

Josh: How much?

..

I paid an extortionate amount of money and made my way to the foyer, where I successfully begged the cloakroom assistant to store the vacuum box. The bustle in the theater foyer was electric. A beautiful chandelier and literal red carpet were the main attractions of a stunning room. I flicked through the program and skimmed over the cast intros. Daphne's face was all over the pamphlet—the director, the actor, the star of the show.

DETECTIVE: *I wonder which one they went on that date with.*
VOLITION: *Doesn't matter, does it?*

DETECTIVE: *True. I'm just curious.*
BIOLOGY: *Human curiosity.*

The call to the theater sounded, the ushers swarmed out like storm troopers, and the audience made their way to their seats. Unsurprisingly, the tout had sold me a seat way up in the gallery, but I was fortunate because this play was to be performed in the round. I had a lovely view, even though I was high up in the rafters. I was also enveloped in darkness, which allowed me to sip the supermarket wine that I had snuck in. The play started. I was excited.

Daphne was mesmerizing. I must have watched the whole thing with my jaw agape. Seeing her act in person was incomparable to slouching in front of one of her movies at home. At times I thought I recognized the Daphne I knew from the therapy room, especially when she gazed up into the darkness of the gallery. There was one occasion when I felt she was looking directly at me, briefly warping me to a limbo existing between the present and the therapy room.

I left the theater to a curtain of rain. Typical Manchester. I decided to take a stroll around the city and assumed that burdening the theater with my vacuum cleaner overnight would be okay. I like walking around a city in the rain; it reminds me of my love for film noir. I'd often let go of worries and pretend I was in *Blade Runner*, *L.A. Confidential*, or *The Big Sleep*. An hour passed as I wandered the streets. I grabbed some falafel from a street vendor and strolled through the Northern Quarter. The lights of bars and restaurants rippled in the petrol-strewn puddles on the roads.

I was getting tired, so I took a left down a narrow alleyway to head home. There must have been another hidden Manchester speakeasy down here because my path was blocked by a wall of dark umbrellas. A group of people were standing outside the fire exit talking, smoking, and sharing each other's shelter.

Josh: Excuse me, please.

The umbrellas parted, revealing a jovial party of people wearing plentiful amounts of what looked like stage makeup. One person passed a cigarette to another, while someone else was regaling the others with an amusing tale that was presumably in the group's sphere of reference. I began to step sideways through the slowly dispersing group.

Josh: Thank you. Have a lovely rest of your evening.

One of the umbrellas twisted around and almost struck me in the face.

Daphne: Josh!

ANXIETY: *This was unexpected.*

Josh: I . . . er . . .

Daphne led me several feet away and shared her large umbrella with me. She was smoking and looked exceptionally cheerful.

Daphne: You out for drinks with friends? I'm so glad we bumped into each other! I recognized your voice immediately.

ANALYTICAL: *Out with a client here, Josh. Be wary.*
COMPASSION: *It's an unusual event. He'll navigate it.*
VOLITION: *Trust in your ability.*

Josh: I, er . . . I was on my way home. I . . .

I wiped my brow as I realized I was dripping with rainwater.

VOLITION: *The truth is the only thing needed here.*

Josh: I'll be honest, Daphne. I came to see your final show. It was a spur-of-the-moment thing.

The umbrella struck my shoulder as she immediately crashed into me and squeezed my back in an embrace.

ANXIETY: *I don't know what to do.*
IRREVERENCE: *You're getting a hug from Daphne! This is bananas!*
INTUITION: *Don't look at me . . .*
VOLITION: *Me either.*

I gave a considered hug back, smiled, and stepped away.

Daphne: I'm so happy you came to watch it. What did you think?

Josh: I thought it was exceptional. Congratulations. I can see why everyone loves it.

Daphne: Care to join us inside? They do outstanding food and drink, and it's all paid for. It's our ending party, and it would be an honor to host you.

Josh: Ah, I wish I could. But you know the rules . . .

Daphne: Yes . . . I know . . . boundaries and things.

She smiled.

COMPASSION: *I'm proud of you. For everything. For being brave enough to challenge and dare to be yourself. You're also an amazing actor.*

INTUITION: *Don't say that. It's patronizing. Pride has been the bone of contention in their unhelpful belief system.*

COMPASSION: *But I really am proud! Unconditionally.*

VOLITION: *Not appropriate.*

ANALYTICAL: *And it could dredge up power-dynamics stuff.*

COMPASSION: *Fine. I'll just feel it instead.*

Josh: I'd better be off, Daphne.

Daphne: Wait, before you go . . .

She ran inside the fire exit into the after-party, leaving me with the umbrella. I stood awkwardly for a moment. A few of the cast members glanced over and smiled politely. I think they were intrigued as to who I was.

Daphne skipped back out of the doorway and joined me once again under the umbrella. I reached out to return it, but Daphne pushed my arm away. Suddenly, she went into a hunched, mechanical posture, standing side on. I recognized it immediately.

Daphne: I'm not going to say the line, because I value my integrity. However . . .

Daphne revealed an old silver Zippo lighter and flicked it to reveal the flame.

IRREVERENCE: *Got a boon for my light?!*

Daphne: It's the original. I got my assistant to find it and send it up here.

Daphne put the lighter into my palm and closed my fingers around it.

Daphne: It's yours. Thank you.

I could have wept there and then. But I saved the tears of gratitude for later when I got home, where I spent the evening flicking and closing the lighter like a gleeful child.

30
Noah

I was sitting in the office severely procrastinating during a window of time that I had labeled "admin" in my calendar. My weapon of choice this afternoon was *The Sims 3*—a PC game where you control the lives of computerized people called Sims with the aim of helping them progress in life . . . or sadistically drown them in swimming pools. I was busy building a doorless four-wall prison for the postman when there was a timid knock on my door. I got up to answer.

Josh: Noah! . . . Hello . . .

ANXIETY: *I feel weird about this.*
ESCAPIST: *He's under the care of psychological services now. You don't need to open a sustained dialogue.*
COMPASSION: *I am a human being and so is he.*

Noah: Hi, Josh. Have you got a moment? Sorry to interrupt—I just thought I'd pop by on the off chance that you would have a few minutes to spare.

I cushioned it as best I could.

Josh: I'm sorry, Noah, but unfortunately, we both know that I am no longer your therapist. You've been assigned one as part of your care team. If you have things on your mind, then it would be appropriate to bring those issues up with them.

IRREVERENCE: *Throw the book at him while you're at it, Josh.*
CRITIC: *Even I thought that was cold.*

Noah: I know . . . I know . . . I . . . just wanted to clear something up. I can leave if it puts you in too much of a predicament. I'm sorry, it wasn't my intention to make you feel uncomfortable.

I felt so conflicted. My internal prejudices were loud in protest at Noah's assault of a young man, and this was a clear violation of professional boundaries, but these voices were matched in pitch by an inner voice of compassion.

CRITIC: *Rapist.*
COMPASSION: *We're not just one thing. We're not defined by single traits.*
CRITIC: *He literally raped a nineteen-year-old.*
COMPASSION: *I don't think it's as cut and dried as that. It wasn't premeditated.*
CRITIC: *You're a rape apologist? It does not excuse his behavior. He is an adult and is responsible for his actions. Rape is not excusable.*
COMPASSION: *It isn't excusable. But do we dismiss the humanity of a person for eternity should they commit a crime? Where's the line? Where's the hope for redemption if all manner of compassion is withdrawn?*
CRITIC: *He'll probably rape again.*
COMPASSION: *I'm not sure about that.*

Josh: Sure, come on in. I've got a few minutes.

We both took a seat. I sat in a chair different from my usual one, so as not to replicate the dynamic of previous therapy sessions, and I could see that Noah noticed.

Noah: I just wanted to let you know that I confessed to the authorities what happened. I also wrote a letter to Jacob—I'm not sure if he'll read it. It wasn't for forgiveness, just to show my deep remorse. I don't expect him to reply or anything. Why would he?

Noah looked nervous. He was blinking fast and struggling to sit still. But he also looked determined to get out what he had come here to say.

Josh: Okay . . . I know you're remorseful, Noah. I respect your wish to put things as right as they can be. That said, I'd strongly suggest that you don't contact Jacob anymore, unless he initiates it. We must respect the boundary—

Noah: That I violated.

I gave a respectful nod of acknowledgment.

DETECTIVE: *I wonder why he's not in a cell.*

Josh: What happened when you spoke to the police, Noah?

Noah: I was discharged from the psychiatric hospital a few days later—the one you came to. The police were waiting to arrest me. I spent twenty-four hours in custody while they gathered evidence: interviewing Jacob and others at the party, as well as me.

He bowed his head and flushed with what looked like shame.

Noah: Apparently, Jacob is not pressing charges. I confessed and was adamant that I did it, but Jacob said he doesn't want to see me charged. Jacob would now be classed as a "hostile witness," and there wasn't enough evidence to detain me further. They felt the attack wasn't malicious enough to warrant me being an immediate threat to the public, and they considered the circumstances. However, I was insistent. I begged them to detain me.

Josh: Why? What did you say?

Noah: Because I did something awful, Josh. I told the Crown Prosecution Service that I am a danger to the public and need to be punished. I am here on bail, until trial. My mum bailed me out.

EMPATHY: *He's punishing himself. He wants to atone in his own way.*

ANALYTICAL: *It's twisted logic.*

Josh: You're seeking some form of atonement? Do you think you'll feel better if you serve a punishment?

Noah: Yes . . .

Josh: How much is this to atone for the crime? And how much is it punishing yourself, Noah? Jacob said he didn't want to press charges. Did you not think about how he felt?

VOLITION: *Easy now . . .*

Noah: I know he didn't press charges because he feels guilty for giving me the drugs in the first place. But it *is* my fault. I assaulted him.

Josh: I respect the desire to be responsible for your actions, but I'm concerned, not only for your well-being but that this situation has become conflated with an inner turmoil that has been going on within you long before the party. I'm concerned you are using this situation to hurt yourself more. Another way to self-harm, even. You're projecting feelings about yourself onto this incident.

He considered what I'd said.

Noah: It's tricky, Josh. I did feel like a weight had been lifted when I confessed to what I had done.

Josh: And the stuff you said to the CPS, about being a danger to the public? Do you really believe that?

Noah: I . . . no, of course not. I would never do anything like that again. I . . . I was just shocked that my confession wasn't enough to outweigh Jacob's decision not to press charges. They were just willing to let me go, Josh. I felt I had to say something for them to do something about it!

Josh: And whom does your going to prison benefit if you believe you are not a danger to anyone?

Noah: I . . . you're right . . . I'm still being selfish. It's all about me. My feelings . . . I just don't want to feel guilty anymore.

Josh: Guilt is part of remorse. And you are truly remorseful. I see it. I just don't see the benefit in your maximizing the punishment on yourself, particularly as you've been in vulnerable mindsets yourself. I'd worry for your well-being if you were stuck in a cell every day.

He looked concerned, as though he hadn't thought all of this through.

Noah: Do you think I'm a bad person?

COMPASSION: *No.*
CRITIC: *Yes.*
ANALYTICAL: *Hmm . . . what you did was bad, but we stay away from definitive language here as best we can.*

Josh: I wouldn't have become a therapist if I believed we are all defined by our worst mistakes. I'm not the judge of morality or the speaker of objective truth, but I do choose to focus on your remorse and the fact that I believe you to be a kind, empathetic person overall. Someone who is struggling with their own troubles, trying to navigate their life. I do think there was an element of misadventure to the incident, but I'm definitely not suggesting that you're free of blame here.

CRITIC: *Rapist sympathizer. Do you know how much damage people like this cause to people? They destroy lives.*
VOLITION: *Enough now.*
COMPASSION: *He can grow from this.*

Josh: You committed a serious crime, and I can hear you wanting to redress it. I'd ask you just to reflect on the reasons behind your desire to be punished. If you're going to weaponize it against yourself, then I don't see how anyone benefits from that. I just see it as another form of self-harm. You tried to take your own life, Noah. And your life is too important to risk by enacting self-punishing ways of placating guilt. Whatever it is you do, though, just remember that you do deserve to live. The inner critic that comes with depression will use it against you. But you have huge opportunities ahead of you to make things right, in their own way.
Noah: I can never make it right for Jacob.
Josh: I know.

There was a long silence. I gestured that it was time to leave, as I didn't want this turning into a prolonged therapy session.

Noah: I will just tell the truth and admit everything, honestly. I'm sorry for messing you around, Josh. Also, if the court summons you for the case and disrupts your work, then I'm sorry for that too.

He got up to leave. I followed him slowly to the door.

Josh: Look after yourself, Noah. And please keep in constant communication with your mental health team and doctor.

Noah: Can I keep you updated?

Josh: It wouldn't be appropriate because it falls outside of our therapy agreement. It isn't personal, Noah.

Noah: Okay . . . Thank you for the sessions. They did help me. I'm . . . I'm on my way to becoming a better version of myself.

Josh: I believe that.

COMPASSION: *Genuinely.*

Josh: Farewell, Noah.

Noah: Goodbye.

I watched him slope down the corridor and press the elevator button. He wiped his eyes and stepped in, then the doors closed softly behind him. I stood in the doorway of my office and squeezed my knuckles tightly, then lightly pummeled the frame with the side of my fist. My feelings swirled in a pool of compassion, worry, anger, disappointment, and self-critical analysis. Was there something I could have done differently? Was I too cruel to Noah? Or too dismissive? People are never simply their worst mistake, but it's hard to remember that when you're still processing the shock of someone's poor choices. The lens of anger and shock warps the picture too much. But even so, I couldn't bring myself to dislike Noah, and I genuinely hoped he could get to a place where he would be content and fully believe he was not doomed to become his father.

31
Levi

A busker had decided to ply his trade outside of my window. It was pleasant at first, until he decided to loop the same five tracks repeatedly. The overly emotional inflections of Ed Sheeran covers now began to irritate me. It felt like the Universe's sweet revenge for my Justin Bieber jukebox prank. I tried to shut the window, but my office had no air-conditioning, and it was only minutes before I began sweating profusely. A little while later, after the fourth rendition of "Galway Girl" and another crack in the foundations of my will to live, a low, bellowing voice interrupted the guitarist.

Levi: Excuse me, young man. I'm enjoying your music and I do love Ed Sheeran. However, I'm aware that my therapy room is just above your head and I feel I'd be tapping my feet along to the music instead of dealing with my issues. If I chuck you a fiver for your talents, would you mind moving down the road a bit?

Busker: Sure. That makes sense. And thank you.

I braced myself for Levi's standard "John Wayne kicking down the saloon door" entrance but was surprised to hear a considered knock instead. I walked over and opened the door, wondering if it was Levi at all, even though I'd just heard him outside.

Levi: Afternoon, Josh.
Josh: Good afternoon, Levi.

ANXIETY: *Thanks for knocking.*
INTUITION: *Don't draw any attention to it.*

We resumed our usual seats.

Josh: How are you doing this week?

Levi twisted one of the many rings on his fingers and caught himself cracking a knuckle. He took a considered breath before he spoke.

Levi: Not great. I'll get straight to it. I've learned that it's no good to beat around the bush in here.

I leaned forward slightly in my chair, adopting a more engaged posture.

Josh: Anything in particular going on?
Levi: I think you know.

DETECTIVE: *The "community." His wife. Radical practices?*

Josh: I'm not going to jump to assumptions.

He looked disheartened and resigned himself to the fact that he would have to talk about this at some point. He decided sooner rather than later.

Levi: I spent the week laying down some rules . . . or, as you say . . . boundaries . . . with Safia and members of the community. I love my community, but some of it is completely batshit crazy. It feels strange. Mandy at work keeps joking with me that it sounds like a cult. But you know when someone keeps saying the same thing to the point where they're only half joking?
Josh: Mhm.
Levi: What do you think?

ANALYTICAL: *Bring attention to the red flags perhaps?*

Josh: You've mentioned some things that have concerned me, Levi. Particularly regarding the ceremonial activities and the self-punishment—or "penance," as you refer to it.

He was giving me his full attention. I could tell he needed clarity in a situation where we felt lost.

Josh: It's also difficult to feel comfortable and accepting of people around you who are influencing your behaviors under a . . . belief . . . that they are channeling the words of some higher spirit or deity. I genuinely think the intrusive thoughts, and what I believe to be OCD, have been misinterpreted by Safia and members of your community as demons. And that makes me . . . concerned for you.

Levi stood up slowly and walked over to the window.

Levi: Do you mind if I stand for a bit? It's difficult to talk about. I find it very intense face to face.
Josh: Of course.
Levi: I've known this for years, it's just difficult . . . It's my wife . . . she's not well.

I remained silent.

Levi: Safia hasn't always been like this. I know Chantale noticed it, but she tries to keep the peace for my sake. Safia has this . . . paranoia . . . and has had it for a few years now. Honestly, I can't stand it, but I love her and I agreed to stick by her through sickness and in health, you know? The thing is, Safia is very powerful with her words and . . . in all honesty . . .

He pressed the end of one finger against the windowpane as if pointing to something in the distance. His voice was soft. Apologetic even.

Levi: I am scared of her.

He paused.

Levi: My intrusive thoughts have been strong this week. I didn't do my ERP exercises and what we talked about. Sorry. It's been too much. I have fallen back into compulsions again.

EMPATHY: *It's extremely hard to manage OCD and intrusive thoughts within a sphere where acute stress and literal threat exist.*

Josh: It's okay. There's no pass and fail in here. You're scared of Safia?
Levi: Mhm.
Josh: Why?
Levi: She's . . . a powerful woman. She has a hold over me. Her words and stare frighten me. She threatens me with things that go beyond physical violence. I'm used to that. It's like . . .

He scrunched his face, trying to find the right words.

Levi: It's like I feel good enough when she sees me as good enough. If that makes sense?

I nodded so that he would continue.

Levi: All this stuff about cleansing, rebirth, forgiveness, and penance. It just gets in my head.

EMPATHY: *Perhaps finding it difficult to forgive ourselves?*

Josh: Do you think that Safia, and the community, hold the key to some form of forgiveness that you're trying to seek?
Levi: Maybe.
Josh: And I don't just mean the intrusive thoughts. I mean in general. You mentioned in a previous session that Safia "saved" you. What do you mean by this?
Levi: I've had a dodgy past, Josh. I've done stuff I'm not proud of. Things I don't want to talk about today. Safia pulled me back from a dark place.

He seemed very confident of this.

Levi: This is going to sound weird, but it's like Safia is the controller of my dark thoughts. Whenever she is angry, or displeased, it's like she is putting them in my head. It's like . . . telepathy. Punishment by telepathy. I know it sounds strange.

ANALYTICAL: *Not surprising, considering intrusive thoughts can be an offshoot of a threat response.*

Josh: It doesn't sound strange. Do you remember when we were talking about the threat response? And how intrusive thoughts can be interpreted as threat?

He nodded.

Josh: With intrusive thoughts and the threat response, it can be like the chicken and the egg scenario: It's arbitrary which one comes first. Sometimes an intrusive thought can trigger threat . . . anxiety . . . but it

also works the other way around. When our threat response is alarmed
by other things, this can bring up intrusive thoughts. It's because the
threat response associates the intrusive thoughts with previous threats
and so presents them to you as a suggestion.

Levi: Are you saying that Safia triggers my threat thingy, so I'm more likely
to experience intrusive thoughts because I'm more anxious?

Josh: I'm proposing it as a possibility. What do you think?

VOLITION: *Ah, that old "back to you"—nice one.*
CRITIC: *You're a walking cliché.*

Levi: Hm.

He walked over to the other window deep in thought. I noticed and
appreciated the consideration and respect Levi displayed compared to his
first few sessions in here.

Levi: I think you're right. When I'm at work, and it's all going to plan, I don't
seem to have the thoughts as much. Yet when I'm in the car driving
home, I feel . . . uneasy . . . and it's like it lets the thoughts in. I feel this
knot in my belly as I get closer to the house.

Josh: What is it about home, do you think, that creates the knot?

Levi: Other than the intrusive thoughts? I think it's . . . Safia. It's my wife.
My fear becomes stronger. Louder. Then it feels like I'm punished even
more with these horrible thoughts. I . . .

A slow and shocking realization appeared to spread over his face.

Levi: The demon is not in me. No. The demon lies in my wife. She has many
demons.

I waited for him to find the words.

Levi: I've believed up until this moment that doing what she says, keeping
her happy, has been helping her. But . . . it's not. It's not been helping her
at all. It was small changes at first. She was always reasonable until she
started to change. I . . . think this cult of weirdos got into her head too.

He turned to me.

Levi: I'm not a stupid man, Josh. I can spot liars, hidden agendas, and I like to think I'm very, er . . . perceptive. But this community gets to you, Josh. It feeds off your sadness.

He turned back to the window. He squeezed the back of his tattooed neck with one of his hands. One of his rings glinted in the sunlight.

Levi: We lost a baby some years back. Cot death. Only lived for a week or so. It really hurt us both. Safia developed what the doctor called . . . ah, what's it now when women suffer mentally after giving birth?
Josh: Postnatal depression?
Levi: Yeah . . . kinda. She started becoming paranoid and having huge mood swings. She'd hear voices from the "angels." The doctors said it was . . . postpartum issues.

He sighed and brushed the back of his hand across his eyes.

Levi: She's never been the same since.

COMPASSION: *Ah, man, this couple have been through a lot.*
EMPATHY: *It must have been so difficult. Not only to lose a child, but to witness the decline in his wife.*

Josh: That's so tragic, Levi. I'm so sorry.

I let my sincere condolences hang in the air for a moment.

ANXIETY: *I'm a bit afraid to ask this next question . . .*

Josh: How did you cope with such a loss?
Levi: You just get on with it, don't you? Buried my head in work, the gym, work on the side, up my own backside. Kept busy. Also found solace in the whiskey now and then.

He clenched an enormous fist as he stared out the window.

Levi: All while Safia suffered in silence at home. Alone. Letting those demons evolve while I was out feeling sorry for myself.

Josh: I don't believe anyone is their best self in the clutches of shock and grief. I'm hearing that you wished to be there for her more, though.

Levi: Aye.

He sat back down.

Levi: She terrifies me, Josh. Some days she's okay, but others she convinces me that she is the master of our lives—a scary messenger sent from God. I know it sounds crazy. When she looks into your eyes and demands something, it feels so . . . consuming. I know, rationally, deep down, she's unwell, but my mind and body seize up when she gets like that.

ANALYTICAL: *Trauma response?*

Josh: Why do you think your threat response triggers so acutely when this happens?

He looked into one corner of the room and reflected on the question.

Levi: She does remind me of my stepmum a lot. She's dead now. But when I was growing up she scared the hell out of me. Used to corner me in rooms, slap me for no reason. She hated me. Evil stepmother, innit? Don't be getting a hard-on for all the parent stuff, Josh. I can see you want to.

I said nothing.

Levi: I admit she does remind me a bit of her. But Safia has a more powerful spell over me. She's made me do loads of stuff I wish I hadn't.

DETECTIVE: *Like what, Levi?*

Josh: Like what?

He bit his bottom lip, then inflated his chest with a huge breath before releasing it all at once.

Levi: She makes me hit myself. The self-flage—what's it called?

He took a shaky sip of water.

Levi: She stops me from eating. She makes me attend ceremonies with the community where people offer gifts to God and express their love for God and each other through some really weird stuff, man. Blood, massive orgies and things. It's fucked up. Sorry . . . I don't like swearing.

ANXIETY: *Whoa.*
ANALYTICAL: *It's coercive abuse.*

Levi: I know I am my own man. Safia's not *making* me do these things. I know that it's my choice, ultimately. But the threat just feels so real. I'm terrified of upsetting her because of what she'll say, what she'll do. To me . . . to herself . . .

VOLITION: *Let him know.*
EMPATHY: *Cushion it. It's not nice to hear about a loved one.*

Josh: It sounds a lot like coercive abuse, Levi. Also, systematic abuse. If what you're telling me is true, then you're in an abusive relationship within an abusive community.

This news didn't seem to surprise him. It was evident he'd been doing a lot of thinking and reflecting recently. He looked troubled.

Levi: I know . . . They're not just abusers, you know? Safia is my wife. She's . . . in there somewhere.

He tapped his temple.

Josh: You mentioned you've put boundaries in at home and with the community?
Levi: Yeah. I've said I'm no longer doing the ceremonies and things. I'm also doing more work so I won't be available for congregation. They didn't like it and it has upset Safia . . . but . . . it's my life, isn't it? They're gonna have to deal with it.
Josh: Why do you stay, Levi?
Levi: I can't leave my wife.

Josh: Have you asked her to leave the community? Suggested she can get help from safer sources?

Levi: Of course I have. But she's terrifying. I'm married to a woman who I worry about but also fear. She doesn't think she's unwell, Josh. If anything, since she became ill, she's *more* convinced of her own experiences. She's more confident than ever. Just confident in the wrong things. The wrong beliefs. Her eyes become possessed, Josh. You should see it when she's looming over me, counting the whips that I lay into my back. Demanding that they're harder . . .

EMPATHY: *A stuck place.*

COMPASSION: *That's so wrong. Levi is in a horrible position here.*

Josh: I get that you feel stuck. It's understandable. But Levi, your wife standing over you insisting that you self-harm is fundamentally wrong. It not only puts you in danger, but you are directly experiencing danger.

ANXIETY: *What if that back becomes infected?*

Josh: What if your back becomes infected?

ANXIETY: *What if you take it too far?*

Josh: What if you take it too far?

VOLITION: *Ground yourself.*

I took a breath. He nodded, then slouched back to the sofa.

Josh: You can always leave, Levi. I know it's easier said than done. I'm extremely concerned for your well-being and even for your safety at this point. Coercive abuse is a murky, confusing place where our own volition can easily slip away from us. Especially when we're dealing with potential OCD and intrusive thoughts.

Levi: I can't leave her, Josh! And that's that! I can't do it to her. I promised her in my vows.

Josh: As admirable as that is, Levi, I don't believe being in this relationship is safe for you. It's harming you, both physically and emotionally. Look at your back, Levi. Look at it as a reminder.

Levi: But I can do it! I can stick by her and help her. I can get her the help. I just need to learn to stop being petrified of her. And screw the community. If they try anything, they'll get a swift one to the nose.

I tried to meet Levi where he was, to accept that he wasn't yet ready to leave, but it was hard not to show how concerned I felt for him.

Josh: Okay . . . I just . . .

COMPASSION: *I worry about you.*

Josh: I worry about you.

Our gazes locked for a few seconds in a shared look of care, compassion, and understanding. He broke the mood with a childlike grin, then stood up from the sofa. He loomed over the therapy room, a towering giant whose shadow was cast across the side wall. His standing was a symbolic announcement. My intuition saw it before I could even form the thought: I was about to lose him.

Levi: You've helped me so much, Josh, but this is the end of the road for me. Some things you can't help me with.

ANXIETY: *Don't go.*
ESCAPIST: *Let him.*

Josh: Don't go, Levi. We can do some more ERP work with your intrusive thoughts. It's important you have a safe space to go, given everything that is happening. I also have the numbers for some domestic abuse organizations. We can get them involved.

Levi: You're a good man, Josh.

He put on his leather jacket.

Levi: I'll be in touch should I need this again. I like this counseling stuff. It just can't help me now. I've remembered everything about ERP and leaning in to uncertainty. I'm really good at willfully tolerating the anxiety when the thoughts come . . . but this issue has become . . . secondary for now. The pressing issue is one I feel I gotta do alone.

ANXIETY: *Wait . . .*
VOLITION: *Respect it.*
ANALYTICAL: *He's aware of the situation. Trust in his ability to know what to do. He's already started to place his own boundaries and put himself at a safer distance.*
ANXIETY: *But he's in danger.*
CRITIC: *You're so needy! Just admit it, you failed him.*
VOLITION: *Let him go, man.*

I stood up and stretched out my hand.

Josh: The door is always open for you to return.

He squeezed my hand, and I noticed how the grip was gentler and more considered than our first crushing handshake.

Levi: Thank you.

And he left. I heard the elevator doors close on Levi for the last time. I would never see him in my office again. No Hollywood ending. No bow with which to wrap it all up. Just a book left half read on a shelf that I couldn't reach.

Endings

No matter how deep the connection a therapist establishes with a client, they can only partially prepare for endings. Despite being trained to navigate the conclusion of a therapeutic relationship, we can't develop total immunity to the feelings we experience when a client leaves the room for the final time.

Endings in therapeutic relationships are often joyful and celebrated. They can feel like the natural conclusion of a journey shared mutually by the client and therapist. However, therapeutic endings can also be unexpected, confusing, and laden with grief. When this happens, I'm often left with the hope that we parted on good terms and a wish that I have had a lasting, positive impact as a therapist. Similarly, when the ending is sudden, unexplained, or even sour, then there's often a feeling of doubt or a sense that I wish I could have done more or said some things differently. I question whether I should have given advice, withheld it, pushed my opinion, or just shut my mouth and listened. I'm a professional who realizes that therapeutic endings don't always look perfect, but I'd be lying if I said it didn't worry me when things don't end smoothly.

There are some beautiful endings in therapy, the kind of endings that you imagine when starting off studying to be a therapist. There's the ending with the client thanking you and expressing the inner confidence and clarity you helped them to access. There are also the endings where you can imagine the client would be a good friend in other circumstances—a testament to the therapeutic growth achieved by working together. I have experienced lots of positive therapy as a client and acknowledge that these feelings are usually signs that I trusted and felt safe with my therapist. Unfortunately, these relationships are also challenging when it comes time to say goodbye. It's bittersweet, but the stories of these journeys must remain in the therapy room, protected by the guardians of time and anonymity. It is a relationship built on the sanctity of confidentiality, and the extraordinary relationship dynamic exists only in this beautiful and unique context.

Endings in therapy require a reserved withholding from the therapist, which is all but impossible to maintain when talking to friends and family. It's tough not to tell a loved one that their job sucks and that they deserve better, that the person they're dating isn't good for them, or that they do suit that new piece of clothing despite doubting themselves. Opinions shared with loved ones often come from a good place built from love, care, and the irresistible feeling that sometimes we think we know better. However, conveying this explicitly in the therapy room involves all sorts of ethical dilemmas. I have worked with countless clients to whom I wish I could have suggested "solutions" or insisted that we work together for longer, but part of the beauty of therapy is that my room is effectively their room. It's not the room of Josh's life advice. Clients can come and go on their terms. And let's not forget that I certainly don't have my own life worked out yet, so, anxiety advice aside, I'm unable to tell you how to shape yours.

A good ending is one of the best parts of being a therapist. Every time a client shares that they feel confident in themselves or have recently been happy, it floods my brain with a cocktail of dopamine and serotonin. This is so rewarding that there is always a temptation to try to speed up that process—to get to the happy ending fueled by my own desire to feel fulfilled, to jump in with instructions sparked from a hunch I've gotten after knowing a client for just a few hours. But that's not what therapy is about. It's not about prioritizing my need for instant fulfillment, for compliments and accolades. It's about you, the client.

A good therapist will think about you when you leave their office for the last time. I certainly think about a lot of my former clients. It usually flitters between genuine interest and hope for their well-being and always a little worry about my impact on their life. Did I say the right things? Did I strike a balance between congruence and professional integrity? Was the modality I drew upon appropriate for this person? Sometimes it feels like a gamble on which approaches to take, and therapists often rely on a combination of our training mixed with on-the-spot intuition. Therapists hope your experiences in our therapy rooms haven't hindered or damaged your life.

I hope you feel proud of yourself for the courageous decision to go to therapy. I hope you leave feeling empowered and motivated and have a greater sense of understanding about yourself and your life. I hope I have helped you believe there are people out there you can trust. There *are* people who will listen, even if it is in a professional context. I hope you fondly look back on our time together and that your experience has left you open to returning to therapy if you need it, whether with another professional or me. Despite my professional demeanor of reservation, I do care what you think of my role as a therapist and, considering that it's a facet of who I am as a person, I care what you think about me.

Therapist self-doubt is a good thing. I used to think this doubt was some form of weakness in me as a therapist, but as I have grown in my role, I realize that it's an invaluable asset. Therapists who doubt and critically analyze themselves when a therapeutic relationship ends do so because they care. In my opinion, the last thing people sharing their vulnerabilities need is an insupportable know-it-all sitting in front of them, basking in an aroma of excessive self-assurance. If your therapist doesn't hold themselves to account, then this signals that their priority is upholding the belief in their faultlessness. To believe this, alongside prioritizing the duty of care for their clients, seems paradoxical. So I try to embrace feelings of nonfulfillment and missed opportunities as a sign that, quite simply, I care about my clients.

If you choose to leave therapy, remember that you will still exist in the space and memory of the person with whom you shared all that complicated stuff. Your vulnerabilities are treated with care, compassion, and nonjudgment as unwavering as the foundations of the space in which you share it. I must see endings as part of my job, and I sincerely hope that my clients see endings with as close an understanding as I have. But I acknowledge that this can be an unfair expectation, and our responsibility as therapists is to frame those expectations throughout therapy. You have come to the end of therapy because it was time, whether because it was professionally contracted or came to its natural conclusion. Whatever the ending, I always hope the lasting imprint is positive: an experience that strengthens your association with therapy and encourages you to talk about and process emotionally challenging experiences should they arise in your life.

Like all endings, saying goodbye can be hard.

32

Harry:
A Skip, a Flutter

June 2013

INTUITION: *Wake up.*
CRITIC: *Why? I've barely slept.*
INTUITION: *You just need to wake up. Trust me.*

I bolted upright in bed. My mouth and eyes were dry from sleeping in a room with hospital air-con. Some daylight tried to creep in through the blinds. Everything was still, sterile, and unhomely. I'd stayed up the previous night sitting with Harry. His latest chemo treatment had hit him hard, and I'd spent most of the night staring hopefully at his vitals monitor, willing it to show improvement. A whole pizza had grown cold and stale on the side. Harry hadn't eaten in days, and I had no appetite either. A corded phone shrilled at the side of the hospital bed.

Josh: Hello?
Nurse: Hi, Josh. It's Zoe here. I think you should come over to the ward.

ANXIETY: *Oh no . . . no, no, no . . .*
ANALYTICAL: *You're always assuming the worst.*
CRITIC: *He really does.*

Josh: Why? What's happening?
Nurse: Just head on down here. Harry needs you now.

SAVIOR: *I've got this.*

I leaped out of bed and threw on some clothes. I jogged down the laby-rinth of elevators and corridors toward Ward 84, realizing my T-shirt was on backwards, but I didn't care.

BIOLOGY: *What about me? Where's my nicotine and caffeine?!*
VOLITION: *We haven't got time for that.*
INTUITION: *We really haven't.*

I was buzzed into the long corridor of Ward 84. I could see that my mum had just arrived outside Harry's room, alongside Harry's dad and his partner. They'd obviously received a similar call. The nurses and doc-tors were in the room with Harry and there was a gray pull-down screen over the glass on the door, obscuring our view. My heart began to pound through my ribs and the tinnitus screamed through my skull.

SAVIOR: *No . . .*
COMPASSION: *No . . .*
ANXIETY: *No . . .*

Josh: The pull-down screen . . .

We'd all spent enough time in the children's ward over the last year to understand the significance of what we were seeing. The screen is a signal of imminent, palliative intervention for the worst that could happen. It is a signal—not just to you, but to the ward—that this room is to be given a wide berth out of respect, because nothing good is happening in there. The pull-down screen was used to spare hopeful patients and their loved ones the brutal realities of an oncology ward. And to us it was the worst possible sign.

Nurse: Hey, the registrar and consultant are in with the nurses now. They're just tending to Harry.
Mum: What's going on?

I could tell she knew the answer. My poor mum.

Josh: Can I just go in and see him?

Rather than wait for the answer, I opened the door into the dark room. The doctors turned as I came in, but they didn't tell me to leave. Harry was unconscious and hyperventilating. The room felt too dark, too miserable. I flung open the blinds.

Josh: That's better.

Registrar: Have you been informed about what is happening with Harry?

Josh: No, but I'm guessing it's not good. We've had loads of these situations before; he always pulls through. Don't you, lad?

Harry didn't answer. He continued to lie to one side, hyperventilating with his head facing toward the opposite wall. I checked the vitals monitor that I had been staring at the night before and was shocked to see that the numbers I had become comfortably used to had halved since last night. Harry's blood oxygen was extremely low. His pulse was dangerously low. All pretending ceased and my relentlessly optimistic illusion shattered.

Josh: He's dying, isn't he?

The nurse walked over and placed a consoling hand on my back. It was all the answer I needed.

Registrar: We'll leave you and your family with Harry. He'll need you now.

My mum was standing next to the door and overheard the conversation; as the doctors left she took her place on the other side of Harry's bed. She smiled at me through her fear for a moment, then held Harry's hand. His dad also joined us and we all watched Harry together.

Harry's breathing was deep, and his frail abdomen inflated and contracted forcefully. He had no hair left on his scarred, pale body. But he was beautiful. He was my brother.

We all stood in silence for a while, not knowing what to do other than stare awkwardly at the vitals monitor. It began sounding an alarm, and the nurse came in to silence it. Harry's blood oxygen plummeted further. Then an alarm. Then a silence. His heart palpitated, then the rate dropped dangerously low. Then another alarm. Harry's body began to convulse and his breathing became painfully labored. We gathered in closer, holding his hands while Mum placed her palm on his head.

Mum: We're all here for you. We love you so much.
Harry's dad: We love you, Harry.

ESCAPIST: *I just want to run.*
COMPASSION: *Well, we're not running. We have never run since all this began.*
VOLITION: *We're here till the end.*

The monitor alarm sounded again.

Josh: What's the point?!

I traced the monitor's power wire to the socket in the wall and un-plugged it. There were no protests.

ANXIETY: *This . . . pain . . .*

I placed my hand on Harry's chest, over his heart, and felt the beats stutter under my touch. His head was turned to one side. I don't know if he could hear us, but I'd like to think he could sense us there.

Josh: Did you hear that, chief? Everyone here loves you. I love you *so* much. It's almost over. I'm so . . . so . . . proud of you.

A skip, a flutter, a final gasp for air. The rolling of his head on the pillow. The stifled cries of his family. Then stillness.

33
Zahra

Zahra: I think I'm ready to talk about my grief. I know I told you what happened to my dad, but I don't think I have allowed myself to truly feel his loss. To explore it more. Recounting the stabbing and what happened with my family helped to open the dialogue, to let the unspoken be said aloud. But I'm ready to do the feelings side of things. It's what I'd like to talk about today.

Josh: Okay. I think that's a great idea.

> **TRIGGER:** *No, you don't. You hate talking about grief.*
> **COMPASSION:** *You have trained for this.*
> **ANALYTICAL:** *You've worked with grief plenty of times in the past.*
> **CRITIC:** *Not with someone for whom you are developing complex feelings.*
> **COMPASSION:** *It won't stop you from doing your job.*
> **CRITIC:** *Wanna bet?*

There was a long silence while Zahra prepared herself to talk about a deeply emotional topic. Someone was laughing on the main road down below. A door closed in a corridor nearby. I remained patient, sitting with my hands on my lap.

Zahra: There's an emptiness in me that I try to ignore. I've only noticed it since the panic attacks have subsided. Is that normal?

Josh: Yeah, it's expected, really. Anxiety and threat always jump to the front of the queue and consume our thoughts and attention—often for a long time. When the anxiety dissipates enough, there is a backlog of emotions that fight their way to the surface.

I took a sip of tea.

Josh: It doesn't surprise me that you're experiencing this given that panic attacks often consume all of our attention.

Zahra: Yes. It's almost impossible to delve into my feelings when I'm living in constant fear of panic. If anything, I used to avoid evocative triggers. Not because of a fear of sadness, but just because of fear itself.

DETECTIVE: *"Used to."*
INTUITION: *Bring attention to it.*

Josh: "Used to"? Isn't that lovely to hear? You've done amazingly with the panic and the exposures. I know we're about to explore a difficult topic today, but just know that feeling confident enough to do that is a testament to how far you have come.

Zahra smiled. She seemed to accept the praise. Her expression changed as she remembered something that she wanted to ask me.

Zahra: How did you do it?
Josh: Do what?
Zahra: Get over your grief?

ANALYTICAL: *Be careful here.*
VOLITION: *Yeah, watch the boundaries.*

Josh: I don't think anyone who loses someone they love "gets over" it, but they learn to grow and adapt in the loved one's absence. In a similar sequence to yours, I developed an anxiety disorder and needed to deal with that first, then I allowed space to face my grief. All grief is personal and subjective to the individual, though.

Zahra: Do you still struggle with grief now?
Josh: I live a happy life. Grief can rear its head from time to time and I accept that.
Zahra: How long did it take you?

VOLITION: *Redirect now.*
IRREVERENCE: *Swap chairs, shall we?*

Josh: It took me a while. Probably would have been sooner if I'd looked after myself a bit more and not avoided talking about the difficult things. I feel as if you're asking me these things as a form of assurance.

Zahra looked embarrassed.

Zahra: I'm just afraid that if I talk about it all, the grief will overwhelm me and I won't be able to handle it.
Josh: That's interesting. You said something similar before getting into the elevator, or before driving to work, or even experiencing panic on the floor in this therapy room. And yet . . .
Zahra: Yeah, yeah, I know . . . but it feels . . . different? It's like I'm afraid the pain *and* the anxiety will consume me at once.

EMPATHY: *A fear of all the emotions happening at once.*

Josh: It won't. I mean, you'll feel them both perhaps, but you will not lose control.

I tried to look reassuring. Zahra tapped her fingers nervously on her knees.

Zahra: The trauma of it all aside . . . I just miss him . . .

TRIGGER: *I miss him.*
COMPASSION: *It's okay, come back here.*
ANALYTICAL: *Try your best to stay in Zahra's frame of reference.*

Josh: What do you miss about him?
Zahra: I miss everything about him. Even the stuff that annoyed me. I miss his presence, I miss his hugs, the smell of him as I was pressed against his chest. I miss his lectures, his guidance, his belief in me . . .

Zahra began to cry as she continued.

Zahra: I miss him joking around with my mum. I loved his calmness and composure in tricky situations. I could do with some of that right now.

COMPASSION: *You're doing well, in my opinion.*

Zahra: He never really took things personally, which made him so patient with my brother. He was so good at it. My mum and I would lose our patience with Babak so easily.

I gently nodded to show her I was following.

Zahra: I . . . loved how he could command a room. Last night I watched one of his lectures on YouTube. He commanded this respect and admiration from his peers. Even I was getting sucked into the lecture. For a moment, I forgot I was sitting in my bedroom watching it on my laptop, fatherless, and not perched on one of the seats in the lecture hall.

She buried her face in her hands and began to weep.

Zahra: I miss him so much. I feel . . . what's that old boat expression?
Josh: Rudderless?
Zahra: Fucking rudderless. I've never been on a boat in my life. But I feel rudderless, Josh. What is a rudder, anyway?
Josh: I'm hearing that your father helped you feel like you had direction.
Zahra: He did. I aspired to be him.

ANALYTICAL: *Let's see if this is healthy or not.*
DETECTIVE: *Do it tastefully, sir. The woman is opening up about her dead pap.*

Josh: He sounds like an amazing man. I can understand the aspiration to be like him.
Zahra: I wish he was here now. To give me wisdom. To tell me what to do next.

She took a tissue and wiped her eyes with it.

Josh: What do you think he'd say to you now?

Zahra sniffled and blew her nose.

Zahra: I know what he'd say. He would tell me I'm doing brilliantly, and that grief is a powerful thing. He'd say not to judge myself so harshly. He was such a sagacious old bastard. He always had the words. He never judged me for failing to meet the goals I set for myself. My mum didn't either.

Josh: Then why do you think you set the goals so high?

Zahra: Because . . . I don't know . . .

Josh: Perhaps you saw safety in the idealism you constructed around your father?

Zahra frowned.

INTUITION: *Too early, Josh.*

Zahra: There's nothing "constructed" about how great he was. He was incredible. He didn't deserve to go. It's a loss to us all. To me, to my family, and to the profession.

Josh: I don't doubt that, Zahra. But I'm hearing that some of your pain is coming from a frustration with yourself. A frustration born from not meeting an ideal, or a rigid standard, that you've set for yourself using your father's achievements and personality as a framework. He is . . . was older . . . more experienced and his own person. As are you, Zahra. You are your own person. I don't see using your father as your only barometer for your own achievement as being healthy. It also sounds like he was proud of who you have become.

Zahra: What do you mean?

INTUITION: *Rein it in.*

Josh: I'm saying don't be so harsh on yourself. I also think it'll be beneficial that one day you focus on all of your qualities. Realize your worth as a person, not just compared to others.

CRITIC: *And you're well aware of all those traits, aren't you, Joshy?!*
BIOLOGY: *She really is beautiful.*
CRITIC: *Can't hide from Biology, mate. You can ignore me as much as you want, but Biology is as congruent as they come.*

Josh: It's okay to miss him. Perhaps you always will. And that's okay. It doesn't always need a reaction.

She looked at me.

Zahra: Is that you speaking from experience?

TRIGGER: *Hmm . . . You do miss your brother.*
VOLITION: *Not your session.*
CRITIC: *You let Zahra down the moment you continued to work with her when you suspected you had feelings for her.*
ANALYTICAL: *This has become convoluted, Josh.*

Josh: Yeah, I suppose I am. But we're not here to talk about my life.
Zahra: It was brave of you to talk about it publicly. Not many men are so open about emotions. I wish more men in my life were like that.
Josh: Well, it's something I like to model to others in case it helps them.

She leaned forward, and I could tell she was about to ask me a question out of genuine interest, and not just to deflect the session away from herself. It put me on alert: I was trying my best to limit my self-disclosure—"trying" being the operative word.

Zahra: I struggle to find the words to describe my grief. How . . . how would you describe yours?

BIOLOGY: *Her face is comforting.*
ANXIETY: *It would be nice to share something. None of your friends and family ask about it.*
VOLITION: *Be very careful . . .*

Josh: How would I describe grief? Hmm . . . It can feel like a heavy emptiness sometimes. Or white noise that's always there. For me, it's the empty seats that bring it up: One less at the table for Sunday dinner. No one leaning across your lap to shout their order at the drive-thru monitor. A second Xbox controller gathering dust. I've found that sometimes grief can fill a room, but on other occasions, when the ghosts of treasured memories decide not to haunt you for a change, they can comfort you instead. In time, grief can occasionally make you smile.

I'd lost Zahra's frame of reference as I dived into my own. I caught myself just in time and turned my focus back to her.

Josh: Zahra, remember that fond memories can remind you of who you are, remind you of *why* you do what you do, and they can give you a reason to honor the memory of someone who lives on through you. The best way to honor that person isn't to emulate them, but by continuing to live a life being yourself as much as possible. Being you! Continue being the person that *they* loved. It's difficult when you can't call, or text, or send a stupid meme, but I'd like to think grief is there to remind you of how important that person was . . . that person *is* to you.

Zahra stared at me but said nothing.

CRITIC: *You idiot. You are blurring boundaries.*
ANALYTICAL: *Going into unethical territory here.*

I stared back. She smiled, warmly. It made me fizz inside. She was radiating beauty. She lifted a strand of hair from in front of her eye, which floated back down again in moments.

BIOLOGY: *Double endorphins with an adrenal twist.*
CRITIC: *Seriously, what are you doing?*
VOLITION: . . .
ESCAPIST: *That felt so lovely to say to her. She makes you feel so good, Josh. You could help each other.*

Josh: I, erm . . . so yeah . . . where were we?
Zahra: My grief feels like a palpable guilt. Why do I get to walk around when my loved one died? Who am I to enjoy this meal, this movie, this beautiful walk through the hills? Why do I get to do it? Why am I . . . the . . . why am I . . . the . . . ?
Josh: Survivor?

I didn't mean to interject. My mouth acted first. I was slowly losing composure, and I felt it in the moment. I needed to ground myself and retrieve my professionalism.

Zahra: Yes . . . survivor. I am the guilty survivor.
Josh: Why do you think the guilt is there?

She paused to consider my question.

Zahra: Because I didn't get to say goodbye or tell him how much I loved him. I sulked that night at the restaurant . . . I made it about myself. I also think that, had I returned to the house with my parents instead of feeling sorry for myself, then things might have been different.
Josh: What would you say to him if he were here now? You don't need to say it to me, but you can pick anything in the room. Someone chose the potted plant once.

She smiled and continued looking at me attentively. Her eyes were locked on mine.

Zahra: I'd say . . . thank you for being a wonderful man. Thank you for guiding me. Thank you for inspiring me. I'm so sorry that we parted on the wrong terms. Don't blame yourself for your brother, Josh.

ANXIETY: *WTF?*

Zahra: Don't blame yourself for my brother, Dad. You poured your heart and soul into helping Babak. He knows that. We know that too. He wasn't to be fixed, Dad. And . . . neither am I. You spent a lot of time letting us know you were proud of us. I'm sorry that I didn't return the kind gestures. They were powerful and more influential than I realized. Also, don't worry about me. You're such a worrier. I will be fine. Mum and I will be fine. She misses Harry too.

ANXIETY: *Am I imagining this?*
IRREVERENCE: *This is even weirding me out.*

Zahra: She misses you too. I know you care about Babak and wouldn't want me to hold it against him. I don't. He's unwell. I'll try my best to support him in any way I can.

Zahra never broke eye contact the entire time. It felt unusual, like she was talking to me, even though I knew rationally that she wasn't. It was intense. I could feel the passion while I tried to tame the maelstrom of emotions swirling around inside me.

Zahra: Don't have any regrets. I love you. I always will. Thank you for being you.

The realness. The unfiltered, congruent nature of her talking to her father was moving, but being the conduit of these emotions was overwhelming, considering the unprofessional feelings that I was rapidly developing toward her.

BIOLOGY: *I want to embrace her. Hold her.*
ESCAPIST: *I want to kiss her.*

Josh: That felt moving. What was it like? To say that aloud?

Zahra broke eye contact and shrugged off her emotional declarations with a sheepish smile.

BIOLOGY: *Holding her hand. Having each other's shoulder to cry on through the hard times.*
ESCAPIST: *Imagine coming home from work to that level of warmth and compassion.*
BIOLOGY: *Not forgetting beauty.*
ANXIETY: *Volition! Where are you!?*
DETECTIVE: *They've been kidnapped by Biology.*

Zahra: Hey . . . this might sound weird . . . but at the end of therapy, when we conclude for good, would you like to grab a coffee now and then? Catch up from doctor to therapist? Of course, I know the boundaries—I'm not expecting you to. I just think . . . it would be nice, you know?

BIOLOGY: *It would be nice. We'd love to.*
ESCAPIST: *I'll buy!*
CRITIC: *Told you. He is and always will be a charlatan. Weak. Suggestible. Pathetic.*
ANXIETY: *Compassion? Where are you?! Analytical?! Help!*
BIOLOGY: *I'm running the show now.*
ESCAPIST: *You'll be getting no complaints from me.*

Zahra: And . . . if you ever wanted a safe space to talk about Harry . . .
    I understand it must be hard. I'm struggling. I hear you still struggle too.

BIOLOGY: *Every part of me wants this beautiful person.*
ESCAPIST: *She makes everything feel better. She can take all the bad feelings away.*
CRITIC: *FFS.*
TRIGGER: *Harry.*

My body shuddered me lucid. I snapped out of the fantasy. I was back in my office. I was me. Why was my heart pounding?

VOLITION: *Wake up! Take a break and collect yourself.*
ANALYTICAL: *What in the ethics-breaking hell is happening here?*
ANXIETY: *Yay! The cavalry has arrived!*

Josh: I'm really sorry to pause this moment, especially while we are
    talking about this sensitive subject, but do you mind if I nip to the toilet?
    Otherwise, my attention will be focused on arguing with my bladder.

She shuffled awkwardly, aware that I had not answered her request.

Zahra: Yes, of course.

••

When I closed the door behind me, my body released into an almighty tremble. I began to sweat and struggled to catch my breath. I walked hastily down the corridor to the restroom. Thankfully, it was empty. I switched the taps to full pressure and splashed cold water on my face. I looked up into the mirror and realized I was crying.

Josh: What on earth am I doing here?

COMPASSION: *Take a breath. Each scenario can be complex. Let's work this one out. Up until now, you have done an excellent job.*
CRITIC: *Has he?*
COMPASSION: *You're not invited here, Critic. Sod off.*
ANALYTICAL: *It appears your feelings for your client have transcended into the personal. Attraction, both emotional and physical, seems to be preventing you from accessing enough empathy and Zahra's frame of reference. You've failed to see that she is idealizing you—projecting the need for comfort from a male authority figure onto you. Very common in grieving. You missed it.*
EMPATHY: *It's true.*
DETECTIVE: *And it is clouding your judgment. Listen, man. You fancy her. There's no going back.*
ESCAPIST: *But, for once, I don't want to leave.*

I was sobbing over the sink. What a state I was in. The squeaking of the restroom door sounded over the running of the taps. I spotted Dr. Patel in the mirror. He looked at me. Concern immediately spread across his face.

DETECTIVE: *Why does he fucking insist on using the upstairs restroom every time?*

I stood up straight.

Josh: Why do you use this restroom? There's one literally outside your office.

He started to chuckle, which temporarily removed the concern from his face.

Dr. Patel: Ah, nothing but my own superstition, Joshua. Once a patient of mine collapsed when I was using the restroom outside of my office. Since then, I've never been able to use it.

Josh: That makes absolutely no sense.

Dr. Patel: You of all people should know that anxiety doesn't wisely make use of rationality.

I nodded and returned the smile.

Dr. Patel: What is going on here, Joshua? Are you okay? You look distraught. Here, have a paper towel.

He passed me a towel to dry my face and eyes.

Josh: I won't bore you with it, Doctor.

Dr. Patel: Your hypocrisy bores me. Emotional conservatism is something you actively campaign against, is it not?

Josh: How do you know?

Dr. Patel: I attended one of your talks.

Josh: Oh . . . wow . . . that's really kind. And also surprising. Thank you . . . Doc.

Dr. Patel: It was interesting. It resonated with me personally. Anyway, why are you crying in the toilet?

I sighed. I was too afraid to tell him. I feared his judgment.

IRREVERENCE: *Dr. Patel can be your new daddy!*
COMPASSION: *I think it's okay to open up.*
VOLITION: *Do it in a way that works for you.*

Josh: I've been taking something I shouldn't have, Doctor. Something that I thought was good for me but soon realized wasn't. It turns out I'm finding it hard to taper off it. I'm scared that it'll hurt if I go cold turkey, you know?

Dr. Patel: Well, which medication is it? Prescribed?

Josh: No, it's not prescribed . . . It's . . . a drug of some sort. I'm embarrassed to say. It makes me feel nice, but it isn't good for me.

Dr. Patel: Ah, I see . . .

He gave me a sympathetic look, as if he had just discovered that I was now a crackhead.

Dr. Patel: Well, how long have you been taking it?

Josh: Not long . . .

Dr. Patel: Well, there's not many drugs that can harm you if stop taking them shortly after you start. Obviously, I'm going off your vague description here, as you appear reluctant to tell me. But if you've just started, I'd say it was in your very best interests to stop as soon as you can. Addiction is a consuming and life-threatening affliction. You're a good therapist, Josh. Try not to jeopardize it. I can signpost you to some helpful services if you'd like.

VOLITION: *"Stop as soon as you can."*

COMPASSION: *"You're a good therapist, Josh. Try not to jeopardize it."*

Josh: Thanks, Doc. I appreciate it. Your bladder must be about to explode. I won't stop you any further.

Dr. Patel: Look after yourself, Joshua. My door is always open.

IRREVERENCE: *Thanks, Dad!*

••

I placed one hand on my therapy-room door, took a deep breath, then entered. Zahra was waiting for me. She looked human again, not the fantastical figure my attraction, grief, and escapism wanted her to be. She was my client. I took my seat and smiled warmly.

Josh: I'm sorry about that.

Zahra: Did you have to leave because of what I said? I'm so sorry if it was pushing boundaries.

Josh: You have nothing to apologize for.

ANALYTICAL: *Congruence and authenticity are two of your main strengths as a therapist. Be brave. Use them.*

COMPASSION: *They don't teach you how to properly get out of these situations in training.*

Josh: I took a break because I was failing to be your therapist for a while. My attention was distracted, and my professionalism was wavering. I apologize.

Zahra: I didn't notice anything. It's okay.

Josh: Zahra . . . I feel . . . I feel that we can no longer work together, because of my own limitations. I have developed feelings that get in the way of my professional judgment. Sometimes this can happen, given the nature of the connections that can happen in the therapy room. It has happened here.

She looked incredulous.

Zahra: Ha. One of the "It's me, not you?!" moments? Am I being dumped by my therapist?

Josh: No. It's an admission that my own personal feelings, and unprocessed emotions from my own life, have managed to infiltrate this therapeutic relationship. I'm so sorry for letting you down like that. It was never my intention.

Zahra: Are you saying I'm triggering emotions in you?

Josh: I'm saying that emotions are coming up that I realize I haven't dealt with properly.

Zahra: Be honest, why is it that you're stopping this? I've done so well. You have helped me so much! Why stop?

Josh: I think I've taken you as far as I can go.

ESCAPIST: *This is sad.*

Josh: You're doing brilliantly. I highly recommend working with some grief and trauma specialists. They'll have more specific training than me.

Zahra: But I want to work with you. Can we not just park it for this week? Have a break and reset? You're being incredibly vague. I think it's because I asked you for coffee, isn't it?

I sighed and frantically tried to search for a way out of this. I hated how I was upsetting her. I was deeply upset myself.

Zahra: Just tell me why.

VOLITION: *Do not tell her why.*
ANALYTICAL: *Don't. Professional integrity.*
EMPATHY: *The last thing she needs is more complexities in her life, like the admission of attraction from her therapist!*
COMPASSION: *She deserves the truth, though, right?*
VOLITION: *No. There are some occasions where it's okay not to disclose. Even in therapy.*

Josh: I'll be honest. It feels horrible to expect honesty from my clients while I myself hold the power to lie to protect myself. We are concluding therapy because of a professional judgment call. It is *not* because you asked me for coffee; that's a kind gesture and a compliment to the genuine connection we have developed in here. It's not the invitation, it's because a large part of me wanted to accept it. That concerned me, Zahra. A therapist who no longer respects their professional boundaries ceases to become a therapist. And I . . . love being a therapist. I'm so sorry.

She smiled.

Zahra: I understand. I appreciate your being open and clear with me.

She leaned over to the side of the sofa and pulled out a gift bag.

Zahra: Before I go, please, would you accept this gift? It was bought as a thank-you. No, it's not a Rolex or anything, just a plant. The ones in here look like they could have some company. Please tell me you will accept it.
Josh: I will. I'll put it on my windowsill. Thank you.

She looked like she might be about to cry. I leaned forward and caught her gaze.

Josh: Thank you for trusting me. You've done amazingly. I don't doubt that you'll continue to. In all aspects of your life.

She managed a smile. I became aware of tears of my own that I was desperately trying to hold back. Zahra got to her feet for the final time in my therapy room. I allowed myself to reflect on the wonderful contrast to the first session, where she was crawling on the floor in panic. She stood tall, assured, and with integrity. I'd miss her.

Zahra: Goodbye, Joshua.

I closed the door softly behind her. The calathea she had given me remained on the coffee table. I lifted it and placed it in a spare pot. Then I gently moved it to the windowsill, so it was often in my line of sight for many an afternoon to come.

34
Keep Calm
and Carry On

Mum: Thanks for getting lunch.
Josh: Thanks for coming into town to see me!
Mum: Are you okay? I know that it's always a difficult day.
Josh: You know me, Mum. I'm fine. How are you doing?
Mum: Okay. I could feel him with us today.

I smiled and nodded. I wasn't sure how to answer, even all these years later.

Mum: Well, I'm going to get the bus back.
Josh: I'll walk you down and wait for it with you.

We had met up to commemorate what would have been Harry's birthday. It had been an expensive lunch, and it didn't taste as nice as I'd have liked. No fault of the chef, just a depressed palate. Mum seems to be more at peace with Harry's passing, perhaps because of her own belief systems. I, however, always seem to struggle at this time of year. But I didn't want to worry her. I waved her goodbye as the bus pulled away and felt a sinking sorrow spread through my abdomen.

ESCAPIST: *It's your brother's birthday. You don't deserve to feel sad. Let's ease the pain.*
CRITIC: *Here he goes. Justifying poor choices in the name of grief.*

I walked down one of the city's quieter streets and discovered the saddest-looking pub I could find. The barman placed a pint of bitter in front of me in the shadowy taproom, and I watched through the window as the tail end of the lunchtime crowd begrudgingly returned to work. My phone vibrated in my pocket. It was a text from Mum.

Mum: Good to see you. Remember he loves you. I love you xxx

I smiled. Then ordered a whiskey. Then another pint. Then a whiskey. I continued this self-destructive pattern until I got bored of my surroundings and stumbled toward a more gentrified district of town. I found refuge in the Crown & Anchor, where an acoustic guitarist was playing popular bangers to the late-afternoon crowd. I sat nearby and sang along noisily to Manchester classics like Oasis, the Stone Roses, James, and David Gray.

COMPASSION: *Josh . . . don't you think it's high time we went home now?*
ESCAPIST: *Ignore him, you deserve to have fun. It's what Harry would want.*
ANXIETY: *If we go home now, we'll have nothing but the silence and our thoughts.*
ESCAPIST: *Exactly.*
BIOLOGY: *You're gonna need some food in your stomach to soak up these boilermakers.*

When the musician took his break I loudly booed him. Thankfully, he took it in jest. The silence afterward felt too intense, so I left the pub in search of sustenance. I bought something horrendous from a kebab takeout and ate it leaning against the shop window.

My next stop was a nearby blues bar that has live music from afternoon till late. Beer didn't cut it now, so I stuck to whiskey. I found a chair and plonked myself down to listen to the blues band, admiring the saxophonist, who was incredible. I oscillated between chuckling in delight and crying. Not because the music was particularly evocative, but because I was pissed.

I crashed through the restroom door, knocking a middle-aged man backward.

Man: Hey! Watch it.
Josh: I'm sorry. I, er . . . lost my balance.

The room spun as I swayed in front of the urinal. A security guy walked in and eyed me up and down.

Security: A bit early for this level of drunk, mate. Think you better head home?
Josh: *(belching)* Seriously, I'm fine. We're both fine. Look at us, we're fine!
  Hey, have you ever played *Portal*?

The security guy gently escorted me out into the night. With a kindness I wasn't expecting, he put me into a cab and told me to get home safely.

Cabdriver: Where to, pal?
Josh: Er . . . take me to someone that . . . take me to somewhere I can, er . . . oh, I know just the place!

.. ..

The lights around me blurred in and out of focus and I had to forcefully lean to one side to maintain my balance. I staggered past a popular bar that had a queue forming outside of it. Across the road was a public bench, which looked appealing to someone whose legs felt like jelly. I bummed a cigarette off a young man who seemed as drunk as I was, lit it, then sat back and began to people watch. I tuned in to the laughter of the punters in the bar queue. They all seemed strangely dressed to me, and I felt old.

I scanned the side of the building, looking at a stunning bee mural that colored the side of the apartments opposite. The bee is a symbol of Manchester that harks back to the Industrial Revolution, when Manchester laborers were referred to as the worker bees. I marveled at the artistic skill until something jarring spoiled my enjoyment. A large blue poster emblazoned with the words "Keep Calm and Carry On" was plastered over the lower part of the bee's wing.

Josh: That's grim. Someone ought to sort that out.

SAVIOR: *You, mate. You should be the one. You're a hero.*

Josh: I am . . . a hero!

The bar queue had grown to the point where it now blocked the entrance to the alleyway where the mural and abhorrent poster were. I bumped my way through the crowd into the alley and gazed up at the monstrosity. It was a big poster.

Josh: Why would anyone paper that stupid saying over this gorgeous mural?
Punter: *(laughing)* You should get rid of it.
Josh: I should!

The "Keep Calm" poster was twelve feet up the wall, but an industrial-sized wheelie bin offered a route to reach it; I just had to climb. So up I went. A drunken, idiotic mess scaling a wheelie bin to the amusement, and encouragement, of a young, intoxicated crowd.

SAVIOR: *I will remove you.*

I stood up straight on top of the bin, now face-to-face with the poster.

SAVIOR: *I have you now.*

I placed my hand on the corner of the poster, but it had been stuck so flush to the wall that I was forced to trace the edges, trying to find a lip. I could hear laughter below me. Encouraging laughter, I hoped.

CRITIC: *They're laughing at you, Josh. What are you doing?*

Infuriatingly, the poster seemed almost painted to the wall. I couldn't find any purchase on any part of it. I began to frantically claw at its surface.

CRITIC: *Ah, man, this isn't good . . .*
IRREVERENCE: *Mate . . .*

I kept clawing. The ends of my fingers started to sting with pain.

SAVIOR: *Almost there—you can save the bee mural from this abomination!*
ANXIETY: *I can't!*

The laughter from below melded into a mixture of mockery and concern. Some passersby had stopped to see what was happening, and the crowd grew larger. My hands started to bleed. I lost my footing but thankfully only fell to my knees on top of the bin. Everything was spinning. I had failed. My chin fell toward my chest. I hiccupped, cried out in anger, then started to weep.

CRITIC: *What a mess.*
ESCAPIST: *You tried to outrun it, mate. Unlucky.*

I just knelt there and wept. I didn't know what to do. People had taken their phones out to record this comic tragedy.

DETECTIVE: *Josh, get up. This could ruin you. This could affect your career.*
COMPASSION: *Listen to them!*

My legs were now lead. I didn't move. Just let them film. Suddenly the crowd parted to reveal two bouncers from the bar. Their silhouettes grew bigger as they marched toward me. I felt both of my arms being gripped tightly, then I was hauled from the top of the bin and taken away down the alleyway.

CRITIC: *Maybe they'll give you a couple of slaps for the inconvenience.*
ESCAPIST: *I don't even care anymore.*

They pulled me through a fire door into a small kitchen room. I hung my head, staring at my shoes in anticipation of some form of verbal or physical grilling. A mug of black coffee was shoved under my face, the sobering vapors hitting my nostrils. I looked up.

Levi: Take it, then! I can't stand here all day.

I was stunned. I took the coffee, awash with confusion, embarrassment, and relief all at once.

Levi: Had one too many, have we, fella?

He looked at his colleague and lifted his chin to suggest he leave.

Levi: Can you give us a minute? I'll be with you again shortly. See you out the front. Give us a shout if I'm needed urgently.

The bouncer nodded and left with a canteen of hot coffee. Levi pulled up a chair alongside me.

Levi: I don't know what's been happening with you, but whatever it is, it doesn't seem right. You're a smarter man than this.
Josh: I . . . I'm . . .

Levi: Don't try and explain, because you're drunk and it'll annoy me. I don't want that to be my lasting memory of you.

I nodded.

Levi: Whatever it is you're going through, just know that . . . you deserve help for it too, you know?

He took a sip of his own coffee.

Levi: You know, someone to help you, like you helped me?

His radio sounded from his top pocket.

Voice from radio: Levi, sorry, mate, but we've got a group here that are stirring up trouble in the line.

Levi sighed and rolled his eyes.

Levi: *(into radio)* Right, coming.

He stood up and walked to the door. Then he stopped and turned back to me.

Levi: Sober up. I'm not going to come back to this room. I'm going to pretend I never saw you. Stay safe. And . . . thank you.

He opened the door and began to step through it. He stopped once again.

Levi: Oh, and I will leave her one day. It's not the same and . . . never will be. I just need to know that I have tried everything first.

The door closed gently behind Levi and he departed back into the night. I sipped the coffee and made my only sensible decision of the night: I rang a taxi to take me home. I feel forever grateful for Levi that night, when I was at my lowest. His compassion, his nonjudgmental attitude, his manner: all the traits you might expect from a great therapist.

The Beauty of Therapy

When therapy works—when you, your therapist, and the modality of treatment match—beautiful things can and often do happen. Even if you are seeing a therapist just to get things off your chest every couple of weeks, when there is empathy, congruence, and unconditional positive regard (thank you, Carl Rogers) in the mix, really good things can happen and it can be incredibly helpful.

I'd like you to imagine that we are all floating through life together, but each of us within our own special bubble. That bubble is created both for and by us, spun into existence by our experiences, our beliefs, our fears, our hopes, and our dreams. Your bubble is both where you exist and who you are. You ride your bubble through time and space, sometimes experiencing joy and serenity, sometimes tossed around in the violent currents of life. Good therapy—beautiful therapy—is like being invited to park your bubble inside someone else's bubble from time to time. Good therapy is a safe space where all of you is welcome. Good therapy is a place where you can open up without fear of judgment. Good therapy can be a vault where you can store your most valuable thoughts, feelings, and experiences, knowing that they will be there when you return, protected from the outside world. It's a wonderful thing when it happens.

Good therapy is the result of trust. When I first went to therapy, it took me a while to let my guard down. I was living as if everyone, and everything, was a threat. But after a while I began to trust my therapist and those sessions became very special places and times for me. I learned to open up. Some of what was said remains locked in that sacred vault. Some I've learned to also share with others in a healthy and productive way. The experience was wonderful. Powerful. Almost spiritual, which is a word I do not often use.

There is a fair amount of research into different therapy methods to indicate that almost every form of therapy "works" in some way once those core conditions are met. Finding a therapist who is empathetic, authentic, and congruent, and completely accepting of you in every way, means that you have a really good chance of getting some benefit from therapy regardless of the theoretical orientation of your therapist. Of course, there are some issues that do respond better to certain treatments (cognitive-behavioral approaches in the case of anxiety disorders, for example), but this research illustrates for us the potential beauty of therapy when there's a good match between you and the professional who sincerely wants to help. A solid therapeutic relationship based on these fundamental principles is going to be beneficial in some way, most of the time. That is a wonderful thing. Therapy works, and it does so because two human beings working together in the spirit of acceptance and understanding is a powerful thing.

Therapy can be beautiful. What, then, is the difference between the beauty and benefit of therapy, and the beauty and benefit of having good friends or close family members in your life? Sometimes we get lucky and we cultivate personal relationships that can provide us with unconditional acceptance, empathy, and authenticity. That can happen. But life is complicated, and each of us has our own beliefs, conditions of self-worth, experiences, and problems. We see the world through our own personal lens. Would you expect your best friend to completely bury their problems and struggles in deference to yours? Of course not. That's not what we want in our friendships. Would you expect your siblings to completely check their own experiences and beliefs at the door to offer you total unconditional acceptance at all times without conflict? That's not realistic. We all experience conflict with our friends and family members. Do we delude ourselves into thinking that our special people are always completely authentic and transparent with us? We may try, but the people close to us are tending to their own lives and therefore are going to arrive at our doorsteps cloaked, or at least clouded, with their own influences and priorities.

This is all normal and expected. It's good stuff. There's nothing at all wrong with personal relationships that exist within these parameters. We're all allowed to be human with each other. We should always have the respect and love of the people close to us, but we simply cannot expect that we will find unconditional positive regard, empathy, and authenticity in our personal relationships at all times, even when everyone has the best of intentions and is trying to create these conditions. Our close, personal relationships are also beautiful, but in their own way.

The beauty and effectiveness of good therapy is an entirely different animal. It all starts with clear, important boundaries. Your therapist is there to help you. There is no expectation that you will help them, or even care about them on a personal level. You don't have to love or even like your therapist. It certainly helps when there is a good connection, but a therapist is not there to be cared for, liked, or validated by you. Remember when I said that we do not expect our friends to ignore their own struggles in deference to ours? That is exactly what a therapist is there to do for you during the therapeutic hour.

A therapist trains for quite some time to learn how to remain anchored in your frame of reference, something a friend is not required—nor should be required—to do. A friend remains in their own frame of reference while interacting with you and therefore cannot help but examine how you are making THEM feel. A therapist may experience feelings during a session but will also work hard to shelve those feelings to remain focused on how YOU feel.

Note the title of the book you're reading right now: There's a reason we associate that phrase with therapy.

Therapy is transactional. This is not a bad thing. The transactional nature of the relationship is where the potential for beauty and positive outcomes is born. You trust your therapist with your money. In exchange, a therapist is there to be authentic and congruent with you, to be empathetic and to provide you with unconditional positive regard. Of course, they are also there to bring their training and expertise to bear on your problems and concerns, but before they ever get to that point, a good therapist starts every session fully accepting that they are there for you, with no expectation of anything in return beyond payment of the agreed fee.

It's hard to be empathetic, authentic, and entirely accepting of and dedicated to another human being. It's tiring. It takes work and dedication. It even takes training. That's okay. That's why therapists exist. They choose to do that for you and with you in one-hour blocks every week or so depending on the situation. A good therapist absolutely cares about you, but the nature of the relationship means they are not there to be your friend. Rather, a good therapist picks up where the relationship with your friends falls short. Good therapy enhances and augments the support you get in your personal relationships. Good therapy is safe and supportive, but also focused and dedicated entirely to YOUR needs. Therein lies the beauty of good therapy.

This seems like a good time to address the idea of being friends with your therapist. It is hard to get to know someone on an intimate, emotional level and not form a bond of friendship. Therapists are human too. Often our clients want to be our friends. It's normal for you to like your therapist. This is where the training and ethical practice of a good therapist becomes important. I was trained to do my very best to avoid what's called a dual relationship with a client. Being both therapist and friend would be a dual relationship that begins to cross the important boundaries we touched on earlier. You need those boundaries. As a therapist, I need those boundaries. We work hard to keep them intact because they exist to ensure that therapy can be effective in ways that friendships cannot.

A well-trained and ethical therapist steers clear of forming friendships with clients because friends are emotionally invested in helping you feel better. Therapists must be invested in the often more difficult task of helping you *be* better. The emotional bond of friendship makes it more challenging for a therapist to do the hard stuff that you need done. We— and you—are best served when we remain firmly rooted in the clearly defined and delineated role of helper. A friend wants to have your back. A friend will tell you that you are not a screwup and are absolutely lovable. A therapist is willing to do the dirty work with you, not telling you that you are lovable, but asking you to elaborate on why you think you are not.

When a therapeutic relationship ends and you feel that you are no longer in need of help from your therapist, you leave. Sometimes that is a sad moment for both of you, but it's also a proud moment. A good therapist will think about you from time to time, wondering how you're doing, but they do not need you to check in with them and they will never check in with you no matter how much they want to. You can cut off all contact with your therapist for two years, then pick up the phone and book a session with no questions asked and no explanations needed. The door remains open without conditions. Try doing that with your friends and you'll probably get quite a different reaction.

If your therapist has backed away from your attempts to develop a friend-ship, don't be offended. It doesn't mean they don't care. It doesn't mean they're in it only for the money. It doesn't mean that something is wrong with you. It just means that your therapist is trying to keep that relationship in a special place where you are safe and supported and where the focus remains on you and what you need. Anyone who has gone through good therapy will look back and think, *I could have been friends with my therapist, but I'm glad I wasn't.* This is what makes the sanctity of therapy so special.

If it were up to me, I would send my family and friends through therapy. Not because they are broken and in need of repair, but because wonderful therapy is not just for times when we feel broken or in need of repair. Good therapy—beautiful therapy—is a life-enhancing experience as much as it is a remedial or mitigating experience. Good therapy is a gift.

35
The Interview

May 2015

The corridor where we had to wait was long and ornamented with oil paintings of figures I presumed to be important people from academic history. They had us sitting on cushioned pews, like in church. I couldn't keep still. This was my chance to start on a master's course to become a psychotherapist. The large Georgian door next to me creaked open and out stepped a relieved-looking interviewee about my age. She shot me a reassuring glance as if to say "good luck" as she made her way down the corridor. A smiling, middle-aged woman appeared in the doorway.

Dr. Phillips: Joshua?
Josh: That's me.
Dr. Phillips: Would you like to come through for your interview now?

I followed Dr. Phillips into a grand, ornate room, every wall covered with shelves of old books. Two professors sat behind a large mahogany table and gestured for me to take a seat across from them. Dr. Phillips joined the interview panel. Although they seemed friendly, my heart was pounding. I was hoping I wouldn't jumble my words or start spewing nonsense that went off on strange tangents. I also tried my best to hide my stimming hands—a tic I've had since childhood. There was a glass of water waiting for me, and I took a shaky sip.

Dr. Perbesi: Welcome, Joshua.
Josh: Hello.
Dr. Phillips: We enjoyed your application, Joshua. Well done for getting this far. We have received an unusually large number of applications this year, so regardless of what happens today, remember that getting this far is indicative of a strong submission.

I nodded and smiled awkwardly. The third professor remained silent, jotting something down on his pad.

Dr. Perbesi: Let's get straight to it, then. Our first question is something that we asked in the written application, but we'd also like to hear the answer from applicants in person. Don't worry if your answer doesn't mirror that of your written submission; this isn't a memory test.

The third professor looked up to retrieve a document that I presumed was my printed application.

Dr. Perbesi: So, let's get started. Can you explain to us why you want to be a psychotherapist?

I felt frozen in my seat, searching the caverns of my mind for the answer that felt the most appropriate. Some familiar voices chimed in with their two cents.

ANXIETY: *I want to be a therapist because it gives me a sense of control over my own anxieties. Also, the world is falling apart and there'll be no shortage of clients come the apocalypse. Being an anxiety therapist means I can study something that I have struggled with and use my experience to help others.*

VOLITION: *I want to study to be a therapist because it's me making an assertive and informed decision for my life, rather than stewing in indecision and hesitating to make big changes. It's also something that requires me to be my authentic self. A bonus is that I can work alone, make my own work choices, and not be told what to do by annoying bosses.*

ANALYTICAL: *I think it makes complete sense that I train to be a therapist. I've got the grades, the willingness, the life experience, and the hunger. Not many people are drawn to the role of listener, whereas I seem to walk toward it. That makes sense to me.*

DETECTIVE: *I'd be a great therapist because I love finding out more about people. That, and I love a good case to solve with a good partner, which would be my clients. I also possess a penchant for long coats and a fedora, and I'm obsessed with evidence.*

COMPASSION: *I'd like to be a therapist because I hold a huge amount of compassion for those who are struggling. I think showing another*

human compassion is one of the most beautiful things anyone
can do, especially in a society that's so easily divided and rife with
personal and systemic prejudice. My compassion will be a caring,
outstretched hand for those who are in emotional difficulty. Anxiety
can be so terrifying. I want my practice to be based on a cornerstone
of compassion.

SAVIOR: I'd love to be a therapist because I want to save people. More
important, I want to help people save themselves. To empower them to
be their own saviors. As Einstein said, only a life lived for others is a life
worthwhile. It isn't just about trying to project a need to save because of
the loss of my brother—though that undoubtedly plays a part; it's always
something I've wanted to do. His loss has given me the propulsion to
take the leap.

CRITIC: I want to be a therapist to fill the emptiness left behind by grief
and poor life choices. Studying hard and helping others will help me to
persuade myself that I have worth. It'll also help to medicate the survivor
guilt I live with every day. I'm also atrocious at manual labour, banal
routines, and being told what to do, so a job where I get to sit on my ass
all day is perfect.

BIOLOGY: I'd like to be a therapist because I believe it would be nurturing
for my own physical and psychological well-being and for those of others.
I would also like to show people that it is okay for the body to process
emotions and it's okay for them to show them. I also find it exciting, and
it's a job that perhaps lacks male practitioners.

EMPATHY: I'd make a great therapist because I can further nurture
my skill in empathy. Ever since I was a kid, I have always been good at
putting myself in other people's shoes. I was always the one who greeted
the new kid at school and wanted them to feel safe. I was always drawn
to those who were upset, and I wanted to know their experiences so I
could obtain more knowledge on how to help them. To have a job where I
could use and develop this skill would be amazing.

ESCAPIST: I'd like to be a therapist because it allows me to step into the
fascinating worlds of others with a bonus that I get to escape mine, but
in a productive way, although the paradox is that I want my job to become
part of my life. It's also an escape from my current career, in which I
feel unfulfilled. Creating my own practice can give me more agency and
provide a happier time outside of work too.

IRREVERENCE: *I'd like to be a therapist so I can go to parties and lie about my job so drunk people don't divulge their entire trauma history to me while I queue for the toilet. The professor on the right has a mustard stain on their lapel.*

TRIGGER: *I want to be a therapist because I've learned that it's okay to walk toward my anxious triggers and not build a life around avoiding them. Since overcoming disordered anxiety, a part of me enjoys the challenge of practicing willful tolerance. I hope to bring this to my role as a therapist.*

INTUITION: *You've got this, Josh.*

Time slowed. The gentle tapping of a late-summer rain shower on the window was the only noise in the room. The sunlight diffracted through the raindrops, creating a small, colorful ring behind the interview panel. I stared at the bright circle, hoping something or someone would appear to give me the answer. Instead, the circle floated gently for a moment before it vanished. A warm, euphoric feeling crept up inside and eased my anxiety. I couldn't help but smile. I went with intuition.

Josh: For my brother . . .

Acknowledgments

Thank you to my partner, Hannah, my mum, my family, and my friends for always being there for me and supporting me as a therapist and an author. I would also like to thank Mauro, Andrew, and the rest of the team at William Morrow, who have shown their belief in me throughout this thrilling journey.

About the Author

Joshua Fletcher is a qualified psychotherapist, specializing in anxiety disorders and based in Manchester, England. He is often referred to as Anxiety Josh (@AnxietyJosh) and uses his popular Instagram and TikTok pages to educate those who struggle with mental health. Fletcher is also the host of the popular podcast *Disordered*, which he cohosts with Drew Linsalata. His practice, the School of Anxiety, is still open, and he enjoys working with clients to this day.